Table of Contents

1. Introduction To Your Living Trust 5
   1.a. Background 5
   1.b. When this Booklet can be Used 5
   1.c. Use of an Attorney 6
   1.d. How to use this Booklet 7

2. Other Estate Planning Documents That You May Need 8

3. Advantages Of A Living Trust 10
   3.a. Management of Assets 10
   3.b. Protection During Illness, Incompetency or Absence 10
   3.c. Continuity 10
   3.d. Probate Avoidance 10
   3.e. Privacy 10
   3.f. Choice of Law 10
   3.g. Less Easily Challenged than a Will 11
   3.h. Coordinated Estate Plan 11
   3.i. Qualification of Trustee 11
   3.j. Estate Tax Savings 11
   3.k. Declaration of Trust 11
   3.l. Saves Capital Gains In Community Property States 12
   3m. Flexibility and Mobility 12
   3.n. Spare your loved ones the hassles of probate 12
   3.o. Speedy transfer of Property to Heirs 12
   3.p. Good Feelings 12

4. What Is Probate -- Why It Is To Be Avoided 13
   4.a. Definition of Probate 13
   4.b. Costs of Probate 13
   4.c. Ways to Avoid Probate 14

5. Other Information On Living Trusts 15
   5.a. Definitions 15
   5.b. The Difference Between a Last Will, Living Trust, and Living Will 15
   5.c. Living Trust 16
   5.d. A Trust is a Contract and Run Similar to a Corporation 16
   5.e. Limited Liability 16
   5.f. Property Transfer Documents 17
   5.h. Economic Recovery Act of 1981 17
   5.i. Stepped-Up Valuation 17
   5.j. How the Living Trust Works 17
   5.k. Dower Law States 18
   5.l. Curtesy Law States 18
   5.m. What the Trust Does Upon Your Death 18

6. Steps For Implementing Your Living Trust 19
   Step One -- Read the Booklet 19
   Step Two -- Charge Up Your Determination 19
   Step Three -- Make sure you have your basic documents in order 19

    Step Four -- Think Through and Fill In The Living Trust Forms...19
    Step Five -- Fill in the Certificate of Trustee's Powers and Abstract of Trust.......................20
    Step Six -- Document Your Property...20
    Step Seven -- Transfer Assets to the Trust...20
    Step Eight -- Execute the Documents...21
    Step Nine -- Make Copies and Process...21
    Step Ten -- Review Your Documents..21

7. How To Operate Your Living Trust..22

    7.a. Funding the Trust..22

    (1) How to Transfer Registered Securities - Stock Certificates and
        Bond Certificates 23
    (2) How to Transfer Unregistered Securities..23
    (3) How to Transfer Street Name Accounts - Holding Securities..............................23
    (4) How to Transfer Real Estate Interest..23
    (5) How to Transfer Tangible Personal Property..24
    (6) How to Transfer Bank Accounts..24
    (7) How to Transfer Life Insurance...25
    (8) How to Transfer Series E Government Bonds..25
    (9) How to Transfer Retirement Benefits...25
    (10) How to Transfer Promissory Notes and Other Accounts Receivable................25
    (11) How to Transfer Receivables Connected With Real Property...........................26
    (12) How to Transfer a Sole Proprietorship Business..27
    (13) How to Transfer Motor Vehicles, Motorcycles, Motor Homes,
         Trailers, Boats and Airplanes...27
    (14) How to Transfer Partnerships..28
    (15) How to Transfer Corporation Business Interests..28
    (16) How to Transfer Mutual Funds..28
    (17) How to Transfer Miscellaneous..28

    7.b. Acquiring Assets in the Living Trust After You Have
         Established the Living Trust..29

    7.c. Identifying the Trust for Taxes...29

    7.d. Protecting Trust Assets..29

    (1) Insuring the Trust Assets..29
    (2) Placing Trust Assets in a Safe Location...29
    7.e. Administering the Trust..29
    7.f. Record-Keeping..30
    7.g. Segregation of Trust Property 30
    7.h. Tax Returns 30
    7.i. Common Mistakes With a Living Trust..30

    Summary...31

8. How To Amend Your Living Trust..32

    8.a. Adding a Paragraph...32
    8.b. Deleting Paragraphs 32
    8.c. Changing The Wording of a Paragraph..32
    8.d. Other Considerations when making an Amendment 33

9. How To Change Trustees Of Your Living Trust..34

_____ TRUST

DATED: _____

Creation and Intention of Trust and Identification of Parties

Effective Date:	County and State Where Trust is Located:
Grantor (Name, Address, and Zip Code):	Primary Trustee (Name, Address, and Zip Code):

Part One

1.1 Trust Property. Concurrently with the execution of this trust, Grantor has conveyed and delivered to Trustee the property described in a schedule of trust assets, and Trustee hereby acknowledges receipt of that property and agrees to hold and dispose of that property and all additions thereto and income therefrom IN TRUST upon the terms and conditions hereinafter set forth. Additional property from time to time may be transferred to Trustee with Trustee's consent by Grantor or by any other person, estate or trust. Any such additional property shall become a part of the trust property and shall be held, managed, invested, reinvested and disposed of on the same terms and conditions as hereinafter provided.

1.2 Identification of Beneficiaries. The names of beneficiaries of this trust, other than the Grantors who have lifetime rights, are:

Name of Beneficiary	Relationship	Per Stirpes (PS) or Per Capita (PC)
a.		
b.		
c.		
d.		
e.		
f.		
g.		
h.		
i.		
j.		

Per Stirpes indicates that Grantor intends that the Beneficiaries' children and other issue receive the Beneficiaries' share on death. Per Capita indicates that Grantor intends that No One except the named beneficiary receive that share on beneficiaries' death.

Where Grantor has indicated a Beneficiary is "Treated like a child", that beneficiary shall receive all distributions, benefits, and considerations that are designated for a child in this trust

1.3   **Designation of Successor Trustees.** The successor trustees are as follows:

The last named successor trustee may designate their successor by mailing a written nomination declaration to that effect to the then income beneficiaries and cotrustee, if any, for the trust.

1.4 **Designation of Advisers.** Until notified in writing to the contrary, the following professionals shall have the responsibility for advising Trustee in the professional area hereinafter designated:

1.4.a Legal Adviser. The last attorney from whom Grantor sought legal advice.

1.4.b Accounting Adviser. The latest accountant whose services have been engaged by Grantor for maintenance of all books of account, preparation of tax reports and returns, and all other accounting matters.

1.4.c Insurance Adviser. The latest life insurance underwriter through whom Grantor has purchased life insurance.

1.4.d Investment Adviser. The latest stockbroker or other investment adviser from whom Grantor has purchased stocks, bonds or other investments.

Trustee is not mandatorily required to follow the advice of these advisers.

1.5 **Trust Objectives.** Grantor intends, by establishing this trust, to have, among other things:

1.5.a A receptacle during the lifetime of Grantor in which, if desired, to deposit assets for management by Trustee.

1.5.b A receptacle for estate planning in the event of the death of Grantor.

1.5.c A trust arrangement within the trust to provide for separate trusts to benefit each child or person designated as a child of Grantor in the event of Grantor's death.

1.5.d A binding legal document to distribute property of Grantor to named individuals or charities promptly on the death of both Grantors without probate court involvement.

1.7 **Broad Investment Directions to Trustee.** Trustee shall have broad investment discretion as set forth hereinafter in the trust.

1.8 **Statement of Wishes.** Grantor provides Trustee with this precatory Statement of Wishes o guide Trustee and reserves the right from time to time for Grantor to give additional written Statements of Wishes to be used as non-mandatory suggestions and guidelines for Trustee:

1.8.a With respect to any distributions to any of the beneficiaries of this trust, Grantor desires that Trustee not exercise distributions to beneficiaries when there is reason to believe they are not working or are unproductive in order to receive benefits from this trust.

1.8.b Grantor does not wish this trust to provide benefits to a beneficiary who is living riotously or irresponsibly; benefits of this trust shall be suspended until such time as the beneficiary changes direction and pursues a responsible lifestyle, either through employment or continued education.

1.8.c At Trustee's discretion, small amounts may be advanced to assist and encourage beneficiaries in business enterprises, educational endeavors, and the purchase of residences and household goods.

1.8.d If I have filled out LawForms' "Statements of Wishes" as part of my Last Will and Testament, I incorporate those into this trust.

1.9 **Minimum Limitation on Separate Trusts' Size.** Irrespective of the other provisions of this trust, if at any time after the death of Grantor the trust estate or any of the separate trusts created hereunder be of the aggregate principal market value of $50,000 or less, any trust may be terminated in the sole discretion of Trustee and distributed to the income beneficiary or beneficiaries in proportion to their income interests; or, if such interests are indefinite, then to the income beneficiaries in such equitable proportions as Trustee shall determine.

1.10 **Trust Name.** This trust shall, for convenience, be known as by the name set forth in the title of this trust, and it shall be sufficient that it be referred to as such in any deed, assignment, bequest or devise.

1.11 **Interpretation.** Inasmuch as the continued welfare of Grantor is of primary and paramount concern, Trustee is directed to liberally construe all provisions of this trust in favor of Grantor, and if there is any doubt or conflict of interest, the rights and interests of Grantor shall be dealt with by Trustee as primary and paramount to the rights and interests of all other beneficiaries.

1.12 **Life Insurance.** Grantor has delivered or may deliver to Trustee certain life insurance policies owned by Grantor and has caused or may cause the Trustee to be designated as beneficiary of them. Those policies, any other policies that may be delivered to Trustee and of which Trustee may be designated as beneficiary, the proceeds of all such policies payable to Trustee, and any other property that may be received by Trustee, shall be held and disposed of as provided herein.

1.13 **Place of Constructive Notice of Trust Revocation, Amendment or Trustee Succession.** The parties to this living revocable trust specifically designate this offical governmental document recording office: _____, as the location where title companies and others may check to ascertain if this trust has been revoked or amended in any material respect to change the Trustees or Successor Trustees or the powers originally granted to the Trustees. A signed Certificate of Trustees' Powers and Abstract of Trust contains certain terms of this trust shall be filed or recorded with that public office as notice of the existence of this trust, its Grantor, Trustees, beneficiaries, powers of the Trustees, and other relevant terms. All parties dealing with this trust may rely on the abstract, amended abstracts, and other documents filed or recorded with that public office in ascertaining the status of this trust and may assume, if there are no official filings or recordings to the contrary, that no material changes have been made to the trust since the last filing or recording.

1.14 **Incorporation of Last Will and Testament.** This trust incorporates by reference the Last Will and Testaments of Grantors, which provides if a Revocable Living Trust, of which he and she is a Grantor, is in existence at the time of his or her death, all the residue of his or her estate and property, wherever situated, including lapsed legacies and devises, but expressly excluding any property over which he or she may have a power of appointment, is devised to the then Trustee under that trust agreement. It is intended by the Grantor of this trust that this is the trust into which the Last Will and Testament pours over as provided for in that Will.

1.15 **Protection Against Dissipation of Trust.** Under no circumstances shall any beneficiary of this trust who is addicted to alcohol, drugs, or other chemical dependencies receive any distributions from this trust in principal or interest directly from Trustee. If Trustee suspects that any beneficiary has any addiction to gambling, alcohol, drugs or other chemical dependency, Trustee shall require periodic tests, no more frequently than monthly, of the beneficiary to insure that the beneficiary is not taking these substances. Trustee shall, upon discovering that these substances are being taken, require periodic checks of the beneficiary for a period of one year before any distributions are made to that beneficiary. Trustee may require at the time the principal distributions are due to any beneficiary that the beneficiary take a test at an accredited laboratory selected by Trustee as a prerequisite for receiving a principal distribution.

Upon discovery of any addiction or dependency, the Trustee may make payments to hospitals, doctors, or other persons or organizations treating or assisting the beneficiary to recover from the addiction or dependency.

The purpose of this provision is to dissuade any beneficiary of this trust from gambling or using harmful substances which are addictive, to assist the beneficiary in recovery from any such addiction or dependency, and to prevent the trust funds, as much as possible, from ever being used to support an addiction or dependency that is harmful to the beneficiary.

Prior to receiving any distributions from this trust, a beneficiary must sign an affidavit that the beneficiary has not smoked or chewed tobacco for longer than twelve months after the effective date of this trust. If a beneficiary of this trust smokes tobacco for longer than one year, then and in that event Trustee shall reduce any distributions to that beneficiary by ten percent and distribute that ten percent pro rata to contingent beneficiaries as if that beneficiary had predeceased the distribution. The purpose of this provision is to recognize that persons who are addicted to tobacco are less likely to live as long as other beneficiaries and will not require the funds as much as the non-smoking beneficiaries, who are statistically projected to live longer, will need.

Grantor shall notify beneficiaries of these provisions forthwith and shall offer any encouragement or assistance the beneficiaries request to avoid losing any benefits from this trust in the future.

■ ■ ■

Part Two
Dispositive Provisions
Lifetime Trust

2.1 Disposition of Income and Principal. Subject to the provisions of paragraph 2.2 (in capacity of Grantor), during the lifetime of Grantor, Trustee shall dispose of the net income and principal of this trust as Grantor may direct Trustee from time to time by a written instrument signed by Grantor and delivered to Trustee.

2.2 Incapacity of Grantor. If, in the opinion of Trustee, Grantor becomes incapacitated through illness, age or other cause, the Trustee may, in Trustee's uncontrolled discretion, from time to time while trustee believes such incapacity continues, apply all or any part of the net income or principal of this trust for the benefit of Grantor in such amount or amounts and in such manner as Trustee may determine without regard to the other means of Grantor.

2.3 Undistributed Net Income. Any net income of this trust which is not disposed of by the terms of the preceding paragraphs of this Part Two shall be added to the principal of the trust at the end of each year.

2.4 Need of Funds by Grantor or Beneficiaries. If, at any time, in the sole discretion of Trustee, Grantor or any child of Grantor, should for any reason be in need of funds for his or her proper care, maintenance, support or education, Trustee may pay to or apply for the benefit of any one or more of these persons any amount from the principal as Trustee may, from time to time, deem necessary or advisable.

Death of Grantor

2.5 Death of Grantor. After all Grantor's death, the trust shall be administered and distributed as follows:

2.5.a <u>Death and Tax Expense of Grantor</u>. Trustee may pay the expenses of the last illness, funeral and burial of Grantor, together with any inheritance, estate, or other death taxes that may, by reason of Grantor's death, be due upon or in connection with the entire trust estate, unless Trustee shall determine, in Trustee's sole discretion, that other provisions have been made for the payment of such expenses and taxes.

2.5.b <u>Special Distributions on Death of All Grantors</u>. If any residence and/or personal property described in the Last Will and Testament of Grantor have been transferred to the trust, then it is the Grantor's intent and the Trustee is instructed to distribute the residence and/or personal property as set forth in the Will or in any codicils to that Will in the LawForms Tangible Personal Property List included with the Will, or in other documents that are incorporated by reference. Further, the following special distributions shall be made on the death of Grantors.

Name of Beneficiary	Money or Property Distributed and Quantity or Percent	Per Stirpes (PS) or Per Capita (PC)
a. _____	_____	_____
b. _____	_____	_____
c. _____	_____	_____
d. _____	_____	_____
e. _____	_____	_____
f. _____	_____	_____
g. _____	_____	_____
h. _____	_____	_____
i. _____	_____	_____
j. _____	_____	_____

If Grantors have previously or subsequently filled out a Tangible Personal Property Inventory Form or other personal property list authorized by Grantors' Wills as part of Grantors' Wills, these are incorporated by reference as additional special distributions.

If any of the above-named beneficiaries with "per stirpes" designated after his/her name, predeceases this special distribution without issue, then this special distribution shall lapse and the sum or property that deceased beneficiary would have received shall be distributed along with other trust assets in accordance with the subsequent provisions of this Part Two.

If any of the above-named beneficiaries who is not designated as "per capita" predeceases this special distribution with issue, such issue shall receive this special distribution per stirpes. If such issue is under the age of 18, then the share allotted to that minor descendant shall be distributed to a trust established for this minor descendant or, if none, to the legal guardian of such minor descendant upon the Trustee receiving bona fide evidence of Letters of Guardianship issued by a court of law.

Children's Trusts

2.6 **Division of Trust.** Trustee shall divide the remaining trust estate into as many equal as may be necessary to apportion one share for each child of Grantor then living, and one share for the then living descendants collectively of each deceased child of Grantor. Trustee shall obtain a separate tax identification number for each trust share and, except as provided elsewhere in this trust document, treat each trust share as a separate tax entity in accordance with proper accounting rules and procedures.

2.6.a <u>Childrens' Shares</u>. The shares for children or persons treated as children shall be: ☐ Equal ☐ As follows:

2.6.b <u>Interim Distributions of Income and Principal from Children's Separate Trusts</u>. Each share apportioned to a child of Grantor shall be held as a separate trust for such child, during which time Trustee shall pay to or apply for the benefit of such child so much of the net income and principal of such share as Trustee, in Trustee's discretion, shall deem necessary or advisable, considering the best interest of the child, for his or her care, maintenance, support and education. Any net income of this trust in any year which is not disposed of by the terms of the preceding paragraphs of this section shall be added to the principal of the trust at the end of each year. After such child attains the age of 21, the Trustee shall pay to or apply for the benefit of such child the entire net income earned from the assets of that trust.

2.6.c <u>Final Distribution of Principal to the Children</u>. Principal shall be distributed to the children as follows:

2.6.d <u>Distribution on Death of Child</u>. Each share apportioned in accordance with paragraph 2.6 (Division of Trust) to a child of Grantor shall on the death of that child be distributed to the living descendants of the deceased child of Grantor and shall be held or distributed in accordance with paragraph 2.7 (Distribution for Grandchildren).

2.6.e <u>No Special Power of Appointment to Children Beneficiaries</u>. No child of Grantor, from and after the date of Grantor's death, shall have the power to appoint by deed or by will the whole or any part of the principal of the trust.

2.6.f <u>Death and Tax Expense of Beneficiary</u>. Upon the death of any beneficiary provided for in paragraph 2.6 (Division of Trust), Trustee shall pay from the share of that beneficiary his or her expenses of last illness, funeral and burial, together with any inheritance, estate or other death taxes that may by reason of such death be due upon or in connection with the share of such beneficiary, unless Trustee determines, in Trustee's sole discretion, that other provisions have been made for the payment of such expenses and taxes.

2.6.g <u>Disclaimer</u>. Any child of Grantor may disclaim, in whole or in part, any property that is to become or has become the vested interest of such child, before such property is distributed to the child. Such disclaimer shall be in writing under any method recognized at law. The property subject to the disclaimer shall then be held or distributed in accordance with paragraph 2.6.d (Distribution on Death of Child). A written signed copy of the disclaimer shall be mailed or delivered to the Trustee.

Grandchildren Trusts

2.7 **Distribution for Grandchildren.** Upon the death of Grantor and upon the disclaimer or death of a child of Grantor, the portion that such child would have received but for his or her death or disclaimer shall be held, administered and distributed by Trustee as follows:

2.7.a <u>Division of Trust</u>. The share that such child would have received but for death or disclaimer shall be divided by Trustee into as many equal shares as may be necessary to apportion one share for each then living child of such child, and one share for the then living descendants collectively of each deceased child of such child to be distributed by right of representation.

2.7.b <u>Interim Distributions of Income and Principal from Grandchild's Separate Trust</u>. Each share apportioned to a grandchild of Grantor shall be held as a separate trust for such grandchild, during which time Trustee shall pay to or apply for the benefit of such grandchild so much of the net income and principal of such share as Trustee, in Trustee's discretion, shall deem necessary or advisable, considering the best interest of the grandchild, for his or her care, maintenance, support and education. Any net income of this trust in any year which is not disposed of by the terms of the preceding paragraphs of this section shall be added to the principal of the trust at the end of each year. After such grandchild attains the age of 21, the Trustee shall pay to or apply for the benefit of such grandchild the entire net income earned from the assets of that trust.

2.7.c <u>Final Distribution of Principal to Grandchildren</u>. Principal shall be distributed to the grandchildren as follows:

2.7.d **Distribution on Death of Grandchild**. If, after the allocation of trust shares in accordance with paragraph 2.7.a, there occurs the death of any grandchild, Trustee shall distribute his or her trust share, as then constituted, to or in trust for the benefit of such person or persons among Grantor's descendants and their spouses, upon such conditions and estates, with such powers, in such manner, and at such time or times as the grandchild appoints and directs by will specifically referring to this special power of appointment. To the extent a deceased grandchild does not effectively exercise his or her power of appointment, his or her share shall be distributed outright to his or her living descendants by right of representation or, if there are none, then to Grantor's then living descendants by right of representation; except that the share distributable to any beneficiary, in default of appointment, may, in Trustee's absolute discretion, be added to in whole or in part and commingled with another trust which primarily benefits that beneficiary and held as if it had been an original part of that other trust.

If any share becomes distributable to any person under the age of 21 years, his or her share shall vest in him or her, but distribution shall be postponed until after he or she attains the age of 21 years. During such time as any beneficiary is under the age of 21 years, Trustee may pay to or for the benefit of such beneficiary so much of the income and principal of the retained share as Trustee may deem necessary or advisable for his or her proper care, maintenance, support and education. Trustee shall add to the principal any undistributed income. If such beneficiary dies before the age of 21, that beneficiary's share shall be paid to his or her estate.

2.7.e. **Death and Tax Expenses of Beneficiary**. Upon the death of any beneficiary provided for in paragraph 2.7.a (division of trust) Trustee shall pay from the share of that beneficiary his or her expenses of last illness, funeral and burial, together with any inheritance, estate or other death taxes that may by reason of such death be due upon or in connection with the share of such beneficiary, unless Trustee determines, in Trustee's sole discretion, that other provisions have been made for the payment of such expenses and taxes.

2.7.f **Separate Trusts for Tax Purposes**. If property becomes administered under this section of this trust agreement for the benefit of a grandchild or grandchildren of Grantor, then the share set aside for each respective grandchild shall be treated as a separate tax-paying trust and entity and administered as a separate tax-paying entity, if this be possible under the revenue laws at the time the trust is administered.

2.7.g **Disclaimer by Grandchild**. Any grandchild of Grantor may disclaim, in whole or in part, any property that is to or has become the vested interest of such grandchild, before such property is distributed to the grandchild. Such disclaimer shall be in writing under any method recognized at law. The property subject to the disclaimer shall then be held or distributed in accordance with paragraph 2.7.d (Distribution on Death of Grandchild). A written signed copy of the disclaimer shall be mailed or delivered to the Trustee.

Contingent Distribution

2.8 **Contingent Distribution.** If all descendants of Grantor predecease the termination of this trust, so that no beneficiary remains to take under the foregoing provisions, then, upon the death of the last surviving beneficiary, the trust shall terminate and be distributed to:

☐ The heirs at law of Grantor in accordance with the laws of succession of the State of _____ as they exist at the time of executing this trust.

☐ To the following named contingent distributees, in the percentages indicated

Name of Beneficiary	**Mailing Address**	**Percent**
a. _____	_____	_____
b. _____	_____	_____
c. _____	_____	_____
d. _____	_____	_____
e. _____	_____	_____
f. _____	_____	_____
g. _____	_____	_____
h. _____	_____	_____
i. _____	_____	_____
j. _____	_____	_____

If one of the above named contingent distributees or their issue predeceases, then that distributee's share shall be allocated to the others pro rata.

If any of the above-named beneficiaries with "per stirpes" designated after his/her name, predeceases this special distribution without issue, then this special distribution shall lapse and the sum or property that deceased beneficiary would have received shall be distributed along with other trust assets in accordance with the subsequent provisions of this Part Two.

If any of the above-named beneficiaries who is not designated as "per capita" predeceases this special distribution with issue, such issue shall receive this special distribution per stirpes. If such issue is under the age of 18, then the share allotted to that minor descendant shall be distributed to a trust established for this minor descendant or, if none, to the legal guardian of such minor descendant upon the Trustee receiving bona fide evidence of Letters of Guardianship issued by a court of law.

2.9.a **Contingent Charities.** However, in the event there are no descendants of Grantor closer in consanguinity than the issue of a common grandparent, or no other contingent distributees remain alive to receive distributions, and in the further event there are state laws applicable to this trust in any state which provide that the property of the trust will escheat to the state because of there being heirs at law of insufficient closeness to qualify for succession, then, if both these conditions occur at the time of distribution, Grantor directs that the remaining assets of the trust be given to the following charities:

Name of Beneficiary	Mailing Address (if known)	%
a.		
b.		
c.		
d.		
e.		
f.		
g.		
h.		
i.		
j.		

Part Three
General Provisions

3.1 **Income Payment Dates.** Income payments which Trustee hereunder is required to make to a beneficiary of the trust shall be made in convenient installments not less frequently than quarterly.

3.2 **Spendthrift Provision.** The interest of a beneficiary in the income or principal of the trust hereunder shall be free from the control or interference of any creditor of the beneficiary or of the spouse of the beneficiary and shall not be subject to attachment, execution, or other process of law or susceptible to anticipation, alienation or assignment, whether voluntarily or involuntarily encumbered, except in those cases where Trustee, in Trustee's sole discretion, approves the credit extended and the assignment of the beneficiary's interest hereunder as collateral therefor. In exercising such discretion, Trustee shall ascertain whether or not it would appear to be in the best interest of the beneficiary that credit be accepted and collateral given. This provision includes obligations to pay alimony or support by any beneficiary or spouse of a married beneficiary. Nothing contained in this paragraph shall be construed as restricting in any way the exercise of any powers or discretions granted hereunder.

3.3 **Incapacitated Beneficiary.** The whole or any part of the income or principal payable to a beneficiary hereunder who is incapacitated through illness, age or other cause may be applied by Trustee for such beneficiary's support and maintenance. Any such application may be made at such time and in such manner as Trustee deems advisable, whether by direct payment of such beneficiary's expenses or by payment to a person selected by Trustee to receive payment for such beneficiary; in each case, the receipt of the person to whom payment is made or entrusted shall be a complete discharge of Trustee with respect thereof. Whenever any payment is required to be made to a minor beneficiary, the interest so required to be paid shall be indefeasibly vested in the minor, but Trustee may retain the amount payable until the minor attains his majority or dies, whichever first occurs, and Trustee may pay the income and principal to the minor in such amount or amounts and from time to time as Trustee may determine, and if the minor lives to attain his majority, Trustee shall pay the then remaining principal and undistributed income to him, and if the minor dies before attaining his majority, then on the minor's death, Trustee shall pay the then remaining principal and undistributed income in accordance with the provisions of Part Two.

3.4 **Cost of Living Increases.** Should the retail cost of living index change, as evidenced by the Consumer Price Index (CPI), as published by the Bureau of Labor Statistics of the United States Department of Labor, then any amounts set forth in this trust as fixed amounts shall be increased or decreased, on an annual basis, by Trustee in the same proportion as the changes in the CPI for the 12-month period following the first month of payment or last CPI adjustment, whichever is applicable. This paragraph shall not apply to any sum which sets limitations in amounts for tax purposes.

If at the time required for the determination of the cost of living adjustment, the CPI is no longer published or issued, Trustee may use such other index as is then generally recognized and accepted for similar determinations of purchasing power fluctuations.

3.5 **Settlement of Disputes.** Any dispute arising out of or in connection with this trust, including disputes between Trustee and any beneficiary or among Co-Trustees, shall be settled by the negotiation, mediation and arbitration provisions of the LawForms Integrity Agreement (Uniform Agreement Establishing Procedures for Settling Disputes). Any decision rendered either in accordance with the LawForms Integrity Agreement (Uniform Agreement Establishing Procedures for Settling Disputes) shall be binding upon the parties as if the decision had been rendered by a court having proper jurisdiction.

In any dispute arising out of this trust, the losing party shall pay to the prevailing party reasonable costs and expenses incurred in connection with any suit or arbitration as determined by the court or arbitrator, including attorneys' fees, court costs and the value of time lost by the prevailing party or any agent or employee of the prevailing party in participating in any arbitration or litigation in connection herewith. This provision shall be binding upon Trustee and any beneficiary who seeks to enforce rights or privileges under this trust.

This provision shall not be interpreted to allow an assessment of attorneys' fees against a disinterested Trustee who acted in good faith. It shall, however, be interpreted to permit the assessment of attorneys' fees against the share of any Trustee who is also a beneficiary, or the share of any beneficiary. The purpose of this clause is to discourage persons with frivolous disputes by putting them on notice that the losing party shall bear these expenses.

3.6 **Governing Law.** Each trust hereunder is a revocable trust, made in that state, and its validity is to be determined, interpreted and construed according to the laws of the effective county and state of execution. Administration of the trust and investments shall be governed by the law of the situs where it is administered.

3.7 **Certified Copies of This Instrument.** To the same effect as if it were the original, anyone may rely upon a copy certified by a notary public to be a true copy of this trust agreement or an abstract of this trust agreement (and of the writings, if any, endorsed thereon or attached thereto). Anyone may rely upon any statement of fact certified by anyone who appears from the original document or a certified copy thereof to be a Trustee hereunder.

3.8 **Notices of Event.** Until Trustee shall receive written notice of any birth, marriage, death or other event, or the existence of any document upon which the right to payments from the trust estate may depend, Trustee shall incur no liability for disbursements made in good faith to persons whose interests may have been affected by that event.

3.9 **Rule Against Perpetuities.** Irrespective of other provisions of this trust, no trust created hereby shall continue for more than 21 years after the death of the last survivor of the Grantor and beneficiaries and such descendants of Grantor and beneficiaries as are in being at the date this trust becomes irrevocable, and if at the expiration of this period any property is still held in trust hereunder, such property shall immediately be distributed to these persons as are then entitled to receive income therefrom, in the same proportion which the income such persons are receiving shall bear to the entire income of the trust.

3.10 **Merger of Trusts.** If at any time Trustee is holding any trust under this instrument for the primary benefit of any person or persons for whose primary benefit Trustee is holding any other trust, upon substantially the same terms, created by Grantor under this or any other instrument or by any member of Grantor's family, Trustee may, in Trustee's discretion, consolidate and commingle them and hold them as a single trust. Trustee shall allot to each separate trust an undivided interest in the mingled funds that shall always be equal to that trust's proportionate contribution (as adjusted from time to time as a result of accumulations of income, payments or principal and additions to principal) to the mingled funds.

3.11 **Creation of New Trusts.** Trustee shall have the power to create a new trust for any beneficiary with terms and conditions which carry out the intent and purposes of this trust and which protect the well-being of that beneficiary. This provision shall be liberally construed, and the exercise of this power shall be left to the absolute discretion of Trustee. The attorney advising Trustee shall be responsible for reviewing the new trust into which distributions from this trust shall pour over or for drafting the new trust with the necessary provisions.

This clause is a recognition that the challenges of the future for each beneficiary cannot be predicted in advance and that, therefore, wide flexibility must be given to Trustee to meet a myriad of future conditions.

3.12 **Persons Dealing with Trustee.** No person dealing with, making payments to, or delivering property to Trustee hereunder needs to inquire into the validity of anything Trustee purports to do, or needs to see to the application of any money paid or any property transferred to, or upon the order of, Trustee.

3.13 **Gifts During Lifetime.** Unless Grantor expresses in writing to the contrary at the time of a gift, gifts of real or personal property, tangible or intangible, if any, which Grantor may make during Grantor's lifetime, before or after the execution of this trust, to any person, shall not be deemed to be an advancement or a satisfaction to be applied to any share of any beneficiary of this trust, and shall not be taken into account in connection with this trust, except as provided for elsewhere in this trust.

3.14 **Separate and Combined Character of Property.** It is very probable, from time to time, that either separate, tenants in common, tenants by the entirety or community property will be placed in this trust. The Trustee is instructed to correctly identify the property as it is placed in the trust and to maintain the character of the property as either community or separate as long as it remains in the trust. Under no circumstances shall Trustee commingle any community property with separate property. Trustee shall keep books of account, so that the community and separate property can be clearly identifiable upon inspection of the trust at any time.

3.15 **Establishment of Incapacity.** In establishing the incapacity of Grantor or a beneficiary of this trust agreement, the statements of three independent licensed Doctors of Medicine shall be sufficient to establish such incapacity or inability to act or to continue to act hereunder, and Trustee, any Successor Trustee and third parties shall be protected in relying upon such statements without any further act or notice.

Part Four
Definitions

4.1 **Beneficiary.** Unless otherwise expressly identified herein, wherever reference is made herein to a beneficiary, such reference shall be deemed to mean a person to whom the Trustee of a separate trust is then directed or authorized to distribute net income or principal or both from the trust estate of such trust, and wherever the facts and context require such construction, the term beneficiary shall be deemed to mean the plural form thereof.

4.1.a <u>Primary Beneficiaries</u>. Primary Beneficiaries are those persons named as beneficiaries to first receive the income or principal distributions.

4.1.b <u>Successor Beneficiaries</u>. Successor Beneficiaries are those beneficiaries who receive income or principal only on the death or disqualification of Primary Beneficiaries.

4.1.c <u>Adult Income Beneficiaries</u>. Adult Income Beneficiaries are those beneficiaries who are 18 years of age or over, are not incapacitated, and to whom Trustee is then directed or authorized to pay income.

4.2 **By Right of Representation.** The term by right of representation denotes that method of dividing an estate by which an equal share is given to all those persons of a class who are related in the same degree to the decedent. For instance, where the deceased has a son with one son (who is a grandson to the deceased) and a daughter with three daughters (who are the granddaughters to the deceased) and the will provides that the deceased's descendants shall share by right of representation and both children predecease the decedent, then each grandchild shall receive an equal one-fourth share of the estate.

4.3 **Child, Children and Issue.** References in this trust to child or children mean lawful blood descendants in the first degree of the parent designated, and references to issue mean lawful blood descendants in the first, second or any other degree of the ancestor designated, provided always, however, that:

4.3.a <u>Child in Gestation</u>. A child in gestation who is later born alive shall be regarded in this instrument as a child in being during the period of gestation in determining whether any person has died without leaving surviving issue, and in determining, on the termination of any trust hereunder, whether such child is entitled to share in the disposition of the then remaining principal and undistributed income of such trust, but for other purposes, such child's rights shall accrue from the date of birth.

4.4 **Descendants.** Except where distribution is directed to the descendants per stirpes of a person, the term descendants includes descendants of every degree, whenever born, whether or not a parent or more remote ancestor of such descendant is living. Where distribution is directed to any person's descendants per stirpes who are living at a designated point of time, the stirpes shall begin with the children of such person, whether or not any child of that person is then living.

4.5 **Education.** The term education shall include all forms of education, including but not limited to public or private schools, primary or secondary, college, advanced college or postcollege, professional, commercial, technical, business, language or artistic studies, or otherwise.

4.6 **Grantor.** In this trust, the term Grantor shall refer to the person designated above in the block titled Grantor.

4.7 **Gross Estate.** The terms gross estate and taxable estate refer to the amounts described by these terms in the Internal Revenue Code in force from time to time.

4.8 **Heirs-at-Law.** As used herein, the term heirs-at-law means those persons other than creditors who would receive the personal property of the person designated under the laws of the state named in the place designated in the heading of this trust, as if said person had died intestate on the date stipulated for distribution, unmarried and domiciled in that state, and in such shares as if that person had owned only the property constituting the trust estate of the trust to be distributed among such heirs-at-law.

4.9 **Issue Designated as Objects of Power to Appoint.** Whenever any person is given hereunder a power to appoint to designated issue, an appointment may be made to issue of the second or more remote degree even though an appointment is also made, or could be made to the parent of such issue.

4.10 **Per Capita.** The term per capita denotes that method of dividing an estate by which an equal share is given to each of a number of persons, all of whom stand in equal degree to the decedent, without reference to their stocks or the right of representation. The term means literally by the head. For instance, where the deceased has a son with one son (who is a grandson to the deceased) and a daughter with three daughters (who are granddaughters to the deceased) and the will provides that the deceased's children shall share per capita and both children predecease the decedent, then the grandchildren receive nothing and the estate passes under the residuary clauses of the trust or will.

4.11 **Per Stirpes.** The term per stirpes denotes that method of dividing an estate where a class or group of distributees take the share to which a deceased would have been entitled, taking thus by their right of representing such ancestor, and not as so many individuals. The term means literally by the branch. For instance, where the deceased has a son with one son (who is a grandson to the deceased) and a daughter with three daughters (who are granddaughters to the deceased) and the will provides that the deceased's children shall share equally per stirpes and both children predecease the decedent, then the grandson shall receive one-half of the estate (the share his father would have received) and the three granddaughters shall share the other one-half (one-sixth each) which their mother would have received.

4.12 **Personal Representative.** Personal Representative includes executor and administrator.

4.13 **Persons.** The term persons includes corporations.

4.14 **Reference to Male Gender.** Reference hereunder to the male gender shall be deemed to include the female and neuter genders, unless otherwise stated or unless the circumstances eliminate such inclusion.

4.15 **Renunciation or Disclaimers.** Any person who is a beneficiary or who is otherwise interested in any separate trust may at any time renounce the whole, or from time to time, any part of an interest in such trust, either as to income or principal or both, by an instrument in writing delivered to Trustee, and thereafter such trust or the part of such trust which shall have been renounced shall be administered and distributed as if such person had died on the date of delivery of the written instrument, and as if such person had not exercised any testamentary power of appointment granted to that person; provided, however, that such renunciation shall not, unless specifically so provided, affect the right of such person to receive subsequent distributions of principal or income from the trust estate of any separate trust upon the death of any other person, upon the renunciation by any other person of any interest in any separate trust or pursuant to the exercise of any power of appointment by any other person.

4.16 **Spouse or Spouses.** References in this instrument to spouse or spouses mean the person or persons who answer such description, on the assumption that all decrees of divorce rendered by a court of record, wherever located, are valid. Furthermore, the decision of the Trustee made in good faith as to whether a person is the described spouse or whether the persons are the described spouses shall be conclusive for all purposes.

4.17 **Support.** The support of a beneficiary shall include his support and maintenance in reasonable comfort, medical care (including but not limited to dental and psychiatric care) and education. Distributions for the support of a beneficiary shall be based upon the standard of living to which such beneficiary shall have been accustomed during the five-year period immediately preceding any such distribution, but shall be made only if and to the extent that the other income and resources known to Trustee to be available to such beneficiary for such purpose (including the income and resources of any person legally obligated to support such beneficiary) are inadequate.

4.18 **Trust Estate.** As used herein, the term trust estate shall include all property received initially by Trustee with respect to any separate trust, all additions thereto received by Trustee from any other source, all investments and reinvestments of such property or such additions thereto and all accrued and undistributed income of such trust.

4.19 **Trustee.** References in this instrument to Trustee shall be deemed to include not only the original Trustee or Co-Trustees but also any additional or Successor Trustee or Co-Trustees, and all the powers and discretions vested in Trustee shall be vested and exercisable by any such additional or Successor Trustee or Co-Trustees.

4.20 **Will.** Will includes last will and testament and codicils.

■■■

Part Five
Trustee's Powers

5.1 **Tax Returns.** Trustee shall have the power to file estate, gift, and income tax returns on behalf of a deceased person having any interest in this trust.

5.2 **Trustee Powers.** In the investment, administration, and distribution of the trust estate and the several shares thereof, the Trustee (subject only to the duty to apply the proceeds and avails of the trust property to the purposes therein specified) may perform every act in the management of the trust estate which individuals may perform in the management of like property owned by them free of trust, and it may exercise every power with respect to each item of property in the trust estate, real or personal, which individuals owners of like property can exercise, including, by way of illustration but not by way of limitation, the following powers:

5.2.a <u>To Have Rights</u>. To have, with respect to all trust property, all the rights, powers and privileges of an owner, including the power to give proxies, pay assessments, abandon stock, or to expend any sums deemed by Trustee to be necessary for the protection of the trust estate, and to participate in voting trusts, pooling agreements, foreclosures, reorganizations, consolidations, mergers and liquidations, and to participate in and deposit securities with any creditors, bondholders, stockholders or other protective committees.

5.2.b <u>To Apportion Principal and Income</u>. To determine what is principal and what is income and to allocate receipts and expenses between them as Trustee shall in good faith determine to be in accordance with the laws of the State of the effective place of this trust or such other laws as shall from time to time exist; provided, however, that notwithstanding any such laws, all dividends payable in shares of a corporation other than the declaring corporation and all capital gains distributions of any investment trust should inure to the principal.

5.2.c <u>To Add Net Income</u>. To add the portion of the net income of this trust in excess of net income distributed to principal and reinvest such amounts at the end of the taxable year of this trust.

5.2.d <u>To Purchase Insurance</u>. To carry insurance against such risks and for such amounts and upon such terms as Trustee deems necessary and for the protection of Trustee or any beneficiary of the trust estate, and to purchase policies of insurance on the life of any beneficiary of any trust, or on the life of any other person in whom any trust may have an insurable interest, and to continue in effect or to terminate any life insurance policy which may be owned or held by any trust; and to pay (from income or principal) any premiums or other charges, and to exercise any and all rights or incidents of ownership in connection therewith.

5.2.e <u>To Pay Costs</u>. To pay all costs, charges and expenses of the trust estate and pay or compromise all taxes pertaining to the administration of the trust estate which may be assessed against it or against Trustee on account of the trust estate or the income thereof, together with a reasonable compensation to Trustee for Trustee's services hereunder, including services in the matter of whole or partial distribution of the trust estate.

5.2.f <u>To Deal Between</u>. To sell or purchase assets from any trust or estate in which the beneficiary of the trust established by Grantor may be interested, including sales by the trust hereby established to any other one of the trusts hereby established; to deal in every way and without limitation or restriction with the personal representative, Trustee or other representative of any trust or estate in which any beneficiary hereunder has any existing or future interest, even though Trustee is acting in such other capacity, without liability for loss or depreciation resulting from such transactions; to purchase from, sell to, or otherwise deal with any corporation, association, partnership or firm with which any of them may be affiliated, or in which any of them may in any other way be interested, as freely as Trustee might or could deal with an independent third party, and without any greater responsibility, all rules or provisions of law to the contrary being hereby expressly waived.

5.2.g <u>To Determine Value</u>. To determine the market value of any investment of the trust estate for any purpose on the basis of such quotations or information as Trustee may deem pertinent and reliable without any limitation whatsoever; to distribute in cash or in kind upon partial or final distribution.

5.2.h <u>To Hold Property</u>. To retain, without liability for loss or depreciation resulting from such retention, original property, real or personal, received by Trustee from Grantor's estate, including but not limited to stock and securities of Trustee, for such time as to Trustee shall seem advisable; although such property may not be of the character prescribed by law or by the terms of this instrument for the investment of other trust assets, and although it represents a large percentage or all of the trust estate, that original property may accordingly be held as a permanent investment.

5.2.i **To Insure and Change**. To insure, improve, repair, alter and partition real estate, erect or raze improvements, grant easements, subdivide, or dedicate property to public use.

5.2.j **To Develop**. To develop, improve, lease, partition, abandon, subdivide, dedicate as parks, streets and alleys, and grant easements and rights-of-way with respect to any real property or improvements of this trust, and to improve, construct, repair, alter, reconstruct, or demolish any such improvements, and to lease for any periods, all or any part of the trust estate upon such terms and conditions and for such considerations as Trustee may deem advisable. Any lease may be made for such period of time as Trustee may deem proper, without regard to the duration of the trust or any statutory restriction on leasing and without the approval of any court.

5.2.k **To Sell**. To sell, lease, pledge, mortgage, transfer, exchange, convert or otherwise dispose of, or grant options with respect to, any and all property at any time forming a part of the trust estate, in such manner, at such time or times, for such purposes, for such prices and upon such terms, credits and conditions as Trustee deems advisable. Any lease made by Trustee may extend beyond the period fixed by statute for leases made by fiduciaries and beyond the duration of the trust.

5.2.l **To Lease**. To lease property upon any terms or conditions and for any term of years although extending beyond the period of any trust hereunder, including week to week, month to month, and year to year rentals.

5.2.m **To Purchase Special Properties**. To purchase or otherwise acquire, and to retain, whether originally a part of the trust estate or subsequently acquired, any and all stocks, bonds, notes or other securities, or any variety of real or personal property, including stocks or interests in investment trusts and common trust funds, as Trustee may deem advisable, whether or not such investments be of the character permissible for investments by fiduciaries, or be unsecured, unproductive, underproductive, overproductive, or of a wasting nature. Investments need not be diversified and may be made or retained with a view to a possible increase in value. Trustee may at any time render liquid the trust estates, in whole or in part, and hold cash or readily marketable securities of little or no yield for such period as Trustee may deem advisable.

5.2.n **To Settle**. To complete, extend, modify or renew any loans, notes, bonds, mortgages, contracts or any other obligations which the trust estate may owe or be a party to or which may be liens or charges against any property of the trust estate, although the trust estate may not be liable thereon, in such manner as Trustee may deem advisable; to pay, compromise, compound, adjust, submit to arbitration, sell or release any claims or demands of the trust estates against others or of others against the trust estates as Trustee may deem advisable, including the acceptance of deeds of real property in satisfaction of bonds and mortgages, and to make any payments in connection therewith which Trustee may deem advisable.

5.2.o **To Hold Partnership Interests**. To act as a general partner or as a limited partner in any general or limited partnership, in the same manner that an individual could act in such capacity.

5.2.p **To Operate Business**. To operate and manage, at the sole risk of the trust estate and not at the risk of Trustee, any property or business received in trust, as long as Trustee may deem advisable; Trustee is authorized to incorporate any unincorporated business received hereunder and to accept beneficial employment with or from any business in which the trust estate may be interested, whether by way of stock ownership or otherwise, and even though the interests of the trust estate in the business shall constitute a majority interest therein, or the complete ownership thereof; and to receive appropriate compensation from such business for such employment.

5.2.q **To Dissolve Corporations**. To enter into an agreement making the trust estate liable for a pro-rata share of the liabilities of any corporation which is being dissolved, and in which stock is held, when, in Trustee's opinion, such action is in the best interests of the trust estate.

5.2.r **To Borrow**. To borrow money for any purpose connected with the protection, preservation or improvement of the trust estate whenever in Trustee's judgment this action is deemed advisable, and as security to mortgage or pledge any real estate or personal property forming a part of the trust estate upon such terms and conditions as Trustee may deem advisable. Money may be borrowed from the banking department of the corporate Trustee.

5.2.s **To Invest**. To invest and reinvest the trust estate, both principal and income if accumulated, in any property or undivided interests therein, wherever located, including bonds, notes (secured and unsecured), stock of corporations (including stock of Trustee corporation), real estate (or any interest therein), and interests in trusts, including common trust funds, without being limited by any statute or rule of law concerning investments of trustees, and to hold on deposit or to deposit any funds in one or more banks, including Trustee bank, in any form of account whether or not interest-bearing; to cause any of the investments which may be delivered to or acquired by Trustee to be registered in Trustee's name or in the name of a nominee; any corporation or its transfer agent may presume conclusively that such nominee is the actual owner of any investment submitted for transfer; to retain any investment received in exchange in any reorganization or recapitalization.

5.2.t **To Acquire Stock Rights.** To acquire stock and securities of the Trustee corporation by the exercise of rights to acquire stock and securities issued in connection with the stock of Trustee comprising a portion of the trust estate, including but not limited to the following: To vote in person or by general or limited proxy with respect to any shares of stock or other securities held by Trustee; to consent, directly or through a committee or other agent, to the reorganization, consolidation, merger, dissolution or liquidation of any corporation in which the trust estate may have any interest, or to the sale, lease, pledge or mortgage of any property by or to any such corporation; and to make any payments and to take any steps which Trustee may deem necessary or proper to enable Trustee to obtain the benefit of such transaction.

5.2.u **To Set Up Reserves.** To set up, out of the rents, profits or other income received, if any, reserves for taxes, assessments, insurance premiums, repayments of mortgage or other indebtedness, repairs, improvements, depreciation, obsolescence and general maintenance of buildings and other property, and for the equalization of payments to or for beneficiaries entitled to receive income, as Trustee shall deem advisable.

5.2.v **To Make Distribution.** To make any distribution or division of the trust property in cash or in kind, or both, and to allot different kinds or disproportionate shares of property or undivided interests in property among the beneficiaries or portions, and to determine the value of any such property; and to continue to exercise any powers and discretions herein given for a reasonable period after the termination of the trust, but only for so long as no rule of law relating to perpetuities would be violated.

5.2.w **To Buy on Margin.** To buy, sell and hypothecate securities on margin; to buy, sell and write "put and call" options; and to transact all types of securities transactions with a brokerage firm that are allowed under SEC regulations.

5.2.x **To Delegate Powers.** To delegate powers, discretionary or otherwise, for any purpose to one or more nominees or proxies with or without power of substitution; to make assignments to and deposits with committees, trustees, agents, depositories and other representatives; and to participate and retain any investment received in exchange in any reorganization or recapitalization.

5.2.y **To Employ Agents.** To employ agents, experts and counsel, investment or legal, even though they may be associates with, employed by, or counsel for Trustee or any beneficiary of the trust estate; and to make reasonable and proper payments to such agents, experts or counsel for services rendered.

5.2.z **To Keep Property in Name of Nominee.** To keep any property in the name of a nominee with or without disclosure of any fiduciary relationship.

5.2.aa **To Designate Signator on Bank Accounts.** To have the power to designate, as signator or joint signator on any trust bank account, any person Trustee desires to designate. This person shall act as agent for Trustee and may sign on the bank account, deposit funds in the bank account, or otherwise deal with the bank account.

5.2.bb **To Guarantee Debts.** To sign guarantees of loans and co-sign or endorse any type of loan document and thus obligate the trust assets for and on behalf of any individual, partnership, corporation, trust, or other type of participating interest or with which the trust is involved in some type of business relationship and to guarantee an indebtedness, co-sign or endorse an indebtedness for and on behalf of one of the named beneficiaries of the trust should Trustee deem it helpful to a beneficiary. This power supplements the power of Trustee to borrow. Grantor contemplates that many times in the business world, it is more advantageous for an individual or trust to make arrangements to guarantee a loan rather than directly borrowing the funds, and then lending the funds from the trust to the business ventures with which the trust may be associated, or from the trust to the beneficiary of the trust.

5.2.cc **To Transfer Situs.** To transfer the situs of the trust estate to some other place; and in so doing, to resign and appoint a substitute Trustee who may delegate any and all trustee powers to the appointing Trustee as agent, and to remove any substitute Trustee appointed pursuant to this paragraph at any time and appoint another, including the appointing Trustee.

5.2.dd **To Receive Additional Assets.** To receive additions to any trusts established under this agreement from any source, and to administer such additions according to the terms of this agreement.

5.2.ee **To Commence or Defend Litigation.** To commence or defend such litigation with respect to the trust or any property of the trust as Trustee may deem advisable, at the expense of the trust; and to compromise, abandon, or otherwise adjust any claims or litigation against or in favor of the trust.

5.2.ff **To Make Joint Investments.** To make joint investments for any two or more trusts hereunder.

5.2.gg **To Reorganize.** To unite with the owners of other securities in carrying out any plan for the reorganization of any corporation; to deposit securities in accordance with any such plan; and to pay any expenses which may be required with reference to any such plan.

5.2.hh **To Make Loans.** To make loans to any person, including any beneficiary, with adequate interest and adequate security.

5.2.ii **To Render Liquid.** To render liquid the trust estate or any trust created hereunder, in whole or in part at any time or from time to time, and hold cash or readily marketable securities of little or no yield for such period as Trustee may deem advisable.

5.2.jj **To Exploit Oil, Gas and Other Mineral Interests.** To drill, mine and otherwise operate for the development of oil, gas and other mineral interests; to enter into contracts relating to the installation and operation of absorption and repressuring plants; to enter into unitization or pooling agreements for any purpose including primary or secondary recovery; to place and maintain pipelines and telephone and telegraph lines; to execute oil, gas and mineral leases, division and transfer orders, grants and other instruments; and to perform such other acts as Trustee deems appropriate, using such methods as are commonly employed by owners of such interests in the community in which the interests are located.

5.2.kk **To Appoint Ancillary Trustee.** To appoint an individual or another corporation as Trustee if the Trustee is unable to act with respect to real and tangible personal property not located in the state of the trust's situs. The appointed Trustee (1) shall have all the powers of the appointing Trustee, to be exercised, however, only with the approval of the appointing Trustee, (2) shall not, unless required by law, make periodic judicial accountings, but shall furnish the appointing Trustee with semi-annual statements, and (3) may delegate any or all trust powers. The appointing Trustee is to require any Trustee so appointed to remit to the appointing Trustee the income and net proceeds of any sale of any property and the appointing Trustee may remove any Trustee appointed pursuant to this paragraph at any time and to appoint another, including the appointing Trustee.

5.3 **Discretionary Power to Purchase Property from Grantor's Estate.** Trustee is authorized to purchase at a fair price securities and other property, real or personal, belonging to the estate of Grantor, and to retain such purchased property as an investment of the trust.

5.4 **Discretionary Power to Make Loans to Grantor's Estate.** Trustee is authorized to make loans out of the trust property to the Grantor's executors, administrators or personal representatives, provided such loans are made on adequate security and for an adequate interest.

5.5 **Treasury Bonds to Pay Estate Tax.** During the lifetime of Grantor, Trustee is authorized to purchase and retain, as assets of the trust estate, United States of America Treasury Bonds which may be redeemed at par in payment of the federal estate tax which will be imposed upon Grantor's estate. Trustee is authorized to borrow funds for the purpose of purchasing such bonds, and is authorized to secure any such borrowing by pledge of the bonds so purchased, by pledge of any other trust assets, or by any other security arrangement which Trustee determines to be feasible. The discretion granted in this paragraph should be freely exercised, at any time or from time to time, when information is received making it appear that Grantor may be seriously ill, or that there may be a substantial and progressive deterioration in Grantor's state of health. In determining the amount of such bonds to purchase, consideration should be given to Grantor's view that it is better to overestimate the amount of such bonds that may ultimately be required than to purchase an inadequate amount of bonds.

If, upon the death of Grantor, the trust estate contains any such treasury bonds, Trustee shall submit for redemption so many of such bonds as may be required to pay in full the federal estate tax imposed by reason of Grantor's death, including additional assessments, penalties and interest, without regard to the apparent adequacy of the assets comprising Grantor's probate estate.

5.6 **"S" Corporation Stock Distribution.** Upon the death of Grantor whose "S" Corporation stock is included in the trust assets, Trustee shall have the power to immediately distribute, in Trustee's sole discretion, all "S" Corporation stock directly to the current trust beneficiaries, if this is necessary to avoid tax problems for the parties.

5.7 **Authority.** No person dealing with Trustee shall be obliged to inquire as to Trustee's powers or to see to the application of any money or property delivered to Trustee. Trustee shall not be required to obtain authority or approval of any court in the exercise of any power conferred hereunder. Trustee shall not be required to make any current reports or accountings to any court nor to furnish a bond for the proper performance of Trustee's duties hereunder. Trustee may execute and deliver any and all instruments in writing which Trustee may deem advisable to carry out any of the foregoing powers. No party to any such instrument in writing signed by Trustee shall be obliged to inquire into its validity, or be bound to see to the application by Trustee of any money or other property paid or delivered to Trustee pursuant to the terms of any such instrument.

5.8 **Additional Powers Given by Law.** The powers enumerated in this Part Five shall be construed as being in addition to any other authority given or conferred upon Trustee by law.

5.9 **Continuation of Powers.** After termination of any trust created herein until the same is finally distributed, Trustee shall have the authority to exercise all powers and authority including any discretionary powers.

5.10 **Successor Power to Successor to Business of Corporate Trustee.** Any successor to the business of the corporate Trustee, whether by reorganization or otherwise, shall succeed as Trustee with the like powers as though originally named as Trustee.

5.11 **Succession of Powers.** Each Successor Trustee under this agreement shall have, exercise, and enjoy all the rights, privileges and powers, both discretionary and ministerial, as are given and granted to the original Trustee, and shall incur all the duties and obligations imposed upon the original Trustee.

5.12 **Transfers to Trustee.** In the event that any beneficiary of this trust has created a trust for the management of his property, or if any minor or incompetent beneficiary has had a trust created for his protection, care, support or general welfare, then Trustee may, in his discretion, make the designated distributions under this trust to that beneficiary by transferring to the Trustee of that beneficiary's trust the share of that beneficiary, instead of distributing the share to the beneficiary directly. Should a beneficiary ask in writing that a share be distributed to a trust by disclaimer, special power of appointment, or otherwise, then such request shall be controlling on Trustee.

5.13 **Pour-Back.** Trustee shall have the express power at any time to pour back assets to the probate estate of Grantor if this is necessary or advantageous.

5.14 **Continuation of Gift Programs.** Trustee shall have the power and duty to continue gifting programs which Grantor may have begun, or to initiate gifting programs to issue of Grantor should Trustees, in their sole discretion, deem these gifts advantageous to the family of Grantor. All gifts shall be pre-approved by the attorney and accountant for the trust to insure that all tax laws are complied with.

5.15 **Power to Transfer Assets to Another Trust.** The Trustee may, in its absolute discretion, transfer all or some of the assets of the trust to another or other valid, legal trusts which provide substantially the same benefits for the same beneficiaries for purposes of convenience, consolidation, greater protection of the assets or for other reasons which Trustee, in its opinion, feels are in the best interest of the beneficiaries.

5.16 **To Make Tax Options, Elections and Allocations.** To make tax options, elections and allocations under any statute or rule of law as the Trustee deems prudent to minimize or eliminate taxes with respect to the combined estates of the Grantors (upon the death of the first Grantor to die) and with respect to the combined estates of the surviving Grantor, the deceased Grantor and any other beneficiary under this instrument (following the death of the surviving Grantor), and no adjustments shall be made with respect to the interests of the beneficiaries to compensate for the effect of the Trustee's tax options, elections and allocations.

■■■

Part Six
Trustee's Rights and Duties

6.1 **Trustee's Rights.** Trustee shall be entitled:

6.1.a <u>To Act Without Bond</u>. To act at any time and in any jurisdiction without bond or other security to ensure the faithful performance of Trustee's fiduciary duties. If a bond is required by law, no surety on such a bond is required.

6.1.b <u>To Rely on Documents</u>. To rely on any document or other paper if believed by Trustee to be genuine and to be signed and delivered by or on behalf of the proper person, firm or corporation, without incurring liability for any action or inaction based thereon.

6.1.c <u>To Use Best Judgment</u>. To use Trustee's best judgment in exercising the powers, discretions and rights conferred by this trust or in performing the duties imposed upon Trustee by law and, in order to feel free in doing so, to be exempt from liability for any action taken or omitted in good faith.

6.1.d <u>To Reimburse</u>. To reimburse Trustee from the trust estate for all reasonable expenses incurred in the administration thereof.

6.1.e <u>To Not Comply</u>. To not be required to comply with any instructions of Grantor which in Trustee's judgment may subject it to liability or expense, or defend any action, unless indemnified in a manner and amount satisfactory to Trustee.

6.1.f <u>To Petition Court for Accounting</u>. To petition at any time any appropriate court to have trust accountings judicially settled.

6.1.g <u>To Keep Property in Certain Place</u>. To keep any or all trust property at any place or places in the county where the Trustee resides or elsewhere within the United States or abroad or with a depository or custodian at such place or places.

6.2 **Jurisdiction of Probate Court.** Except for disputes to be settled under provision 3.5 (Settlement of Disputes) of this trust the Trustee or any beneficiaries or interested parties may seek the assistance of the probate court to have accountings judicially settled or otherwise clarified.

6.3 **Adequate Records.** Trustee shall be the custodian of the assets and funds constituting the trust estate; and shall be responsible for the maintenance of adequate records showing the condition of the trust estate and the income and expenses thereof, and for the preparation and filing of all required accounting, reports and tax returns. The records pertaining to any trust herein created shall be open at all reasonable times to inspection by Trustee, by any beneficiary of any trust, or by the representatives of any such person; and any such person shall have the right to demand annual accountings showing the administration of the trust.

6.4 **Separate and Combined.** Trustee may combine for investment purposes all or any part of the funds held in all or any of the trust estates, or may hold the funds of all such trust estates in a combined trust fund; but Trustee shall be responsible for the maintenance of full records showing the receipts and disbursements, and the funds held for the benefit of each separate and distinct trust estate, and showing the allocable proportion of any such combined trust fund which belongs to each such separate and distinct trust estate.

6.5 **Compensation to Trustee.** The compensation of the Trustee shall be a reasonable amount as is customary for trustees of corporate fiduciaries in the county and state where the trust is administered.

6.6 **Keep Informed.** The Trustee shall use its best efforts to keep informed of called bonds, subscription rights, reorganizations and other matters of similar nature which may affect the securities on deposit, and upon receipt of any notice in connection therewith, Trustee shall forward the same to Grantor. Proxies, circulars, financial statements and similar material are not to be so forwarded unless, in the judgment of Trustee, the matter is of unusual importance and should be brought to the attention of Grantor to aid Grantor in investment judgment.

6.7 **Consider Current Beneficiaries.** Trustee is directed to regard the income beneficiary or beneficiaries at any given time as having primary rights under this agreement, and Trustee is directed to consider only the welfare of income beneficiaries in the exercise of discretionary powers and to disregard the interests of any successor beneficiaries. Any discretionary right to use principal shall include the right to exhaust principal for such purpose. No beneficiary shall have any right to compel Trustee to make any discretionary payment or expenditure or question the propriety of any discretionary payment or expenditure made by Trustee. Any discretionary determination made by Trustee shall be final as to all beneficiaries.

6.8 **Current Fair Market Value.** Trustee shall, when dividing or distributing any trust fund, make such divisions or distributions wholly or partly in kind by allotting and transferring specific securities or other personal or real property or undivided interests therein as a part or the whole of any one or more shares or payments at current fair market values.

■■■

Part Seven
Rendition of Accounts

7.1 **During Grantor's Lifetime.** During the lifetime of Grantor, Trustee shall render a copy of an account of income and principal to Grantor whenever requested to do so by Grantor or any income beneficiary. The Grantor's written approval of this account shall, as to all matters and transactions covered by the account, be binding upon all who are then or who may thereafter become entitled to the income or principal. Failure to disapprove an account within 10 days of the mailing of the account shall be deemed to be approval.

7.2 **Mandatory Pay-Out of Income.** After the death of Grantor, with respect to each separate trust under which the income is required to be paid out, Trustee shall render annually an account of income and principal to the person or persons to whom the income of the trust is required to be paid, or to the guardian or guardians of such person or persons. The written approval of such person (or his guardian) or such persons (or their guardians) shall as to all matters and transactions covered by that account, be binding upon all who then are or who may thereafter become entitled to the income or principal, provided always, however, that nothing contained in this paragraph shall be deemed to give such person (or his guardian) or such persons (or their guardians), acting in conjunction with Trustee, the power to amend or revoke such trust.

7.3 **Discretionary Pay-Out of Income.** After the death of Grantor, with respect to any separate trust under which the income may be paid out or accumulated in the discretion of the Disinterested Trustee, Trustee shall render annually an account of income and principal to the oldest person to whom such income could be paid, or to such person's guardian. The written approval of such person (or such person's guardian) shall as to all matters and transactions covered by that account be binding upon all who are then or who may thereafter become entitled to the income or principal, provided always, however, that nothing contained in this paragraph shall be deemed to give such person (or such person's guardian), acting in conjunction with Trustee, the power to amend or revoke such trust.

7.4 **Payments.** All payments of income or principal shall be made to the respective beneficiaries in person or upon their personal receipts, or may at their discretion be deposited in any bank to the credit of such beneficiary in any account carried in the beneficiary's name or jointly with another or others. Payments or distributions to an incompetent beneficiary may nevertheless be made by Trustee for the benefit of such beneficiary in such of the following ways as in Trustee's opinion will be most desirable:

a. directly to such beneficiary;

b. to beneficiary's legal representative;

c. to some near relative or friend; or

d. by Trustee using such payments directly for the benefit of such beneficiary.

A beneficiary shall be determined to be incompetent in the same manner as prescribed in Part Eight for determining a Trustee to be incompetent or if a beneficiary is a minor or under legal disability declared by a court of competent jurisdiction, or if a beneficiary shall be incapacitated so as to make it impossible or impracticable for such person to give prompt and intelligent consideration to business matters. Trustee may act upon such evidence of the competency or incompetency of any person as Trustee shall deem appropriate and reliable without liability by reason thereof.

■■■

Part Eight
Resignation and Removal of Trustee and Appointment of Successor Trustee

8.1 **Resignation of Trustee.** Trustee may resign by giving 30 days written notice to Grantor during Grantor's lifetime, or after Grantor's death, to each of the adult income beneficiaries.

8.2 **Removal of Trustee.** Trustee may be removed at any time during the life of Grantor by written notice to Trustee. After Grantor's death, Trustee may be removed at any time by all adult income beneficiaries then entitled to benefits under this trust or, if there are no adult income beneficiaries, a majority of the legally appointed guardians of the other beneficiaries who are then currently entitled to benefits under this trust, by written notice to Trustee. Until the accounts of Trustee are settled and Trustee discharged, Trustee shall continue to have all the powers and discretions granted to Trustee hereunder or conferred by law, except as limited by provisions of this document so limiting the Trustee.

8.3 **Appointment of Successor Trustee.** Except as may be otherwise provided in Part One, in case of resignation or removal of Trustee, the Grantor or, after the death of Grantor, all adult income beneficiaries or, if there are no adult income beneficiaries, a majority of the legally appointed guardians of the other beneficiaries who are then currently entitled to benefits under this trust, may, by instrument signed and acknowledged, appoint a Successor Trustee. If a Successor Trustee is not appointed within 30 days after the giving of notice of resignation or removal, Trustee may apply to a court of competent jurisdiction for the appointment of a successor. Trustee shall be entitled to reimbursement from the trust estate for all expenses incurred in connection with the settlement of Trustee's accounts and the transfer and delivery of the trust estate to Successor Trustee. If Trustee is removed, Trustee shall be entitled to full compensation as if the trust had terminated while Trustee was still acting. If Trustee resigns, Trustee shall be entitled to retain the compensations theretofore taken and to take any compensations then accrued but unpaid. In no event may Grantor appoint himself as Successor Trustee.

8.4 **Powers of Successor Trustee.** Successor Trustee, upon executing an acknowledgment acceptance to the trusteeship and upon the settlement of the accounts and discharge of the prior Trustee, shall be vested, without further act on the part of anyone, with all the estate, title, powers, duties, immunities and discretions granted to the predecessor Trustee. The prior Trustee shall, however, execute and deliver such assignments or other instruments as shall be deemed advisable.

8.5 **Transfer of Trust.** If a majority of the beneficiaries of this trust move to another city, then Trustee, upon written request signed by these beneficiaries, shall transfer this trust to a Successor Trustee, which shall be a corporate Trustee in the banking or financial field of comparable size and stature, located in the state where the majority of the beneficiaries reside. Trustee shall make the selection of the Successor Trustee and, having exercised such discretion to nominate the Successor Trustee, shall have no further liability by reason of this selection, after the assets of this trust have been transferred to that Successor Trustee and after Successor Trustee has accepted the assets and the terms of the trust.

8.6 **Incapacity of Trustee.** If Trustee or any Successor Trustee has become unable to discharge his duties as Trustee of this trust by reason of accident, physical or mental illness, progressive or intermittent physical or mental deterioration or other similar cause, as certified by three independent licensed physicians affirming that each has examined Trustee and that each has concluded, based upon such examination, that Trustee is unable to discharge his duties as Trustee, then, in that event, Trustee shall thereupon cease to be Trustee in the same manner as if he had resigned on the date that the third certificate from the disinterested physician is attached to an Affidavit of Succession signed by Successor Trustee and recorded with the County Recorder where Trustee resides. Successor Trustee shall deliver a true copy of that Affidavit of Succession, with the attached certificates, to Trustee forthwith after recordation of the original. The independent physicians shall be selected one by the spouse or oldest child of Trustee, and the other two by the other Trustees or Successor Trustees and the president of the Medical Association in the county where Trustee resides. Should the spouse or child not be available, then the disinterested doctor shall be selected by one of the income beneficiaries. If none of these persons is available, then all shall be selected by the other Trustees and the president of the Medical Association of the county in which Trustee resides. The standard that shall be used in determining incapacity for purposes of succession is the same as that defined for the appointment of a conservator under the present laws of the state in which Trustee resides.

8.7 **Notice of Incapacity.** To give proof of the incapacity of the incompetent Trustee, in order for the other or Successor Trustee to act on behalf of the trust, the latter must mail, by certified mail, return receipt requested, or by direct delivery, a copy of the Affidavit of Succession to the incompetent Trustee. The purpose of this provision is to permit the Successor Trustee to act on behalf of the incompetent Trustee without the necessity of the Successor Trustee filing court proceedings.

8.8 **Restriction on Liability of Successor Trustee.** No Successor Trustee shall be liable for the acts or defaults of any predecessor Trustee, nor for any loss or expense from anything done or neglected to be done by any predecessor Trustee, but such Successor Trustee shall be liable only for his own willful wrongdoing or gross negligence with respect to property received by him as Trustee. Any Successor Trustee who shall be then acting as Trustee pursuant to a notice of vacancy shall not be guilty of any wrongdoing merely because he is acting as Successor Trustee if it shall later be discovered that another has been designated as Successor Trustee pursuant to any provisions herein.

8.9 **Criminal Charges, Convictions or Bankruptcy of Trustee.** Should any Trustee be convicted of a felony or file bankruptcy, Trustee shall be deemed immediately terminated as Trustee as of that date. Should a Trustee be subjected to a charge of committing a felony or to the filing of an involuntary bankruptcy, then all his powers as a Trustee shall be suspended until the determination of the proceedings.

Part Nine
Co-Trustees - Effect Upon Operation

9.1 **Operation of Trust.** If there is more than one Trustee, the following provisions shall be controlling and take precedence over any other provisions relating to Trustee:

9.1.a <u>Definition</u>. The use of the term Trustee or Co-Trustee shall be used interchangeably throughout this agreement and shall mean, for all purposes, the duly authorized Trustees under this trust.

9.1.b <u>Corporate Trustees Unable to Act</u>. If any corporate Trustee at any time resigns or is unable or refuses to act, another corporation, authorized under the laws of the United States or of any state to administer trusts, may be appointed as Trustee by an instrument delivered to it and signed by the beneficiaries, at the time of appointment.

9.1.c <u>Acts of Trustees</u>. If there are two Trustees, both must consent and act to bind the trust. If there are three or more Trustees, approval of a majority of the Trustees shall be necessary to constitute the act of the trust.

9.1.d <u>Power of Attorney</u>. Any one Co-Trustee may give another Co-Trustee of this trust or anyone else a general or special power of attorney to act for him as Trustee under this trust. The use of such a power of attorney shall not relieve either Trustee of his liability for breach of any fiduciary duties.

9.2 **Delegation of Powers.** A Trustee hereunder may, by an instrument in writing, delegate all or any of his powers and discretions to a Co-Trustee.

9.3 **Acts of Co-Trustees.** If there are two or more Co-Trustees, one Co-Trustee shall not be responsible for the acts or omissions of another Co-Trustee or for allowing another Co-Trustee to have custody or control of the funds, securities or property. Each Trustee shall be responsible for his own acts or omissions in bad faith.

9.4 **Other Conflicts of Interest.** Trustees shall disclose to the other Trustees any conflict of interest they may have with respect to any act. The other Trustees shall seek legal counsel and if the Trustees after seeking legal counsel decide there is a conflict of interest, then the Trustee with the conflict shall not vote on that decision. Whenever a Trustee disqualifies himself for a vote or is disqualified by the other Trustees for a vote, a written memorandum of this decision to disqualify and the reasons for it shall be written and placed in the files of the trust.

9.5 **One Trustee Authority to Sign Insurance Applications and Tax Documents.** If any insurance is purchased by the Trustees of this trust, any one of them may sign life, property and casualty or other insurance applications and other paperwork necessary to purchase and process the policies. The reason for this special authority to any one of the Trustees is that sometimes speed is necessary in obtaining insurance coverages and damages may be caused to the trust by the unnecessary delays of finding one Trustee. Any one of the Trustees may sign tax applications, returns and other tax and governmental forms and paperwork that may be required from time to time.

Part Ten
Insurance Provisions

10.1 **Insurance as Trust Res.** Insurance policies may be the subject property of this trust, and Grantor may cause Trustee to be designated as beneficiary of certain policies of insurance on the life of Grantor, listed in Schedule A or another schedule of assets for the trust attached hereto, which policies may remain in the custody of Grantor or may be deposited with Trustee for safekeeping. Grantor and Trustee hereby agree that such policies and the proceeds therefrom, together with any other property which Grantor may hereafter add or cause to be made payable to this trust, and the investments and reinvestments thereof shall be managed, controlled and disposed of for the uses and purposes and upon the terms and conditions as provided herein.

10.2 **Power in Grantor with Respect to Insurance.** Grantor reserves the right, by Grantor's act alone, without the consent or approval of Trustee, to sell, assign or hypothecate any policies of insurance upon the life of Grantor made payable to Trustee hereunder, to exercise any option or privilege granted by such policies, including, but without limitation of the generality of the foregoing, the right to change the beneficiary of such policies, and to receive all payments, dividends, surrender values, benefits or privileges of any kind which may accrue on account of such policies during Grantor's lifetime. Furthermore, Trustee agrees to deliver to Grantor, on Grantor's written request, any of such policies deposited with Trustee hereunder.

When the ownership of life insurance policies has been transferred to the trust, then Trustee shall have all rights in the life insurance policies that are given to the owner of each policy, except as to any restrictions on those rights, if any, as may be set forth in the document effectuating the transfer of ownership. One of the reasons for transferring ownership of life insurance policies to this trust shall be to allow Trustee to exercise the rights of the owner under those policies during the period of time when Grantor may be incapacitated and cannot act for himself in exercising rights under the policies.

10.3 **Duties of Trustee with Respect to Insurance.** Trustee shall use Trustee's best efforts to collect the proceeds of any policies of insurance upon the life of Grantor which are made payable to Trustee hereunder when any of such policies shall, to the knowledge of Trustee, have matured, but shall not be required to take legal proceedings until indemnified to Trustee's satisfaction against all expenses and liabilities to which Trustee might be subjected. Any release of Trustee to any insurance company shall fully and completely discharge it for any payment so made and shall be binding upon every beneficiary under this trust agreement. Trustee shall have no responsibility with respect to any policies for payment of premiums, payment of assessments, or otherwise, except to hold any policies received by Trustee in safekeeping.

10.4 **Designation of Trust as Beneficiary of Disability and Salary Continuation Policies.** It is contemplated that from time to time this trust may be designated as the beneficiary of disability or salary continuation policies which provide for income to the named insured while the named insured is incapacitated or disabled as defined in the policies. The reason for designating the trust as the beneficiary of these policies is to allow a receptacle for the administration of these funds, should the disabled Grantor be unable to manage the funds because of incapacity or disability.

10.5 **Notice to Insurance Company.** No insurance company shall be required to inquire into or take notice of any of the provisions of this trust agreement or to see to the application or disposition of the proceeds of such policies.

■■■

Part Eleven
Power to Amend or Revoke

11.1 **Power in Grantor During Lifetime of Grantor.** In addition to any powers reserved to the Grantor elsewhere in this trust, Grantor reserves the right at any time or times to amend or revoke this instrument and the trusts hereunder, in whole or in part, by an instrument or instruments in writing, signed by Grantor and delivered in Grantor's lifetime to Trustee. If one of two Co-Grantors dies, then the surviving Co-Grantor shall not have power to amend or revoke this trust.

11.2 **Power in Grantor by Last Will and Testament.** Grantor reserves the right to amend or revoke this instrument and the trusts hereunder, in whole or in part, by a will which specifically refers to this instrument and specifically directs what amendments are to be made or states that the instrument is revoked. If this instrument is revoked in its entirety by a will of Grantor, Trustee shall deliver to Grantor's estate, or as his will may direct, all the trust property.

11.3 **Correlation of Grantor's Last Will and This Instrument.** Grantor's will may provide for additions to the trust property hereunder, and consequently Grantor's will should be examined in connection with the making of any amendment or revocation of this instrument or of the trusts hereunder to determine what changes, if any, should be made in Grantor' will in the light of such amendment or revocation.

Part Twelve
Optional Provisions

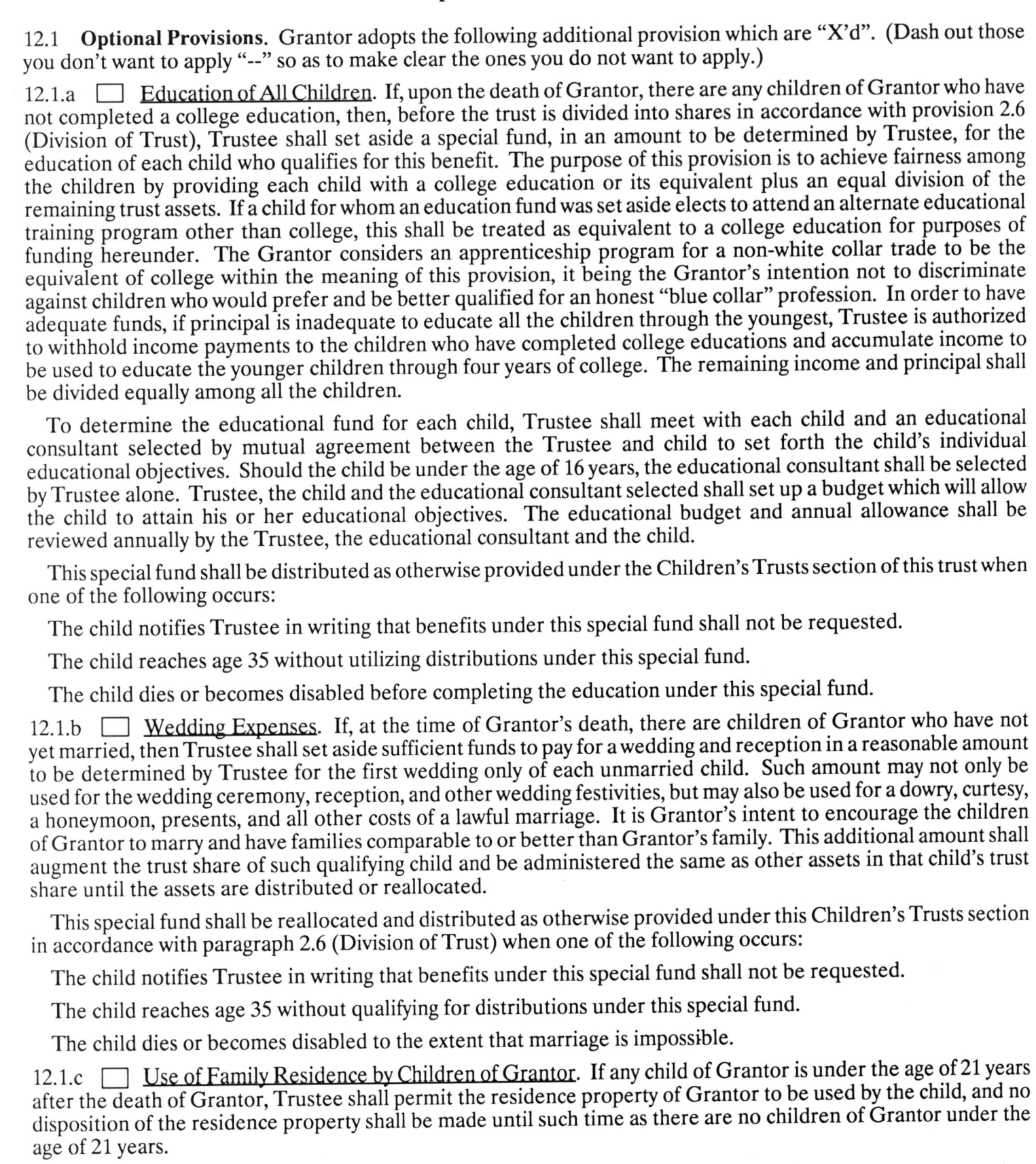

12.1 Optional Provisions. Grantor adopts the following additional provision which are "X'd". (Dash out those you don't want to apply "--" so as to make clear the ones you do not want to apply.)

12.1.a ☐ <u>Education of All Children</u>. If, upon the death of Grantor, there are any children of Grantor who have not completed a college education, then, before the trust is divided into shares in accordance with provision 2.6 (Division of Trust), Trustee shall set aside a special fund, in an amount to be determined by Trustee, for the education of each child who qualifies for this benefit. The purpose of this provision is to achieve fairness among the children by providing each child with a college education or its equivalent plus an equal division of the remaining trust assets. If a child for whom an education fund was set aside elects to attend an alternate educational training program other than college, this shall be treated as equivalent to a college education for purposes of funding hereunder. The Grantor considers an apprenticeship program for a non-white collar trade to be the equivalent of college within the meaning of this provision, it being the Grantor's intention not to discriminate against children who would prefer and be better qualified for an honest "blue collar" profession. In order to have adequate funds, if principal is inadequate to educate all the children through the youngest, Trustee is authorized to withhold income payments to the children who have completed college educations and accumulate income to be used to educate the younger children through four years of college. The remaining income and principal shall be divided equally among all the children.

To determine the educational fund for each child, Trustee shall meet with each child and an educational consultant selected by mutual agreement between the Trustee and child to set forth the child's individual educational objectives. Should the child be under the age of 16 years, the educational consultant shall be selected by Trustee alone. Trustee, the child and the educational consultant selected shall set up a budget which will allow the child to attain his or her educational objectives. The educational budget and annual allowance shall be reviewed annually by the Trustee, the educational consultant and the child.

This special fund shall be distributed as otherwise provided under the Children's Trusts section of this trust when one of the following occurs:

The child notifies Trustee in writing that benefits under this special fund shall not be requested.

The child reaches age 35 without utilizing distributions under this special fund.

The child dies or becomes disabled before completing the education under this special fund.

12.1.b ☐ <u>Wedding Expenses</u>. If, at the time of Grantor's death, there are children of Grantor who have not yet married, then Trustee shall set aside sufficient funds to pay for a wedding and reception in a reasonable amount to be determined by Trustee for the first wedding only of each unmarried child. Such amount may not only be used for the wedding ceremony, reception, and other wedding festivities, but may also be used for a dowry, curtesy, a honeymoon, presents, and all other costs of a lawful marriage. It is Grantor's intent to encourage the children of Grantor to marry and have families comparable to or better than Grantor's family. This additional amount shall augment the trust share of such qualifying child and be administered the same as other assets in that child's trust share until the assets are distributed or reallocated.

This special fund shall be reallocated and distributed as otherwise provided under this Children's Trusts section in accordance with paragraph 2.6 (Division of Trust) when one of the following occurs:

The child notifies Trustee in writing that benefits under this special fund shall not be requested.

The child reaches age 35 without qualifying for distributions under this special fund.

The child dies or becomes disabled to the extent that marriage is impossible.

12.1.c ☐ <u>Use of Family Residence by Children of Grantor</u>. If any child of Grantor is under the age of 21 years after the death of Grantor, Trustee shall permit the residence property of Grantor to be used by the child, and no disposition of the residence property shall be made until such time as there are no children of Grantor under the age of 21 years.

12.1.d ☐ Use of Family Residence by Guardian. If Grantor dies leaving a child or children under the age of 18, then, in that event, Grantor specifically directs that the guardian of Grantor's minor child or children be allowed to reside in Grantor's home rent-free for as long as the guardian serves in this capacity.

12.1.e ☐ Incentives to Children or Grandchildren. Grantors give the following special or earlier distributions to Grantors' children or grandchildren if they perform the following acts or satisfy the following conditions:

12.1.f ☐ Disincentives to Children or Grandchildren. Grantors limit, take away or penalize children or grandchildren if they do the following acts or fail to satisfy the following conditions:

12.1.g ☐ Other Additional Provisions as Follows:

■■■

Part Thirteen
Execution and Certification

13.1 **Effective Date.** This legal instrument has been executed by the parties intending that it be effective on the effective date set forth on the caption page. The parties recognize that they effectuated a meeting of the minds among themselves on that effective date and intended that this instrument take effect on that date even though, because of the exigencies of the modern world, the mechanics of drafting, the convenience of the parties, and the economy of travel, it may have been necessary to actually sign the document at a later time.

13.2 **Effective Place of Execution.** The parties intend that the place of execution be that county and state that is set forth in the caption of this instrument. The effective place of execution is the place that the parties intend this instrument to have been executed incorporating all laws, for purposes of conflicts of laws, which apply to that effective place of execution. The parties recognize that, due to the exigencies of the modern world, the mechanics of drafting, the convenience of the parties, and the economy of travel, this instrument may be executed by one or all the parties at some other geographic location and possibly at multiple places. However, in spite of this, they intend that it be deemed executed at the effective place of execution.

13.3 **Interlineations and Initials.** The parties recognize that because of the exigencies of the modern world, the mechanics of drafting, the convenience of the parties, and the economy of costs, they may have in their own handwriting made minor changes in this instrument. These minor changes have been initialed by all the parties, if any changes have been made, fore and aft of the change on all originals to prevent any extension or alteration of that change by any of the parties or others. Unless otherwise indicated by the placement of a date beside the change, these changes were intended by the parties to have occurred as of the effective date of this instrument. Any interlineated changes made by the parties after the effective date of this instrument shall be initialed by all parties, dated and have the date itself initialed fore and aft by all parties to this instrument.

13.4 **Execution.** All parties named in the caption as parties shall sign below and at least one of the parties shall initial all pages of all original copies of this instrument. Furthermore, all documents such as schedules, exhibits and like documents which are expressly incorporated herein shall be initialed by the parties and either exchanged or attached to the originals which are given to any party named on the caption page of this instrument. It is the intent of the parties that all pages be initialed on all originals that are exchanged in order that no substituted pages or misunderstanding shall ever become possible to create problems in satisfying the intended objectives of this instrument.

13.5 **Acknowledgment.** The Notary Publics who have acknowledged the signatures of the various parties as designated in the acknowledgments hereof certify that this instrument was acknowledged by the signing party before the notary on the date of the notarization. If the instrument was subscribed by any of the parties in a representative capacity, then the notary ascertained that the signing party signed for the principal named and in the capacity in which that party indicated he signed.

* * *

IN WITNESS WHEREOF, the parties execute this legal instrument intending that it be effective on the Effective Date and at the Effective Place of Execution.

....

....
Signature of Grantor   Signature of Trustee

The foregoing trust was at the date thereof by the named Grantor signed, sealed, published and declared to be a trust which incorporates the Last Will and Testament of the Grantor and serves as a receptacle to receive the pour over of assets. This trust was signed in the presence of us who, at the request and in the presence of Grantor and in the presence of each other, have signed the same as witnesses thereto.

....   _____
Signature of Witness   Address of Witness

....   _____
Signature of Witness   Address of Witness

....   _____
Signature of Witness   Address of Witness

STATE OF _____)
) ss.
County of _____)

    On this day, _____, before me, the undersigned Notary Public, personally appeared the above-subscribed Grantor, Trustee and witnesses, respectively, known to me or satisfactorily proven to be the persons whose names are subscribed to the foregoing instrument, who being first duly sworn, did hereby declare to the undersigned Notary Public that the Grantor and Trustee signed and executed the instrument with the formality of a Last Will and that Grantor and Trustee executed it as their free and voluntary act for the purposes therein expressed, and that each of the witnesses, in the presence of the Grantor and Trustee, signed the trust as witnesses and that to the best of their knowledge, the Grantor and Trustee were at the time 18 or more years of age, of sound mind, and under no constraint or undue influence; and this trust was subscribed, sworn to and acknowledged before me on the date hereinabove written.

_____   ....
Notary Expiration Date   Signature of Notary

This instrument was recorded at request of:

The recording official is directed to return this instrument or a copy to the above person.

Space Reserved For Recording Information

Certificate of Trustee's Power and Abstract of Trust of the

_____
TR-2 © LawForms 6-90

Effective Date:	County and State where Trust is Located:
Grantor (Name, Address and Zip Code):	Primary Trustee (Name, Address and Zip Code):

    The following provisions are found in that certain trust agreement named and described above, by and between the above-designated Grantor and Trustee, and may be relied upon as a full statement of the matters covered by such provisions by anyone dealing with Trustee or any successor Trustee. However, in the unlikely event there is a clerical error causing a discrepancy between the original trust and this certificate and abstract of the trust, the original trust document will control the interpretation and administration of the trust.

    Names and Addresses of Beneficiaries. In compliance with applicable state and federal statutes, we disclose only the names and addresses of the beneficiaries of this trust, other than the Grantors, who have a lifetime beneficial interest, as follows:

Name of Beneficiary   **Mailing Address and Zip Code**

a. _____   _____

b. _____   _____

c. _____   _____

d. _____   _____

e. _____   _____

f. _____   _____

g. _____   _____

h. _____   _____

i. _____   _____

j. _____   _____

1.1 **Trust Property**. Concurrently with the execution of this trust, Grantor has conveyed and delivered to Trustee the property described in a schedule of trust assets, and Trustee hereby acknowledges receipt of that property and agrees to hold and dispose of that property and all additions thereto and income therefrom IN TRUST upon the terms and conditions hereinafter set forth. Additional property from time to time may be transferred to Trustee with Trustee's consent by Grantor or by any other person, estate or trust. Any such additional property shall become a part of the trust property and shall be held, managed, invested, reinvested and disposed of on the same terms and conditions as hereinafter provided.

1.3 **Designation of Successor Trustees**. The Successor Trustees of the trust are as follows:

1.13 **Place of Constructive Notice of Trust Revocation, Amendment or Trustee Succession.** The parties to this trust designate this governmental office: _____, as the location where title companies and others may check to ascertain if this trust has been revoked or amended in any material respect to change the Trustees or Successor Trustees or the powers originally granted to the Trustees. A signed abstract of certain terms of this trust shall be filed or recorded with that public office as notice of the existence of this trust, its Grantor, Trustee, beneficiaries, powers of the Trustee, and other relevant terms. All parties dealing with this trust may rely on the abstract, amended abstracts, and other documents filed or recorded with that public office in ascertaining the status of this trust and may assume, if there are no official filings or recordings to the contrary, that no material changes have been made to the trust since the last filing or recording.

4.19 **Trustee.** References in this instrument to Trustee shall be deemed to include not only the original Trustee or Co-Trustees but also any additional or Successor Trustee or Co-Trustees, and all the powers and discretions vested in Trustee shall be vested and exercisable by any such additional or Successor Trustee or Co-Trustees.

5.2 **Trustee Powers.** In the investment, administration, and distribution of the trust estate and the several shares thereof, the Trustee (subject only to the duty to apply the proceeds and avails of the trust property to the purposes therein specified) may perform every act in the management of the trust estate which individuals may perform in the management of like property owned by them free of trust, and it may exercise every power with respect to each item of property in the trust estate, real or personal, which individual owners of like property can exercise, including, by way of illustration but not by way of limitation, the following powers:

    5.2.a <u>To Have Rights</u>. To have, with respect to all trust property, all the rights, powers and privileges of an owner, including the power to give proxies, pay assessments, abandon stock, or to expend any sums deemed by Trustee to be necessary for the protection of the trust estate, and to participate in voting trusts, pooling agreements, foreclosures, reorganizations, consolidations, mergers and liquidations, and to participate in and deposit securities with any creditors, bondholders, stockholders or other protective committees.

    5.2.b <u>To Apportion Principal and Income</u>. To determine what is principal and what is income and to allocate receipts and expenses between them as Trustee shall in good faith determine to be in accordance with the laws of the State of the effective of this trust or such other laws as shall from time to time exist; provided, however, that notwithstanding any such laws, all dividends payable in shares of a corporation other than the declaring corporation and all capital gains distributions of any investment trust should inure to the principal.

    5.2.c <u>To Add Net Income</u>. To add the portion of the net income of this trust in excess of net income distributed to principal and reinvest such amounts at the end of the taxable year of this trust.

    5.2.d <u>To Purchase Insurance</u>. To carry insurance against such risks and for such amounts and upon such terms as Trustee deems necessary and for the protection of Trustee or any beneficiary of the trust estate, and to purchase policies of insurance on the life of any beneficiary of any trust, or on the life of any other person in whom any trust may have an insurable interest, and to continue in effect or to terminate any life insurance policy which may be owned or held by any trust; and to pay (from income or principal) any premiums or other charges, and to exercise any and all rights or incidents of ownership in connection therewith.

    5.2.e <u>To Pay Costs</u>. To pay all costs, charges and expenses of the trust estate and pay or compromise all taxes pertaining to the administration of the trust estate which may be assessed against it or against Trustee on account of the trust estate or the income thereof, together with a reasonable compensation to Trustee for Trustee's services hereunder, including services in the matter of whole or partial distribution of the trust estate.

    5.2.f <u>To Deal Between</u>. To sell or purchase assets from any trust or estate in which the beneficiary of the trust established by Grantor may be interested, including sales by the trust hereby established to any other one of the trusts hereby established; to deal in every way and without limitation or restriction with the personal representative, Trustee or other representative of any trust or estate in which any beneficiary hereunder has any existing or future interest, even though Trustee is acting in such other capacity, without liability for loss or depreciation resulting from such transactions; to purchase from, sell to, or otherwise deal with any corporation, association, partnership or firm with which any of them may be affiliated, or in which any of them may in any other way be interested, as freely as Trustee might or could deal with an independent third party, and without any greater responsibility, all rules or provisions of law to the contrary being hereby expressly waived.

5.2.g **To Determine Value**. To determine the market value of any investment of the trust estate for any purpose on the basis of such quotations or information as Trustee may deem pertinent and reliable without any limitation whatsoever; to distribute in cash or in kind upon partial or final distribution.

5.2.h **To Hold Property**. To retain, without liability for loss or depreciation resulting from such retention, original property, real or personal, received by Trustee from Grantor's estate, including but not limited to stock and securities of Trustee, for such time as to Trustee shall seem advisable; although such property may not be of the character prescribed by law or by the terms of this instrument for the investment of other trust assets, and although it represents a large percentage or all of the trust estate, that original property may accordingly be held as a permanent investment.

5.2.i **To Insure and Change**. To insure, improve, repair, alter and partition real estate, erect or raze improvements, grant easements, subdivide, or dedicate property to public use.

5.2.j **To Develop**. To develop, improve, lease, partition, abandon, subdivide, dedicate as parks, streets and alleys, and grant easements and rights-ofway with respect to any real property or improvements of this trust, and to improve, construct, repair, alter, reconstruct, or demolish any such improvements, and to lease for any periods, all or any part of the trust estate upon such terms and conditions and for such considerations as Trustee may deem advisable. Any lease may be made for such period of time as Trustee may deem proper, without regard to the duration of the trust or any statutory restriction on leasing and without the approval of any court.

5.2.k **To Sell**. To sell, lease, pledge, mortgage, transfer, exchange, convert or otherwise dispose of, or grant options with respect to, any and all property at any time forming a part of the trust estate, in such manner, at such time or times, for such purposes, for such prices and upon such terms, credits and conditions as Trustee deems advisable. Any lease made by Trustee may extend beyond the period fixed by statute for leases made by fiduciaries and beyond the duration of the trust.

5.2.l **To Lease**. To lease property upon any terms or conditions and for any term of years although extending beyond the period of any trust hereunder, including week to week, month to month, and year to year rentals.

5.2.m **To Purchase Special Properties**. To purchase or otherwise acquire, and to retain, whether originally a part of the trust estate or subsequently acquired, any and all stocks, bonds, notes or other securities, or any variety of real or personal property, including stocks or interests in investment trusts and common trust funds, as Trustee may deem advisable, whether or not such investments be of the character permissible for investments by fiduciaries, or be unsecured, unproductive, underproductive, overproductive, or of a wasting nature. Investments need not be diversified and may be made or retained with a view to a possible increase in value. Trustee may at any time render liquid the trust estates, in whole or in part, and hold cash or readily marketable securities of little or no yield for such period as Trustee may deem advisable.

5.2.n **To Settle**. To complete, extend, modify or renew any loans, notes, bonds, mortgages, contracts or any other obligations which the trust estate may owe or be a party to or which may be liens or charges against any property of the trust estate, although the trust estate may not be liable thereon, in such manner as Trustee may deem advisable; to pay, compromise, compound, adjust, submit to arbitration, sell or release any claims or demands of the trust estates against others or of others against the trust estates as Trustee may deem advisable, including the acceptance of deeds of real property in satisfaction of bonds and mortgages, and to make any payments in connection therewith which Trustee may deem advisable.

5.2.o **To Hold Partnership Interests**. To act as a general partner or as a limited partner in any general or limited partnership, in the same manner that an individual could act in such capacity.

5.2.p **To Operate Business**. To operate and manage, at the sole risk of the trust estate and not at the risk of Trustee, any property or business received in trust, as long as Trustee may deem advisable; Trustee is authorized to incorporate any unincorporated business received hereunder and to accept beneficial employment with or from any business in which the trust estate may be interested, whether by way of stock ownership or otherwise, and even though the interests of the trust estate in the business shall constitute a majority interest therein, or the complete ownership thereof; and to receive appropriate compensation from such business for such employment.

5.2.q **To Dissolve Corporations**. To enter into an agreement making the trust estate liable for a pro-rata share of the liabilities of any corporation which is being dissolved, and in which stock is held, when, in Trustee's opinion, such action is in the best interests of the trust estate.

5.2.r **To Borrow**. To borrow money for any purpose connected with the protection, preservation or improvement of the trust estate whenever in Trustee's judgment this action is deemed advisable, and as security to mortgage or pledge any real estate or personal property forming a part of the trust estate upon such terms and conditions as Trustee may deem advisable. Money may be borrowed from the banking department of the corporate Trustee.

5.2.s **To Invest**. To invest and reinvest the trust estate, both principal and income if accumulated, in any property or undivided interests therein, wherever located, including bonds, notes (secured and unsecured), stock of corporations (including stock of Trustee corporation), real estate (or any interest therein), and interests in trusts, including common trust funds, without being limited by any statute or rule of law concerning investments of trustees, and to hold on deposit or to deposit any funds in one or more banks, including Trustee bank, in any form of account whether or not interest-bearing; to cause any of the investments which may be delivered to or acquired by Trustee to be registered in Trustee's name or in the name of a nominee; any corporation or its transfer agent may presume conclusively that such nominee is the actual owner of any investment submitted for transfer; to retain any investment received in exchange in any reorganization or recapitalization.

5.2.t **To Acquire Stock Rights**. To acquire stock and securities of the Trustee corporation by the exercise of rights to acquire stock and securities issued in connection with the stock of Trustee comprising a portion of the trust estate, including but not limited to the following: To vote in person or by general or limited proxy with respect to any shares of stock or other securities held by Trustee; to consent, directly or through a committee or other agent, to the reorganization, consolidation, merger, dissolution or liquidation of any corporation in which the trust estate may have any interest, or to the sale, lease, pledge or mortgage of any property by or to any such corporation; and to make any payments and to take any steps which Trustee may deem necessary or proper to enable Trustee to obtain the benefit of such transaction.

5.2.u **To Set Up Reserves**. To set up, out of the rents, profits or other income received, if any, reserves for taxes, assessments, insurance premiums, repayments of mortgage or other indebtedness, repairs, improvements, depreciation, obsolescence and general maintenance of buildings and other property, and for the equalization of payments to or for beneficiaries entitled to receive income, as Trustee shall deem advisable.

5.2.v **To Make Distribution**. To make any distribution or division of the trust property in cash or in kind, or both, and to allot different kinds or disproportionate shares of property or undivided interests in property among the beneficiaries or portions, and to determine the value of any such property; and to continue to exercise any powers and discretions herein given for a reasonable period after the termination of the trust, but only for so long as no rule of law relating to perpetuities would be violated.

5.2.w **Broad Securities Brokerage and Margin Powers**. To buy, sell and hypothecate stocks, bonds, commodities and securities of every nature on margin; to buy, sell and write "put and call" options; to engage in buying options, long and covered option writing; and, in connection therewith, to borrow money and to pledge any and all stocks, bonds and securities, to execute any and all agreements on behalf of the trust which any broker may require to establish a margin account or otherwise deal in stocks; and to transact all types of securities transactions with a brokerage firm that are allowed under SEC regulations.

5.2.x **To Delegate Powers**. To delegate powers, discretionary or otherwise, for any purpose to one or more nominees or proxies with or without power of substitution; to make assignments to and deposits with committees, trustees, agents, depositories and other representatives; and to participate and retain any investment received in exchange in any reorganization or recapitalization.

5.2.y **To Employ Agents**. To employ agents, experts and counsel, investment or legal, even though they may be associates with, employed by, or counsel for Trustee or any beneficiary of the trust estate; and to make reasonable and proper payments to such agents, experts or counsel for services rendered.

5.2.z **To Keep Property in Name of Nominee**. To keep any property in the name of a nominee with or without disclosure of any fiduciary relationship.

5.2.aa   **To Designate Signator on Bank Accounts.** To have the power to designate, as signator or joint signator on any trust bank account, any person Trustee desires to designate. This person shall act as agent for Trustee and may sign on the bank account, deposit funds in the bank account, or otherwise deal with the bank account.

5.2.bb   **To Guarantee Debts**. To sign guarantees of loans and co-sign or endorse any type of loan document and thus obligate the trust assets for and on behalf of any individual, partnership, corporation, trust, or other type of participating interest or with which the trust is involved in some type of business relationship and to guarantee an indebtedness, co-sign or endorse an indebtedness for and on behalf of one of the named beneficiaries of the trust should Trustee deem it helpful to a beneficiary. This power supplements the power of Trustee to borrow. Grantor contemplates that many times in the business world, it is more advantageous for an individual or trust to make arrangements to guarantee a loan rather than directly borrowing the funds, and then lending the funds from the trust to the business ventures with which the trust may be associated, or from the trust to the beneficiary of the trust.

5.2.cc   **To Transfer Situs**. To transfer the situs of the trust estate to some other place; and in so doing, to resign and appoint a substitute Trustee who may delegate any and all trustee powers to the appointing Trustee as agent, and to remove any substitute Trustee appointed pursuant to this paragraph at any time and appoint another, including the appointing Trustee.

5.2.dd   **To Receive Additional Assets**. To receive additions to any trusts established under this agreement from any source, and to administer such additions according to the terms of this agreement.

5.2.ee   **To Commence or Defend Litigation**. To commence or defend such litigation with respect to the trust or any property of the trust as Trustee may deem advisable, at the expense of the trust; and to compromise, abandon, or otherwise adjust any claims or litigation against or in favor of the trust.

5.2.ff   **To Make Joint Investments.** To make joint investments for any two or more trusts hereunder.

5.2.gg   **To Reorganize**. To unite with the owners of other securities in carrying out any plan for the reorganization of any corporation; to deposit securities in accordance with any such plan; and to pay any expenses which may be required with reference to any such plan.

5.2.hh   **To Make Loans**. To make loans to any person, including any beneficiary, with adequate interest and adequate security.

5.2.ii   **To Render Liquid**. To render liquid the trust estate or any trust created hereunder, in whole or in part at any time or from time to time, and hold cash or readily marketable securities of little or no yield for such period as Trustee may deem advisable.

5.2.jj   **To Exploit Oil, Gas and Other Mineral Interests**. To drill, mine and otherwise operate for the development of oil, gas and other mineral interests; to enter into contracts relating to the installation and operation of absorption and repressuring plants; to enter into unitization or pooling agreements for any purpose including primary or secondary recovery; to place and maintain pipelines and telephone and telegraph lines; to execute oil, gas and mineral leases, division and transfer orders, grants and other instruments; and to perform such other acts as Trustee deems appropriate, using such methods as are commonly employed by owners of such interests in the community in which the interests are located.

5.2.kk   **To Appoint Ancillary Trustee**. To appoint an individual or another corporation as Trustee if the Trustee is unable to act with respect to real and tangible personal property not located in the state of the trust's situs. The appointed Trustee (1) shall have all the powers of the appointing Trustee, to be exercised, however, only with the approval of the appointing Trustee, (2) shall not, unless required by law, make periodic judicial accountings, but shall furnish the appointing Trustee with semi-annual statements, and (3) may delegate any or all trust powers. The appointing Trustee is to require any Trustee so appointed to remit to the appointing Trustee the income and net proceeds of any sale of any property and the appointing Trustee may remove any Trustee appointed pursuant to this paragraph at any time and to appoint another, including the appointing Trustee.

5.7 **Authority.** No person dealing with Trustee shall be obliged to inquire as to Trustee's powers or to see to the application of any money or property delivered to Trustee. Trustee shall not be required to obtain authority or approval of any court in the exercise of any power conferred hereunder. Trustee shall not be required to make any current reports or accountings to any court nor to furnish a bond for the proper performance of Trustee's duties hereunder. Trustee may execute and deliver any and all instruments in writing which Trustee may deem advisable to carry out any of the foregoing powers. No party to any such instrument in writing signed by Trustee shall be obliged to inquire into its validity, or be bound to see to the application by Trustee of any money or other property paid or delivered to Trustee pursuant to the terms of any such instrument.

5.11 **Succession of Powers.** Each Successor Trustee under this agreement shall have, exercise, and enjoy all the rights, privileges and powers, both discretionary and ministerial, as are given and granted to the original Trustee, and shall incur all the duties and obligations imposed upon the original Trustee.

7.4 **Payments.** All payments of income or principal shall be made to the respective beneficiaries in person or upon their personal receipts, or may at their discretion be deposited in any bank to the credit of such beneficiary in any account carried in the beneficiary's name or jointly with another or others. Payments or distributions to an incompetent beneficiary may nevertheless be made by Trustee for the benefit of such beneficiary in such of the following ways as in Trustee's opinion will be most desirable:

a. directly to such beneficiary;

b. to beneficiary's legal representative;

c. to some near relative or friend; or

d. by Trustee using such payments directly for the benefit of such beneficiary.

A beneficiary shall be determined to be incompetent in the same manner as prescribed in Part Eight for determining a Trustee to be incompetent or if a beneficiary is a minor or under legal disability declared by a court of competent jurisdiction, or if a beneficiary shall be incapacitated so as to make it impossible or impracticable for such person to give prompt and intelligent consideration to business matters. Trustee may act upon such evidence of the competency or incompetency of any person as Trustee shall deem appropriate and reliable without liability by reason thereof.

9.1.c <u>Acts of Trustees</u>. If there are two Trustees, both must consent and act to bind the trust. If there are three or more Trustees, then the act of a majority of the Trustees shall constitute the act of the trust. Unanimous approval of Trustees shall be necessary only when expressly provided for elsewhere in this trust.

9.5 **One Trustee Authority to Sign Insurance Applications and Tax Documents.** If any insurance is purchased by the Trustees of this trust, any one of them may sign life, property and casualty or other insurance applications and other paperwork necessary to purchase and process the policies. The reason for this special authority to any one of the Trustees is that sometimes speed is necessary in obtaining insurance coverages and damages may be caused to the trust by the unnecessary delays of finding one Trustee. Any one of the Trustees may sign tax applications, returns and other tax and governmental forms and paperwork that may be required from time to time.

11.1 **Power in Grantor During Lifetime of Grantor.** In addition to any powers reserved to the Grantor elsewhere in this trust, Grantor reserves the right at any time or times to amend or revoke this instrument and the trusts hereunder, in whole or in part, by an instrument or instruments in writing, signed by Grantor and delivered in Grantor's lifetime to Trustee.

In confirmation and affirmation of the foregoing, the undersigned, as Grantor and Trustee, hereby state that the assertion by any Trustee hereinabove designated that (a) he or she is acting alone or with another as a qualified Trustee, or (b) he or she is acting with full delegated powers from a Co-Trustee, shall be sufficient on its face, and no person shall be put to further inquiry into the right of such Trustee to so act.

Reproductions of this executed original (with reproduced signatures) shall be deemed to be original counterparts of this Certificate and Abstract.

IN WITNESS WHEREOF, the parties execute this legal instrument intending that it be effective on the Effective Date and at the Effective Place of Execution.

....

Signature of Grantor   Signature of Trustee

STATE OF _____)
                                                  ss.)   ACKNOWLEDGEMENT OF GRANTOR
County Of _____)

On this date, _____, before me, the undersigned Notary Public, personally appeared _____, who acknowledged himself/herself/themselves to be the person named herein and executed the within instrument of the purposes contained therein.

IN WITNESS WHEREOF, I hereunto set my hand and official seal.

_____   ....
Notary Expiration Date   Notary Public

STATE OF _____)
                                                  ss.)   ACKNOWLEDGEMENT OF TRUSTEE
County of _____)

This instrument was acknowledged before me this date, _____,
by ,_____ who acknowledged himself/herself/themselves to be the acting Trustee, being authorized to so do, executed the within instrument for the purposes therein contained by signing for that trust as such Trustee.

IN WITNESS WHEREOF, I hereunto set my hand and official seal.

_____   ....
Notary Expiration Date   Notary Public

SCHEDULE OF ASSETS TRANSFERRED TO TRUST

TR-3 © LawForms 5-15, 6-90

Name of Grantors of Trust:

Name of Trust and Date of Formation:

No.	Date of Transfer	Assets Transferred (For Real Property use Common Name or Address)	Form of Ownership	Tax Base at Time of Transfer (If Known)	Fair Market Value on Date of Transfer (If Known)

(Continued on Reverse Side)

No.	Date of Transfer	Assets Transferred (For Real Property use Common Name or Address)	Form of Ownership	Tax Base at Time of Transfer (If Known)	Fair Market Value on Date of Transfer (If Known)

The undersigned Grantors have reviewed the Schedule of Assets and approve the form of ownership of property as set forth above this date:

....
Signature of Grantor   Signature of Grantor

AFFIDAVIT OF SUCCESSION OF TRUSTEE FOR TRUST

TR-4 © LawForms 6-90

Effective Date of Trust:	Name of Trust:

Amendments to Trust and Effective Dates of Amendments		Names of Original Grantors:
Amendment Number	Effective Date of Amendment	
		Names of Original Primary Trustees:

Public Places Where Trust or Abstract of Trust Has Been Filed or Recorded:	Places Where Originals of Trust and Amendments Are Located:

1. **Circumstances Warranting Succession of Trustees.** Trustee: _____ has:
   ☐ Died as evidenced by death certificate attached.
   ☐ Became disabled as evidenced by statements of 3 physicians attached.
   ☐ Resigned as evidenced by written resignation attached.
   ☐ Recovered as a former disabled Trustee as evidenced by statements of 3 physicians attached.

2. **Affirmation of Successor Trustee.** The undersigned successor trustee affirms that the above facts are true and the documents are genuine. And that successor trustee is designated in the trust document as the next successor trustee. Successor trustee is willing to assume the responsibilities of successor trustee.

3. **Public Notice of Succession.** Executed copies of this Affidavit will be recorded in the County where the terminated Trustee resides and in all counties where real property belonging to the trust is situated, to wit:

4. **Notice to Persons Concerned With the Trust.** A copy of this Affidavit shall be mailed or delivered to all beneficiaries of the trust, to all persons known to have copies of the trust, and, as soon as these are ascertained, to all persons known to have business relationships with the trust.

5. **Verification.** We have read the foregoing and know, of our own knowledge, that the facts stated therein are true and correct, and execute this Affidavit for the purpose set forth herein.

6. THIS AFFIDAVIT IS MADE TO NOTIFY ALL PERSONS concerned with the trust that the undersigned is, as of this date, a Successor Trustee of this trust.

....
Signature of Successor Trustee   Signature of Successor Trustee

STATE OF	**Verification of Successor Trustee.** On this date, before me, a Notary Public, personally appeared:	Signature of Notary Public:
COUNTY OF	_____,	
Date of Verification:	who, being duly sworn upon oath, stated that he had read this document and knows of his own knowledge that the facts stated within are true and correct, except for those matters based on information which he believes to be true.	Notary Expiration Date:

THE _____ AMENDMENT
_____ TRUST

TR-5 © LawForms 5-90

Effective Date of Trust: Amendment Effective Date: Effective Place of Execution:

Grantors: Primary Trustees:

(Hereinafter referred to as Grantors)   (Hereinafter referred to as Trustees)

The above-described trust, by and between the above-named Grantors and Trustees, is amended by substituting provisions, adding provisions, or deleting proovisions as follows:

(Continued on Reverse Side)   Page 1

THE _____ AMENDMENT
_____ TRUST

(Continued)

(Continued on Next Page)

THE _____ AMENDMENT
_____ TRUST

(Continued)

THE _____ AMENDMENT _____ TRUST

TR-5 © LawForms 5-90

(Continued)

Incorporation by Reference. All provisions of the above-named trust are incorporated by reference herein with the exception of the provisions expressly changed by this Amendment.

IN WITNESS WHEREOF, the parties hereto have duly executed this Amendment to the above named Trust.

....

....
Signature of Grantor   Signature of Trustee

The foregoing amendment was at the date thereof by the named Grantors signed, sealed, published and declared to be an amendment to a trust which incorporates the Last Wills and Testaments of the Grantors and serves as a receptacle to receive the pour over of assets. This trust amendment was signed in the presence of us who, at the request and in the presence of Grantors and in the presence of each other, have signed the same as witnesses thereto.

1..   1._____

2..   2._____

3..   3._____
Signature of Witness   Address of Witness

STATE OF COUNTY OF Date of Acknowledgement:	**Acknowledgement of Grantor.** On this date, before me, a Notary Public, personally appeared: 1. 2._____, known to me or satisfactorily proven to be the person whose name is subscribed to this instrument and acknowledged that he executed the same. If this person's name is subscribed in a representative capacity, it is for the principal named and in the capacity indicated.	Signature of Notary Public: Notary Expiration Date:
STATE OF COUNTY OF Date of Acknowledgement:	**Acknowledgement of Trustee.** On this date, before me, a Notary Public, personally appeared: 1. 2._____, known to me or satisfactorily proven to be the person whose name is subscribed to this instrument and acknowledged that he executed the same. If this person's name is subscribed in a representative capacity, it is for the principal named and in the capacity indicated.	Signature of Notary Public: Notary Expiration Date:

STATEMENT OF WISHES
AS A SUPPLEMENT TO WILLS AND TRUSTS

TR-6 © LawForms 2-81, 4-81, 6-90

I, _____ , having previously executed certain wills, trusts or other documents, set forth hereafter this statement of wishes to guide my designated personal representatives, trustees, conservators and/or guardians in carrying out my wishes.

I intend this statement of wishes as advisory only and not mandatory. It is written to assist, but not control my fiduciaries.

My wishes are that:

SIGNED this date: _____ ....

Signature

AFFIDAVIT TERMINATING THE
REVOCABLE LIVING TRUST

TR-7 © LawForms 6-90

1. I am over 18 and otherwise competent to testify in a court of law of the United States or its several states and make this Affidavit without being under fraud, duress or undue influence from any person.

2. **Identification of Trust.** We are the Grantor(s) of the _____,
dated _____, by between _____,
as Grantors, and _____, as Trustees.

3. The Beneficiary(ies) of the Trust are:

4. **Revocation**. The trust is hereby revoked:

☐ in accordance with paragraph 11.1 of the trust.(Power in Grantor During Lifetime of Grantor to Revoke)
☐ as a result of all assets of the trust being distributed out of the trust.
☐ pursuant to a court order, a copy of which is attached.

5. **Recorded Information on Trust** The names and address of the Grantor, trustees and beneficiaries of the trust the identity of the trust and the relevant provisions of the trust have been disclosed in the Certificate of Trustees' Powers and Abstract of Trust which is recorded at:

_____

6. **Notice of Recording**. As evidence of such termination, a signed oriiginal of this Affidavit shall be recorded with the county recorders office in the following counties:

7. **Notice to Beneficiaries**. A copy of this Affidavit Terminating the Revocable Living Trust has been mailed to the above named beneficiaries this date of this Affidavit.

I have read the foregoing and know of my own knowledge that the facts stated herein are true and correct.

....
Signature of Grantor   Signature of Grantor

STATE OF	**Verification of Grantor.** On this date, before me, a Notary Public, personally appeared: 1.	Signature of Notary Public:
COUNTY OF	2._____,	
Date of Verification:	who, being duly sworn upon oath, stated that he had read this document and knows of his own knowledge that the facts stated within are true and correct, except for those matters based on information which he believes to be true.	Notary Expiration Date:

This instrument was recorded at request of:

The recording official is directed to return this instrument or a copy to the above person.

Space Reserved For Recording Information

SPECIAL WARRANTY DEED TO TRUST
TR-8 © LawForms 10-76, 12-85, 6-90

Effective Date:	County and State where Real Property is Located:
Grantor (Name, Address and Zip Code):	Grantee (Name, Address and Zip Code):
Subject Real Property (Address or Location):	Legal Description Proofed by Persons Whose Initials Appear to the Right 1. 2. 3.

Subject Real Property (Legal Description):

(Continued on Reverse Side)

SUBJECT TO all taxes and other assessments, reservations in patents and all easements, rights of way, encumbrances, liens, covenants, conditions, restrictions, obligations and liabilities as may appear of record or in the most recent title insurance policy on the subject real property. It is the intent of the parties to maintain and not waive all rights under the most recent title insurance policy on the subject real property.

1. Recorded Information on Trust. The names and addresses of the grantor, trustees and beneficiaries of the trust, the identity of the trust and the relevant provisions of the trust have been disclosed in the Certificate of Trustee's Powers and Abstract of Trust which is recorded at: _____ .

2. Effect of Transfer. Any transfers effectuated by this document transferring real property interests to a trust, involve the transfer of real property by the legal owners to a Revocable Living Trust, which will have the same IRS identification number as the transferor, and will not be an Irrevocable transfer until the death of the transferors and as such shall not warant the triggering of "due on sale" clauses in any related documents, or the imposition of taxes, or tax reassessments, imposed when there is a completed transfer of real property ownership.

3. Conveyance. This special warranty deed made by the assignor, hereby grants, sells and conveys the above described property to the above named assignee, for true and actual consideration in the amount of 10.00 dollars to have and to hold the same, with all appurtenances thereon, to assignee and assignee's heirs and assigns forever. I/We covenant that I/we convey and warrant specially the title against all persons claiming under me.

1...   ....

2...   ....
Signatures of Witnesses   Signatures of Grantor

STATE OF COUNTY OF Date of Acknowledgement:	**Acknowledgement of Grantor.** On this date, before me, a Notary Public, personally appeared: _____, known to me or satisfactorily proven to be the person whose name is subscribed to this instrument and acknowledged that he executed the same. If this person's name is subscribed in a representative capacity, it is for the principal named and in the capacity indicated.	Signature of Notary Public: Notary Expiration Date:
STATE OF COUNTY OF Date of Acknowledgement:	**Acknowledgement of Witnesses.** On this date, before me, a Notary Public, personally appeared: 1. 2._____, known to me or satisfactorily proven to be the person whose name is subscribed to this instrument and acknowledged that he executed the same. If this person's name is subscribed in a representative capacity, it is for the principal indicated.	Signature of Notary Public: Notary Expiration Date: TR-8 © LawForms

This instrument was recorded at request of:	
The recording official is directed to return this instrument or a copy to the above person.	Space Reserved For Recording Information

BILL OF SALE TO TRUST

(Household Goods and Personal Effects)

TR-9 © LawForms 10-71, 1-83, 7-87, 6-90

Effective Date:	County and State where property is located:
Seller (Name, Address and Zip Code):	Buyer (Name, Address and Zip Code):

Address and Location of Property Sold:

Property Sold (List of Personal Property by Description, Serial Number and Other Identifying Characteristics):

All right, title and interest of Seller in, and to, all household furnishings, fixtures, equipment, works of art, silverware, chinaware, artifacts, collections, musical instruments, antiques, jewelry, furs and all personal property, and personal effects located in and about the residence of Sellers at _____ as of this date and as may be hereinafter acquired in this residence or in later acquired residences of Seller.

1. **Conveyance.** For valuable consideration, receipt of which is acknowledged, Seller sells and conveys to Buyer the Property Sold, to have and to hold the Property Sold to Buyer and the heirs, executors, administrators and assigns of Buyer forever, and Seller and the heirs, executors, administrators and assigns of Seller warrant to defend the sale of the Property sold unto Buyer and the heirs, executors, administrators and assigns of Buyer, against all and every person whomsoever lawfully claiming or to claim the same.

2. **Recorded Information on Trust.** The names and addresses of the grantor, trustees and beneficiaries of the trust, the identity of the trust and the relevant provisions of the trust have been disclosed in the Certificate of Trustee's Powers and Abstract of Trust which is recorded at: _____ .

....
Signature of Seller   Signature of Seller

STATE OF COUNTY OF	**Acknowledgement of Seller.** On this date, before me, a Notary Public, personally appeared: _____,	Signature of Notary Public:
Date of Acknowledgement:	known to me or satisfactorily proven to be the person whose name is subscribed to this instrument and acknowledged that he executed the same. If this person's name is subscribed in a representative capacity, it is for the principal indicated.	Notary Expiration Date:

This instrument was recorded at request of:

The recording official is directed to return this instrument or a copy to the above person.

Space Reserved For Recording Information

BILL OF SALE TO TRUST

(General)

TR-10 © LawForms 10-71, 1-83, 7-87, 6-90

Effective Date:

County and State where property is located:

Assignor (Name, Address and Zip Code):

Assignee (Name, Address and Zip Code):

Address or Location of Property Sold:

Property Sold (List of Personal Property by Description, Serial Number and Other Identifying Characteristics):

1. Conveyance. For valuable consideration, receipt of which is acknowledged, Seller sells and conveys to Buyer the Property Sold, to have and to hold the Property Sold to Buyer and the heirs, executors, administrators and assigns of Buyer forever, and Seller and the heirs, executors, administrators and assigns of Seller warrant to defend the sale of the Property sold unto Buyer and the heirs, executors, administrators and assigns of Buyer, against all and every person whomsoever lawfully claiming or to claim the same.

2. Recorded Information On Trust. The name and addresses of the grantor, trustees and beneficiaries of the trust, the identity of the trust and the relevant provisions of the trust have been disclosed in the Certificate of Trustee's Powers and Abstract of Trust which is recorded at: _____ .

....
Signature of Seller

....
Signature of Seller

STATE OF
COUNTY OF

Date of Acknowledgement:

Acknowledgement of Buyer. On this date, before me, a Notary Public, personally appeared:
_____,
known to me or satisfactorily proven to be the person whose name is subscribed to this instrument and acknowledged that he executed the same. If this person's name is subscribed in a representative capacity, it is for the principal indicated.

Signature of Notary Public:

Notary Expiration Date:

This instrument was recorded at request of:

The recording official is directed to return this instrument or a copy to the above person.

Space Reserved For Recording Information

DEED, BILL OF SALE AND ASSIGNMENT

(Omnibus)

TR-11 © LawForms 10-71, 1-83, 7-87, 6-90

Effective Date:	County and State where property is located:
Assignor (Name, Address and Zip Code):	Assignee (Name, Address and Zip Code):

1. Effort to Transfer. The Assignor has made every effort to transfer all assets belonging to Assignor to the above named Trust for the purpose of avoiding unnecessary costs or adverse consequences at time of Assignor's death, therefor the property assigned by this document is located wherever it may be at the time of Assignor's death should it not have been previously assigned to the above named trust.

2. Intention of Assignor. For valuable consideration receipt of which is acknowledged, assignor intends by this legal instrument to transfer to Assignee, as of the effective date, all right, title and interest in all property or property rights, tangible or intangible, which may now be owned or may hereafter accrue to Assignor unless there are written documents executed by Assignor stating a contrary intent in the language of the documents themselves dated after this date.

3. Transfer Without Additional Documents. Assignor intends that this document by itself shall effectuate the transfer without any necessity of additional transfer documents, and directs and consents that this document may be recorded or filed in any public agency to evidence the transfer of any property or property right which may vest title in the ownership of Assignor.

4. Power to Assignee to Make Transfer. However, if by reason of law, regulation, custom or other requirement, additional documents are necessary to mechanically evidence the transfer, the Assignee is given the express power by Assignor to prepare and sign, on behalf of both parties, whatever additional documents are necessary to mechanically carry out the intent of this omnibus transfer.

5. Purpose of Omnibus. The purpose of this document is to carry out the intent of Assignor that all Assignor's property (not otherwise transferred to a partnership, corporation, retirement plan or other trust) be owned by Assignee trust, in order to make unnecessary the costs, inconvenience and other adverse consequences of probate and other court proceedings which would otherwise be required if property is owned by Assignor at the time of Assignor's death.

6. Specific Examples. Specific examples of property to which this transfer applies would be: (1) causes of action in the nature of legal claims against other persons; (2) property rights accrued by reason of unwritten contracts or commitments; (3) inheritances which result in property being owned by Assignor by operation of law or documents that Assignor is not aware of; (4) devises from Wills of relatives; (5) distributions from trusts; and (6) real or personal tangible or intangible property that was inadvertently forgotten or omitted from transfer to Assignee.

(Continued on Reverse Side)

7. Preparation of Documents. Assignee directs and consents that Assignee may prepare whatever document may be necessary to carry out the purpose and intent of this Deed, Bill of Sale and Assignment.

8. Recorded Information on Trust. The names and addresses of the grantor, trustees and beneficiaries of the trust, the identity of the trust and the relevant provisions of the trust have been disclosed in the Certificate of Trustee's Powers and Abstract of Trust which is recorded at: _____ .

9. Conveyance by Special Warranty Deed. If a transfer of Real Property is made, then the above named Assignor conveys by special warranty deed hereby the following described property to the above named Assignee, for true and valuable consideration in the amount of $10.00 dollars, to have and to hold the same, with all appurtenances thereon to Assignee and Assignee's heirs and assigns forever. We covenant that we convey and warrant specially the title against all persons claiming under me. Any conveyance of Real Property shall be subject to all taxes and other assessments, reservations in patents and all easements, rights of way, encumbrances, liens, covenants, conditions, restrictions, obligations and liabilities as may appear of record or in the most recent title insurance policy on the subject real proeprty. It is the intent of the parties to maintain and not waive all rights under the most recent title insurance policy on the subject real property.

10. Effect of Transfer. Any transfers effectuated by this document transferring real property interests to a trust, involve the transfer of real property by the transfer of real property by the legal owners to a Revocable Living Trust which will have the same IRS identification number as the transferor, and will not be an Irrevocable transfer until the death of the transferors, and as such shall not warrant the triggering of "due on sale" clauses in any related documents, or the imposition of taxes, or reassessments, imposed when there is a completed transfer of real property ownership.

....
Signature of Assignor   Signature of Assignor

1... _____

2... _____
Signatures of Witness   Address of Witness

STATE OF	**Acknowledgement of Assignor.** On this date, before me, a Notary Public, personally appeared:	Signature of Notary Public:
COUNTY OF	_____,	
Date of Acknowledgement:	known to me or satisfactorily proven to be the person whose name is subscribed to this instrument and acknowledged that he executed the same. If this person's name is subscribed in a representative capacity, it is for the principal indicated.	Notary Expiration Date:

LETTER OF INSTRUCTION TO MOTOR VEHICLE DEPARTMENT REGARDING TRANSFERRING ALL OF THE UNDERSIGN'S MOTOR VEHICLES INTO THE TRUST

TR-12a © LawForms 6-90

To whom it may concern:

This is a letter informing you of the formation by the undersigned Grantors of_____ Trust, dated _____, with_____ as trustees.

We are sending you this letter on the suggestion of LawForms, Inc. It has been drafted by the staff of attorneys which produce the LawForms documents and is for the purpose of informing the Motor Vehicle Department of certain rights which are created by the formation of the Revocable Living Trust.

We want to make certain that there are no complications in making investments using the trust which we have implemented as part of our estate plan.

We provide you with all the relevant information pertaining to the trust in the Certificate of Trustee's Powers and Abstract of Trust which has been attached. This Certificate sets forth the "vital statistics" of the trust in an abbreviated form providing you with the information you need to deal with the trust -- much like a driver's license or passport is used to identify an individual:

1. **Owner of Automobiles**. Please change the title(s) of any vehicle(s) into the name of the above named Trust. The trustees will sign on behalf of the trust.

2. **Beneficiary Designations**. All beneficiary designations which may be necessary are set forth in the attached Certificate.

3. **Tax ID Numbers**. Revocable living trusts are not required to have a separate tax number and the social security numbers of the grantors/trustees may be used.

4. **Copies to Us**. We would appreciate your sending us copies of the documentation which evidences that the instructions set forth in this letter have been carried out.

5. **Further Information**. Should you require more information or explanation, please call us anytime. We would be happy to assist you.

It is our desire to make an easy transition of ownership and control to the Trust. We appreciate your help in making that possible.

Yours truly,

....
Signature of Grantor/Trustee   Signature of Grantor/Trustee

Enc. Copy of the Certificate of Trustees' Powers and Abstract of Trust.

# LETTER OF INSTRUCTION REGARDING INTEGRATING THE FAMILY TRUST INTO INVESTMENT PORTFOLIO, STOCK AND BROKERAGE ACCOUNTS AND OTHER INVESTMENT ASSETS

To whom it may concern:

This is a letter informing you of the formation by the undersigned Grantors of _____ Trust dated _____ with _____ as trustees.

We are sending you this letter on the suggestion of LawForms, Inc. It has been drafted by the staff of attorneys which produce the LawForms documents and is for the purpose of informing the Brokerage institution of certain rights which are created by the formation of the Revocable Living Trust.

We want to make certain that there are no complications in making investments using the Trust which we have implemented as part of our estate plan.

We provide you with all the relevant information pertaining to the trust in the Certificate of Trustee's Powers and Abstract of Trust which has been attached. This Certificate sets forth the "vital statistics" of the trust in an abbreviated form providing you with the information you need to deal with the trust -- much like a driver's license or passport is used to identify an individual.

1. **Stock Brokerage Accounts and Money Market Accounts.** These accounts should be place in the ownership of the Trust designating named trustees of the revocable living trust. This means that the account name would include the Title of the Trust, date of creation and the names of the trustees. All this relevant information may be found in the attached Certificate.

2. **Beneficiary Designations.** All beneficiary designations which may be necessary are set forth in the attached Abstract.

3. **Stocks and Bonds Issued by Certificate.** Any stocks and bonds issued by certificate should be issued in the name of the Trust.

4. **Tax ID Numbers.** Revocable living trusts are not required to have a separate tax number and the social security numbers of the grantors/trustees may be used.

5. **IRA Accounts.** The beneficiary designations of the IRA Accounts should be the surviving spouse as the primary beneficiary and the Trust as the contingent beneficiary variable. In the event there is no spouse, the primary beneficiary should be the Trust.

6. **Copies to Us.** We would appreciate your sending us copies of the documentation which evidences that the instructions set forth in this letter have been carried out.

7. **Further Information.** Should you require more information or explanation, please call us anytime. We would be happy to assist you.

It is our desire to make an easy transition into investing with a family trust. We appreciate your help in making that possible.

Yours truly,

....
Signature of Grantor/Trustee   Signature of Grantor/Trustee

Enc. Copy of the Certificate of Trustees' Powers and Abstract of Trust.

LETTER OF INSTRUCTION REGARDING BANKING WITH A FAMILY TRUST

TR-12c © LawForms 6-90

To whom it may concern:

This is a letter informing you of the formation by the undersigned Grantors of _____ Trust, dated _____ with _____ as trustees.

We are sending you this letter on the suggestion of LawForms, Inc. It has been drafted by the staff of attorneys which produce the LawForms documents and is for the purpose of informing the Banking institution of certain rights which are created by the formation of the Revocable Living Trust.

We want to make certain that there are no complications in banking with the trust which we have implemented as part of our estate plan.

We provide you with all the relevant information pertaining to the trust in the Certificate of Trustee's Powers and Abstract of Trust which has been attached. This Certificate sets forth the "vital statistics" of the trust in an abbreviated form providing you with the information you need to deal with the trust -- much like a driver's license or passport is used to identify an individual.

We have segmented this letter according to the particular aspect of banking with a trust to which the paragraph relates.

1. **Bank Accounts.** The family bank account or any other ancillary accounts (this excludes bank accounts for family corporations, partnerships or nonpersonal accounts) are to be placed into the ownership of the Trust dated as of the effective date indicated on the Certificate of Trustee's Powers and Abstract of Trust.

This means that we have the option of (1) changing only the signature card(s) or (2) changing the signature cards as well as actually titling the checks in the name of the trust.

   a. **Trust Name on Face of Check.** If the name of the Trust is to appear on the face of the checks, then both the signature card(s) on file at the bank and the checks must carry the name of the Trust and the trustees.

The name on the check matches the name of the account. The trust document permits the trustee to designate agents to act for a trustee and to designate signatories on bank accounts so it is not necessary that one or all the trustees sign on the account. Any one of them could be designated as a signatory. A trustee could designate his wife, son, secretary or other trusted person to sign on the account for convenience.

It is not necessary to have the names of all the trustees printed on the face of the check in addition to the name of the trust. Sometimes trustees designate the checks with the name of the trust, sometimes the name of the trust and both trustees. They may also designate on the checks sub accounts such as "Business Matters," "Household" or other designations.

Where the trustees are a husband and wife, most clients set up a trust household checking account, a trust investment checking account, and a trust savings account. Many times they will designate the wife as being responsible for the household account, the husband being responsible for the investment account, and either of them responsible for the savings account.

   b. **Trust Name only on Signature Cards.** If the name of the Trust is not to appear on the face of the checks, you need only redo the signature cards.

In order to set up a bank account in this manner, you change the signature card over to the ownership of the trust and continue using the same checks for the account as before.

Even though the name of the trust is not on the checks, the ownership of the account, as designated on the signature card, will permit the account to remain in the ownership of the trust even if one of the trustees dies.

(Continued on Reverse Side)

2. **Beneficiary Designations.** All beneficiary designations which may be necessary are set forth in the attached Abstract.

3. **Safe Deposit Boxes.** The ownership of safe deposit box(es) will also be placed in the name of the Trust.

4. **Tax ID Numbers on Accounts.** Revocable living trusts are not required to have a separate tax number and the social security numbers of the grantors/trustees may be used.

5. **Savings Accounts, Money Market Accounts and CD's.** These should all be owned by the Trust. The trustees will be designated on the ownership and/or signature documents.

6. **IRA Accounts.** The beneficiary designations of the IRA Accounts should be the surviving spouse as the primary beneficiary and the Trust as the contingent beneficiary.

7. **Copies to Us.** We would appreciate your sending us copies of the documentation which evidences that the instructions set forth in this letter have been carried out.

8. **Further Information.** Should you require more information or explanation, please call us anytime. We would be happy to assist you.

It is our desire to make an easy transition into banking with a family trust. We appreciate your help in making that possible.

Yours Truly,

....
Signature of Grantor/trustee   Signature of Grantor/trustee

Enc. Copy of the Certificate of Trustees' Powers and Abstract of Trust

LETTER OF INSTRUCTION REGARDING REAL ESTATE TRANSACTIONS WITH A REVOCABLE TRUST

TR-12d © LawForms 6-90

To whom it may concern:

This is a letter informing you of the formation by the undersigned Grantors of _____ Trust dated _____ with _____ as trustees.

We are sending you this letter on the suggestion of LawForms, Inc. It has been drafted by the staff of attorneys which produce the LawForms documents and is for the purpose of informing the Real Estate Agency of certain rights which are created by the formation of the Revocable Living Trust.

We want to make certain that there are no complications with real property transactions using the Trust which we have implemented as part of our estate plan.

We provide you with all the relevant information pertaining to the trust in the Certificate of Trustees' Powers and Abstract of Trust which has been attached. This Certificate sets forth the "vital statistics" of the trust in an abbreviated form providing you with the information you need to deal with the trust -- much like a driver's license or passport is used to identify an individual.

1. **Real Estate Purchases and Sales**. Any purchases of real property should be made in the name of the trust dated by trustees of that Trust. Any sale of real property should be made through that same trust. This means all Deeds of Trusts, Promissory Notes and any other documentation, part of the purchase or sale, be made in the name of Trust.

2. **Beneficiary Designations**. All beneficiary designations which may be necessary are set forth in the attached Certificate.

3. **Recordation of Abstract of Trust**. A certified copy of the Certificate of Trustees' Powers and Abstract of Trust has to be recorded in every county where the real property is owned. This means if property is purchased in a county where we have never owned property, a Certificate of Trustee's Powers and Abstract of Trust must be recorded in that same county.

4. **Tax ID Numbers**. Revocable living trusts are not required to have a separate tax number and the social security numbers of the grantors/trustees may be used.

5. **Copies to Us**. We would appreciate your sending us copies of the documentation which evidences that the instructions set forth in this letter have been carried out.

6. **Further Information**. Should you require more information or explanation, please call us anytime. We would be happy to assist you.

It is our desire to make an easy transition in using our Trust for real estate transactions. We appreciate your help in making that possible.

Yours truly,

....
Signature of Grantor/Trustee   Signature of Grantor/Trustee

Enc. Copy of the Certificate of Trustees' Powers and Abstract of Trust

AFFIDAVIT OF TRUSTEE
FOR TRANSFER OF MOTOR VEHICLE
INTO NAME OF TRUST

TR-13 © LawForms 6-90

1. **Competency.** I am over the age of 21 years, a resident of the State of _____, and otherwise competent to testify in a court of law. I make this Affidavit without being under fraud, duress or undue influence from any person.

2. **Description of Trust.** I am a Trustee of the following-described revocable, living declaration of trust:

   Name of Trust: _____

   Date of Trust: _____

   Grantor: _____

   Trustee: _____

3. **Description of Motor Vehicle.** Concurrently with the submission of this Affidavit to the State Motor Vehicle Department, I have submitted an Application for Certificate of Title and Registration to transfer the ownership of the following-described motor vehicle to the above-described trust:

   _____

4. **Registration and Title.** This vehicle is to be titled and registered in the name of the family trust identified above and not in a business or commercial trust.

I have read the foregoing and know of my own knowledge that the facts stated therein are true and correct.

Signature of Trustee	Signature of Trustee

STATE OF	Verification of Trustee. On this date, before me, a Notary Public, personally appeared: 1.	Signature of Notary Public:
COUNTY OF	2. _____, who, being duly sworn upon oath, stated that he had read this document and knows of his own knowledge that the facts stated within are true and correct, except for those matters based on information which he believes to be true.	
Date of Verification:		Notary Expiration Date:

STOCK POWER AND ASSIGNMENT APART FROM

CERTIFICATE TO TRUST

TR-14 © LawForms 8-74, 6-90

Effective Date:	County and State:
Assignor (Name, Address and Zip Code):	Assignee (Name, Address and Zip Code):

Stock Assigned (Corporation - Type)	Number of Shares	Certificate Numbers

Attorney in Fact of Assignor (Name, Address and Zip Code):

1. Transfer of Stock. For value received, assignor assigns the stock carried in the name of assignor on the books of the designated corporation and appoints irrevocably the above named attorney-in-fact to transfer that stock on the books of the corporation, with full power of substitution in the premises, to assignee.

2. Recorded Information of Trust. The names and addresses of the grantor, trustees and beneficiaries of the trust, the identity of the trust and the relevant provisions of the trust have been disclosed in the Certificate of Trustee's Powers and Abstract of Trust which is recorded at: _____ .

3. Affirmation of Signature. I affix hereto my signature exactly as it appears on the certificates without alteration, change or enlargement.

Name, Address and Zip Code of commercial bank, trust company, or firm which guarantees signature of assignor:	
	.... Signature of Assignor

GUARANTY OF SIGNATURE

I am an officer of a commercial bank or trust company having its principal office OR a correspondent in the City of New York, Midwest, American or Pacific Coast Stock Exchanges, and I know and certify that the above signature is valid and guarantee it as the true signature of assignor.

Date of Guaranty of Signature	Signature and Title of Officer

**BOND POWER AND ASSIGNMENT
APART FROM CERTIFICATE TO TRUST**

TR-15 © LawForms 8-74, 6-90

Effective Date:	County and State:
Assignor (Name, Address and Zip Code):	Assignee (Name, Address and Zip Code):

BONDS ASSIGNED

(Issuer and Type)	Amount of bonds	Certificate Numbers

Attorney in Fact of Assignor (Name, Address and Zip Code):

1. Conveyence of Bond Power. For value received assignor assigns the stock carried in the name of assignor on the books of the designated corporation and appoints irrevocably the above name attorney in fact to transfer that stock on the books of the corporation, with full power of substitution in the premises, to assignee.

2. Recorded Information. The names and addresses of the grantor, trustees and beneficiaries of the trust, the identity of the trust and the relevant provisions of the trust have been disclosed in the Certificate of Trustee's Powers and Abstract of Trust which is recorded at:

_____.

3. Affirmation of Signature. I affix hereto my signature exactly as it appears on the certificates without alteration, change or enlargement.

Name, Address and Zip Code of commercial bank, trust company, or firm which guarantees signature of assignor:	
	....
	....
	Signature of Assignor

GUARANTY OF SIGNATURE

I am an officer of a commercial bank or trust company having its principal office OR a correspondent in the City of New York, Midwest, American or Pacific Coast Stock Exchanges, and I know and certify that the above signature is valid and guarantee it as the true signature

Date of Guaranty of Signature:	Signature and Title of Officer:

This instrument was recorded at request of:

The recording official is directed to return this instrument or a copy to the above person.

Space Reserved For Recording Information

ASSIGNMENT OF PARTNERSHIP INTEREST TO TRUST.
TR-16 © LawForms 10-71, 1-83, 7-87, 6-90

Effective Date:	County and State where property is located:
Assignor (Name, Address and Zip Code)	Assignee (Name, Address and Zip Code)

Partnership Interests Assigned (Address or Location of Documentation of Articles of Partnership):

Partnership Interests Assigned (Legal Description):

All right, title and interest of Assignors in undivided percentage or units equal to _____ in the limited partnership, _____ , a partnership of the state of _____ , _____ , including all Assignor's right and interest in that partnership and any successor partnership and all Assignor's rights and interests in and under the partnership agreement relating thereto, and proceeds of any of the above.

1. General Partner Approval. By their signatures below, the General Partners of the limited partnership signify their approval of this assignment of interest on the dates set forth.

.... Dated: _____
Signature of General Partner

.... Dated: _____
Signature of General Partner

.... Dated: _____
Signature of General Partner

.... Dated: _____
Signature of General Partner

(Continued on Reverse Side)

2. Recorded Information on Trust. The names and addresses of the grantor, trustees and beneficiaries of the trust, the identity and the relevant provisions of the trust have been disclosed in the Certificate of Trustees' Powers and Abstract of Trust which is recorded at:
_____

3. Assumption of Partnership Agreement. Assignees below acknowledge that they have read and are familiar with the Agreement of Partnership and have received a copy of same, and agree to be bound by its terms as a limited partner.

4. Conveyance. For valuable consideration, receipt of which is acknowledged by Seller, Seller sells and conveys to Buyer the Property Sold, to have and to hold the Property Sold to Buyer and the heirs, executors, administrators and assigns of Buyer forever, and Seller and the heirs, executors, administrators and assigns of Seller warrant to defend the sale of the Property sold unto Buyer and the heirs, executors, administrators and assigns of Buyer, against all and every person whomsoever lawfully claiming or to claim the same.

....	....
Signatures of Assignor	Signatures of Assignee

STATE OF COUNTY OF Date of Acknowledgement:	**Acknowledgement of Assignor.** On this date, before me, a Notary Public, personally appeared: _____, known to me or satisfactorily proven to be the person whose name is subscribed to this instrument and acknowledged that he executed the same. If this person's name is subscribed in a representative capacity, it is for the principal named and in the capacity indicated.	Signature of Notary Public: Notary Expiration Date:
STATE OF COUNTY OF Date of Acknowledgement:	**Acknowledgement of Assignee.** On this date, before me, a Notary Public, personally appeared: _____, known to me or satisfactorily proven to be the person whose name is subscribed to this instrument and acknowledged that he executed the same. If this person's name is subscribed in a representative capacity, it is for the principal indicated.	Signature of Notary Public: Notary Expiration Date:

This instrument was recorded at request of:

The recording official is directed to return this instrument or a copy to the above person.

Space Reserved For Recording Information

ASSIGNMENT AND BILL OF SALE

OF SOLE PROPRIETORSHIP PROPERTY TO TRUST

TR-17 © LawForm 10-71, 1-83, 7-87, 6-90

Effective Date:	County and State where property is located:
Seller/Assignor (Name, Address and Zip Code):	Buyer/Assignee (Name, Address and Zip Code):

Address or Location of Property Sold and Assigned:

Property Sold and Assigned (List of Property by Description, and/or Other Identifying Characteristics):

All furniture and fixtures, equipment, personal property, and all other tangible assets of that certain sole proprietorship of _____ _____ known as _____ which are presently being used in the business or may be hereafter acquired, which are located at: _____ and
which are: ☐ listed hereafter ☐ listed on attached inventory ☐ contained at that location.

(Continued on Reverse Side)

Intangible Property Assigned (files, customer lists):

All accounts receivable, notes receivable, funds receivable, good will, trade name, trademarks and all other intangible assets, both present and future, of that certain business which is known as _____ , located at _____ _____ as entered on the books, records, and files of said business and which are: ☐ listed hereafter ☐ listed on attached inventory ☐ contained at that location.

1. Conveyance of Tangible Property. For valuable consideration, receipt of which is acknowledged by Seller, Seller sells and conveys to Buyer the tangible Property Sold, to have and to hold the Property Sold to Buyer and the heirs, executors, administrators and assigns of Buyer forever, and Seller and the heirs, executors, administrators and assigns of Seller warrant to defend the sale of the Property Sold unto Buyer and the heirs, executors, administrators and assigns of Buyer, against all and every person whomsoever lawfully claiming or to claim the same.

2. Conveyance of Intangible Property. For valuable considerations, receipt of which is acknowledged by Assignor, Assignor assigns all of his right, title and interest in the Property Assigned to Assignee.

3. Recorded Information on Trust. The names and addresses of the grantor, trustees and beneficiaries of thetrust, the identity of the trust and the relevant provisions of the trust have been disclosed in the Certificate of Trustees' Powers and Abstract of Trust which is recorded at: _____ .

....
Signatures of Assignor/Seller   Signatures of Assignee/Seller

STATE OF _____	**Acknowledgement of Assignor/Seller.** On this date, before me, a Notary Public, personally appeared:	Signature of Notary Public:
COUNTY OF _____	_____, known to me or satisfactorily proven to be the person whose name is subscribed to this instrument and acknowledged that he executed the same. If this person's name is subscribed in a representative capacity, it is for the principal indicated.	
Date of Acknowledgement:		Notary Expiration Date:

This instrument was recorded at request of:

The recording official is directed to return this instrument or a copy to the above person.

Space Reserved For Recording Information

ASSIGNMENT AND BILL OF SALE

OF SOLE PROPRIETORSHIP PROPERTY TO TRUST

TR-17 © LawForm 10-71, 1-83, 7-87, 6-90

Effective Date:	County and State where property is located:
Seller/Assignor (Name, Address and Zip Code):	Buyer/Assignee (Name, Address and Zip Code):

Address or Location of Property Sold and Assigned:

Property Sold and Assigned (List of Property by Description, and/or Other Identifying Characteristics):

All furniture and fixtures, equipment, personal property, and all other tangible assets of that certain sole proprietorship of _____ known as _____ which are presently being used in the business or may be hereafter acquired, which are located at: _____ and

which are: ☐ listed hereafter ☐ listed on attached inventory ☐ contained at that location.

(Continued on Reverse Side)

Intangible Property Assigned (files, customer lists):

All accounts receivable, notes receivable, funds receivable, good will, trade name, trademarks and all other intangible assets, both present and future, of that certain business which is known as _____ , located at _____ _____ as entered on the books, records, and files of said business and which are: ☐ listed hereafter ☐ listed on attached inventory ☐ contained at that location.

1. Conveyance of Tangible Property. For valuable consideration, receipt of which is acknowledged by Seller, Seller sells and conveys to Buyer the tangible Property Sold, to have and to hold the Property Sold to Buyer and the heirs, executors, administrators and assigns of Buyer forever, and Seller and the heirs, executors, administrators and assigns of Seller warrant to defend the sale of the Property Sold unto Buyer and the heirs, executors, administrators and assigns of Buyer, against all and every person whomsoever lawfully claiming or to claim the same.

2. Conveyance of Intangible Property. For valuable considerations, receipt of which is acknowledged by Assignor, Assignor assigns all of his right, title and interest in the Property Assigned to Assignee.

3. Recorded Information on Trust. The names and addresses of the grantor, trustees and beneficiaries of the trust, the identity of the trust and the relevant provisions of the trust have been disclosed in the Certificate of Trustees' Powers and Abstract of Trust which is recorded at: _____ .

.... | ....
Signatures of Assignor/Seller | Signatures of Assignee/Seller

STATE OF	**Acknowledgement of Assignor/Seller.** On this date, before me, a Notary Public, personally appeared:	Signature of Notary Public:
COUNTY OF	_____,	
Date of Acknowledgement:	known to me or satisfactorily proven to be the person whose name is subscribed to this instrument and acknowledged that he executed the same. If this person's name is subscribed in a representative capacity, it is for the principal indicated.	Notary Expiration Date:

This instrument was recorded at request of:	
The recording official is directed to return this instrument or a copy to the above person.	Space Reserved For Recording Information

ASSIGNMENT AND ASSUMPTION OF LEASE

TR-18 © LawForms 10-76, 12-85, 6-90

Effective Date:	County and State where Real Property is Located:			
Assignor (Name, Address and Zip Code):	Assignee (Name, Address and Zip Code):			
Subject Leased Premises (Address or Location):	Legal Description Proofed by Persons Whose Initials Appear to the Right	1.	2.	3.

Leased Premises Assigned (Legal Description of parcel on which leased premises are located):

Lessor (Name, Address, and Zip Code):	Lessee (Name, Address, and Zip Code):
Date of Lease:	Recording Number if Recorded:

1. **Conveyance**. For valuable consideration, receipt of which is acknowledged, Assignor, Assignor assigns to Assignee all right, title and interest of Assignor as ☐ Lessor ☐ Lessee in the Lease Assigned and the property rights of Assignor in the Leased Premises assigned as prescribed in the Lease Assigned.
2. **Assumption by Assignee**. Assignee assumes all terms of the Lease Assigned which were the obligations of Assignor as of the Effective Date. The below parties consent to this assignment.
3. **Recorded Information on Trust**. The names and addresses of the grantor, trustees and beneficiaries of the trust, the identity of the trust and the relevant provisions of the trust have been disclosed in the Certificate of Trustee's Powers and Abstract of Trust which is recorded at: _____

....
Signature of Lessor   Signature of Lessee

....
Signature of Assignor   Signature of Assignee

This instrument was recorded at request of:	The recording official is directed to return this instrument or a copy to the above person.

ASSIGNMENT OF PROMISSORY NOTE RECEIVABLE TO TRUST

Effective Date:	County and State where property is located:
Assignor (Name, Address and Zip Code):	Assignee (Name, Address and Zip Code):
Promissory Note Assigned (Address or Location of Original):	Legal Description Proofed by Persons Whose Initials Appear to the Right			

Promissory Note Assigned (Legal Description):

Promissory Note Assigened (Description):

All right, title and interest of Assognor in and to that certain Commercial Negotiable Prommissory Note dated _____,
in the principal amount of _____ by and between _____
as maker and Assignor as payee.

☐ Receivable Assigned (Description):

The Debt owing to Assignor by _____ the Debtor for the principal sum of $_____ which is evidenced
by a:

1. **Assignment of Title**. For valuable considerations, receipt of which is acknowledged by Assignor, Assignor assigns all of his right, title and interest in the Promissory Note assigned to Assignee.

2. **Recorded Information on Trust**. The names and addresses of the grantor, trustees and beneficiaries of the trust, the identity of the trust and the relevant provisions of the trust have been disclosed in the Certificate of Trustee's Powers and Abstract of Trust which is recorded at: _____

....
Signature of Assignor   Signature of Assignor

STATE OF	**Acknowledgement of Assignor.** On this date, before me, a Notary Public, personally appeared:	Signature of Notary Public:
COUNTY OF	_____,	
Date of Acknowledgement:	known to me or satisfactorily proven to be the person whose name is subscribed to this instrument and acknowledged that he executed the same. If this person's name is subscribed in a representative capacity, it is for the principal.	Notary Expiration Date:

This instrument was recorded at request of:

The recording official is directed to return this instrument or a copy to the above person.

Space Reserved For Recording Information

ASSIGNMENT OF MORTGAGE TO TRUST

Effective Date:

County and State where property is located:

Assignor (Name, Address and Zip Code):

Assignee (Name, Address and Zip Code):

Mortgage Assigned (Address or Location of Real Property):

Legal Description Proofed by Persons Whose Initials Appear to the Right			

Mortgage Assigned (Legal Description):

All right, title and interest of Assignor in and of that certain mortgage agreement dated _____ , by and between _____ as mortgagor and Assignors as mortgagee for the original principal amount of $_____ upon the following described real property:

1. Conveyance. Any transfers effectuated by this document transferring real property interests to a trust, involve the transfer of real property by the transfer of real property by the legal owners to a Revocable Living Trust which will have the same IRS identification number as the transferor, and will not be an Irrevocable transfer until the death of the transferors, and as such shall not warrant the triggering of "due on sale" clauses in any related documents, or the imposition of taxes, or tax reassessments, imposed when there is a completed transfer of real property ownership. The names and addresses of the primary beneficiaries of the trust at the time of this transfer, the disclosure of which may be required by "anti blind trust" laws in force or which may be later enacted, are:

2. Assignment of Title. For valuable considerations, receipt of which is acknowledged by Assignor, Assignor assigns all of his right, title and interest in the Property Assigned to Assignee.

3. Recorded Information on Trust. The names and addresses of the grantor, trustees and beneficiaries of the trust, the identity of the trust and the relevant provisions of the trust have been disclosed in the Certificate of Trustee's Powers and Abstract of Trust which is recorded at: _____ .

....
Signature of Assignor

....
Signature of Assignor

STATE OF COUNTY OF Date of Acknowledgement:	**Acknowledgement of Assignee.** On this date, before me, a Notary Public, personally appeared: _____ , known to me or satisfactorily proven to be the person whose name is subscribed to this instrument and acknowledged that he executed the same. If this person's name is subscribed in a representative capacity, it is for the principal indicated.	Signature of Notary Public: Notary Expiration Date:

This instrument was recorded at request of:

The recording official is directed to return this instrument or a copy to the above person.

Space Reserved For Recording Information

DEED AND ASSIGNMENT OF INTEREST IN DEED OF TRUST TO TRUST

TR-21 © LawForms 4-82, 1-89, 6-90

Effective Date:	County and State where Real Property is located:
Assignor (Name, Address and Zip Code):	Assignee (Name, Address and Zip Code):
Trustee of Deed of Trust (Name, Address and Zip Code):	Deed of Trust Date:
	Name of Original Trustor:
	Name of Original Beneficiary:
Subject Real Property (Address or Location):	Legal Description Proofed by Persons Whose Initials Appear to the Right			

Subject Real Property (Legal Description):

(Continued on Reverse Side)

SUBJECT TO all taxes and other assessments, reservations in patents and all easements, rights of way, encumbrances, liens, covenants, conditions, restrictions, obligations and liabilities as may appear of record or in the most recent title insurance policy on the subject real property. It is the intent of the parties to maintain and not waive all rights under the most recent title insurance policy on the subject real property.

1. **Recorded Information on Trust.** The names and addresses of the grantor, trustee and beneficiaries of the trust, the identity of the trust and the relevant provisions of the trust have been disclosed in the Certificate of Trustee's Powers and Abstract of Trust which is recorded at:_____

2. **Assignment.** Assignor assigns to Assignee all right, title and interest of Assignor in that certain above described Deed of Trust of Subject Real Property.

3. **Consideration.** For valuable consideration receipt of which is acknowledged, Assignor Specially Warrants to Assignee all right, title and interest of Assignor in Subject Real Property together with all rights and privileges appurtenant or to become appurtenant to Subject Real Property on effective date.

Assignee accepts this Deed and Assignment and receives ownership of the interest transferred as trustee for the _____
_____

4. **Effect of Transfer.** Any transfers effectuated by this document transferring real property interests to a trust, involve the transfer of real property by the transfer of real property by the legal owners to a Revocable Living Trust which will have the same IRS identification number as the transferor, and will not be an Irrevocable transfer until the death of the transferors, and as such shall not warrant the triggering of "due on sale" clauses in any related documents, or the imposition of taxes, or tax reassessments, imposed when there is a completed transfer of real property ownership.

☐ This is an Assignment of the interest of the Beneficiary of the subject Deed of Trust. Assignee herein is granted the right to receive and accept any and all sums due under that agreement and to enforce that agreement according to its terms.

☐ This is an Assignment of the interest of the Trustor of the subject Deed of Trust. Assignee herein assumes and accepts all obligations of that agreement and shall pay and fully discharge that agreement, holding Assignor harmless from any further liability thereon.

5. **Conveyance by Special Warranty Deed.** This special warranty deed made by the above named assignor, hereby grants, sells and/or conveys the above described property to the above named assignee, for true and actual consideration in the amount of 10.00 dollars, to have and to hold the same, with all appurtenance thereon, to assignee and assignee's heirs and assigns forever. I/We covenant that I/we convey and warrant specially the title against all persons claiming under me.

Signatures of Assignor	Signatures of Assignee

1... _____

2... _____
Signatures of Witness   Address of Witness

STATE OF	Acknowledgement of Assignor. On this date, before me, a Notary Public, personally appeared:	Signature of Notary Public:
COUNTY OF	_____,	
Date of Acknowledgement:	known to me or satisfactorily proven to be the person whose name is subscribed to this instrument and acknowledged that he executed the same. If this person's name is subscribed in a representative capacity, it is for the principal named and in the capacity indicated.	Notary Expiration Date:
STATE OF	Acknowledgement of Assignee. On this date, before me, a Notary Public, personally appeared:	Signature of Notary Public:
COUNTY OF	_____,	
Date of Acknowledgement:	known to me or satisfactorily proven to be the person whose name is subscribed to this instrument and acknowledged that he executed the same. If this person's name is subscribed in a representative capacity, it is for the principal capacity indicated.	Notary Expiration Date:

This instrument was recorded at request of:

The recording official is directed to return this instrument or a copy to the above person.

Space Reserved For Recording Information

DEED AND ASSIGNMENT OF INTEREST IN REALTY AGREEMENT FOR SALE OF REAL PROPERTY TO TRUST
TR-22 © LawForms 8-81, 6-90

Effective Date:	County and State where Real Property is Located:
Assignor (Names, Address and Zip Code):	Assignee (Names, Address and Zip Code):

Subject Realty Agreement For Sale:

Subject Realty Agreement For Sale is entitled:_____

and is dated _____ and numbered_____, if any, wherein the original Grantor/Seller is:

_____

and the Grantee / Buyer is:

Subject Real Property (Address or Location):	Legal Description Proofed by Persons Whose Initials Appear to the Right	1.	2.	3.

Subject Real Property (Legal Description):

(Continued on Reverse Side)

SUBJECT TO all taxes and other assessments, reservations in patents and all easements, rights of way, encumbrances, liens, covenants, conditions, restrictions, obligations and liabilities as may appear of record or in the most recent title insurance policy on the subject real property. It is the intent of the parties to maintain and not waive all rights under the most recent title insurance policy on the subject real property.

Assignor assigns to Assignee all right, title and interest of Assignor in subject Realty Agreement as follows:

☐ This is an Assignment of the interest of the Grantor/Seller of the subject Realty Agreement. Assignee herein is granted the right to receive and accept any and all sums due under that agreement and to enforce that agreement according to its terms.

☐ This is an Assignment of the interest of the Grantee/Buyer of the subject Realty Agreement. Assignee herein assumes and accepts all obligations of that agreement and shall pay and fully discharge that agreement, holding Assignor harmless from any further liability thereon.

1. Conveyance by Special Warranty Deed. Additionally and for valuable consideration, the above named Assignor conveys by special warranty deed hereby the following described property to the above named Assignee, for true and valuable consideration in the amount of $10.00 dollars, to have and to hold the same, with all appurtenances thereon to Assignee and Assignee's heirs and assigns forever. We covenant that we convey and warrant specially the title against all persons claiming under me.

2. Assignment. This assignment and deed is made to Assignee, as Trustee under Subject Trust, for Assignee to hold, sell, convey, mortgage or pledge, or otherwise handle as permitted and/or required under Subject Trust, and to do all things necessary or incidental for carrying out its purposes.

3. Recorded Information on Trust. The names and addresses of the grantor, trustees and beneficiaries of the trust, the identity and the relevant provisions of the trust have been disclosed in the Certificate of Trustees' Powers and Abstract of Trust which is recorded at:

_____

4. Effect of Transfer. Any transfers effectuated by this document transferring real property interests to a trust, involve the transfer of real property by the transfer of real property by the legal owners to a Revocable Living Trust which will have the same IRS identification number as the transferor, and will not be an Irrevocable transfer until the death of the transferors, and as such shall not warrant the triggering of "due on sale" clauses in any related documents, or the imposition of taxes, or tax reassessments, imposed when there is a completed transfer of real property ownership

....	....
....	....
Signatures of Assignor	Signatures of Assignee

1.. _____

2.. _____
Signatures of Witness   Address of Witness

STATE OF	**Acknowledgement of Grantor.** On this date, before me, a Notary Public, personally appeared: 1._____ 2._____, known to me or satisfactorily proven to be the person whose name is subscribed to this instrument and acknowledged that he executed the same. If this person's name is subscribed in a representative capacity, it is for the principal named and in the capacity indicated.	Signature of Notary Public:
COUNTY OF		
Date of Acknowledgement:		Notary Expiration Date:
STATE OF	**Acknowledgement of Trustee.** On this date, before me, a Notary Public, personally appeared: 1._____ 2._____, known to me or satisfactorily proven to be the person whose name is subscribed to this instrument and acknowledged that he executed the same. If this person's name is subscribed in a representative capacity, it is for the principal named and in the capacity indicated.	Signature of Notary Public:
COUNTY OF		
Date of Acknowledgement:		Notary Expiration Date:

This instrument was recorded at request of:

The recording official is directed to return this instrument or a copy to the above person.

Space Reserved For Recording Information

DEED AND ASSIGNMENT OF BENEFICIAL INTEREST IN REALTY TRUST TO TRUST

TR-23 © LawForms 4-82, 1-89, 6-90

Effective Date:	County and State where Real Property is located:
Assignor (Name, Address and Zip Code):	Assignee (Name, Address and Zip Code):

Trustee (Name, Address and Zip Code):

Trust Number: Trust Date:

Assignor Is:
☐ First Beneficiary or Successor of First Beneficiary
☐ Second Beneficiary or Successor of Second Beneficiary

1. Conveyance. For valuable consideration, receipt of which is acknowledged Assigner conveys to Assignee all of Assignors right, title, interest, powers, privileges, and benefits created or reserved to Assignor in this Trust.

2. Acceptance of Trustee Actions. This Deed and Assignment of Beneficial Interest is given and accepted with the understanding and agreement that Assignor and Assignee ratify, confirm, and approve all actions heretofore taken by Trustee and all disbursements heretofore made by Trustee, and is given and accepted with the understanding and agreement that the interest and the property held under this Trust which is conveyed and assigned is subject to all terms and conditions of this Trust Agreement, and subject to all obligations and liabilities under this Trust Agreement heretofore accrued or hereafter arising under the terms therof and the Assignee agrees to accept and be bound by all of the terms, conditions, stipulations and obligations thereof. Trustee is authorized to substitute the Assignee in place of Assignor under this Trust as of the effective date.

3. Assumption and Acceptance by Assignee. Assignee accepts this deed and assignment and approves all terms and conditions and agrees to be bound by and to comply with all obligations of the Trust, and receive ownership of the interest transferred as: ☐ Sole and separate property; ☐ Community Property; ☐ Not as Community Property or as Tenants in Common but as Joint Tenants with Rights of Survivorship; Not as Community Property but as Tenants in Common.

4. Approval by Trustee. Trustee acknowledges and approves this assignment and receipts that a copy has been filed with the Trustee.

(Continued on Reverse Side)

5. **Recorded Information on Trust.** The names and address of the grantor, trustees and beneficiaries of the trust, the identity of the trust and the relevant provisions of the trust have been disclosed in the Certificate of Trustees' Powers and Abstract of Trust which is recorded at:
_____

....	....	....
Signatures of Assignor	Signatures of Assignee	Signatures of Trustee
STATE OF COUNTY OF Date of Acknowledgement:	**Acknowledgement of Assignor.** On this date, before me, a Notary Public, personally appeared: _____, known to me or satisfactorily proven to be the person whose name is subscribed to this instrument and acknowledged that he executed the same. If this person's name is subscribed in a representative capacity, it is for the principal named and in the capacity indicated.	Signature of Notary Public: Notary Expiration Date:
STATE OF COUNTY OF Date of Acknowledgement:	**Acknowledgement of Assignee.** On this date, before me, a Notary Public, personally appeared: _____, known to me or satisfactorily proven to be the person whose name is subscribed to this instrument and acknowledged that he executed the same. If this person's name is subscribed in a representative capacity, it is for the principal named and in the capacity indicated.	Signature of Notary Public: Notary Expiration Date:
STATE OF COUNTY OF Date of Acknowledgement:	**Acknowledgement of Trustee.** On this date, before me, a Notary Public, personally appeared: _____, known to me or satisfactorily proven to be the person whose name is subscribed to this instrument and acknowledged that he executed the same. If this person's name is subscribed in a representative capacity, it is for the principal indicated.	Signature of Notary Public: Notary Expiration Date:

This instrument was recorded at request of:

The recording official is directed to return this instrument or a copy to the above person.

Space Reserved For Recording Information

AFFIDAVIT OF REVOCABLE LIVING TRUST DISCLOSURE

TR-25 © LawForms 10-76, 12-85, 6-90

Effective Date: of Trust:	County and State where Real Property is Located:
Grantor (Name, Address and Zip Code):	Trustee (Name, Address and Zip Code):
Trust Name (Exact Name as Set Forth in Trust):	Location of Trust. The Trust Document or Abstract Can be Located: At Docket _____, Pages _____, at the County Recorder's Office for the above set forth county.

Subject Real Property (Address or Location):	Legal Description Proofed by Persons Whose Initials Appear to the Right	1.	2.	3.

Subject Real Property (Legal Descriptiono):

Beneficiaries (List all Beneficiaries and state their present Addresses and Zip Codes):

The above is a list of the Primary Beneficiaries. Additional, Contingent or Successor Beneficiaries may also be named in the Trust.

(Continued on Reverse Side)

TERMS

1. Intent. In recording this Affidavit, it is Trustee's intent to comply with state requirements by placing in the records of the above described county the names of all Beneficiaries and their addresses and the identification of the Trust, as this information pertains to the above described Real Property. This Affidavit may serve to provide this information in relation to all past transactions concerning the Trust, or to the current transfer with which this Affidavit is recorded.

2. Beneficiaries. The above list sets forth the names and addresses of all Beneficiaries under this Trust. Depending on the nature and type of Trust, these Beneficiaries may be subject to change. However, as of the date of this Affidavit, the above list is a true and accurate list of the Beneficiaries under the Trust.

3. Real Property. The Subject Real Property completely describes all property held by the Trustee as Trustee pursuant to the Trust. This property may be comprised of all property transferred prior to this Affidavit, or the property which is being transferred under the Deed with which this Affidavit is being recorded.

4. Trustee. The below signed Trustee swears that: he has capacity to make this Affidavit; that he is the Trustee of the above described Trust, or is an Officer of the Trustee with the authority to execute such Affidavits on behalf of Trustee; and that all the information set forth in this Affidavit is true and correct to the best of Trustee's knowledge, information and belief.

....
Signature of Trustee   Signature of Trustee

STATE OF COUNTY OF	Acknowledgement of Trustee. On this date, before me, a Notary Public, personally appeared: _____, known to me or satisfactorily proven to be the person whose name is subscribed to this instrument and acknowledged that he executed the same. If this person's name is subscribed in a representative capacity, it is for the principal indicated.	Signature of Notary Public:
Date of Acknowledgement:		Notary Expiration Date:

ASSIGNMENT OF OWNERSHIP OF LIFE INSURANCE
AND INSTRUCTIONS TO INSURER
TR-26 © LawForms 8-76, 6-90

Effective Date:

County and State of Transaction:

Insurer (Name, address and zip code):

Assignor (Present policy owner's name, address & zip code):

Policy Numbers:	Face Amounts:	Life Insured:

Assignee (New policy owner's name, address and zip code. If a trust, designate name of Trustee as Assignee with name, date and Grantors of Trust.):

Owner's Designee Of Assignee (Name, address and zip code):

(Continued on Reverse Side)

1. **Consideration.** For valuable consideration, the parties, all being of legal age, execute this Assignment according to the terms hereinafter set forth.
2. **Assignment.** Assignor assigns to Assignee all right, title and interest in the above-described insurance policies, and all dividends, benefits and advantages to be had or derived therefrom, subject to the conditions of the policies, the rules and regulations of Insurer, and any indebtedness to Insurer against the policies.
3. **Ownership.** Assignees shall hold ownership to these policies in trust.
4. **Owner's Designee.** Subject to Assignee's power to modify this designation, Assignee instructs Insurer that, in the event of Assignee's death before the death of the Insured, the persons designated as the Owner's Designee of Assignee shall become owner of the policies.
5. **Beneficiaries.** In connection with this Assignment, Insurer is notified that all previous beneficiary designations are revoked and new beneficiaries are set forth on the attached Change of Beneficiary.
6. **Insurance Premiums.** Assignee assumes all responsibility for all future payments and agrees that Insurer shall look solely to Assignee for payment of these premiums.
7. **Effect on Policy.** The other provisions of the policy shall remain in full force and effect. The right to change beneficiaries or to transfer or assign ownership is transferred to Assignee.
8. **More Than One Policy.** If more than one policy is involved, the changes effected shall apply to all policies listed by number and face amount.
9. **Endorsement of Change.** If the policies require Endorsement of Assignment, Assignor requests that Insurer waive all such requirements and attach a copy of this instrument to Insurer's file copy of the policy.
10. **Effective Date.** This Assignment, upon being filed with Insurer, will take effect as of the date of this notice, except as to any payment made by Insurer before the notice is received by Insurer.
11. **Instructions to Insurer.** One copy of this Assignment has been attached to Assignee's copy of the policy. Assignor requests that you attach this Assignment to your copy of the policy and otherwise record this change. You are also instructed to notify Assignor and Assignee immediately if additional procedures or documents are needed to effect this Assignment. Assignor and Assignee acknowledge that you are assuming no responsibility for the validity of this Assignment.
12. **Trust Terms and Revocation.** If a Trust is involved, Insurer shall not be obligated to inquire into the terms of the Trust and shall be fully discharged from all liability after the death proceeds are paid to the last designated beneficiary of Assignee.
13. **Verification of Trust.** In the event a Trust is involved, Trustee, by signing below as either Assignor or Assignee, certifies that the Trust as described above is in full force and effect.
14. **Assignee's Rights.** Nothing stated herein shall be construed to limit Assignee's right to change beneficiaries, assign his ownership interests, modify the Owner's Designee, or any other right or interest in these policies.
15. **Payment and Settlement Options.** Assignee expressly authorizes any beneficiary **after** death of insured, to elect any payment or settlement option that may be available under the terms of this policy. It is the intent of this provision to give the beneficiaries of the policy, after the death of the insured, the greatest amount of flexibility in dealing with the insurer when faced with the many and varied circumstances that the beneficiary may have at the time of the insured's death.

Signature of Assignor

Signature of Assignee

STATE OF COUNTY OF Date of this acknowledgement:	**Acknowledgement of Assignor.** On this date, before me, a Notary Public, personally appeared:: 1. 2._____, known to me or satisfactorily proven to be the person whose name is subscribed to this instrument and acknowledged that he executed the same. If this person's name is subscribed in a representative capacity, it is for the principal named and in the capacity indicated.	Signature of Notary Public: Notary Expiration Date:
STATE OF COUNTY OF Date of this acknowledgement:	**Acknowledgement of Assignee.** On this date, before me, a Notary Public, personally appeared:: 1. 2._____, known to me or satisfactorily proven to be the person whose name is subscribed to this instrument and acknowledged that he executed the same. If this person's name is subscribed in a representative capacity, it is for the principal named and in the capacity indicated.	Signature of Notary Public: Notary Expiration Date:

ASSIGNMENT OF OWNERSHIP OF LIFE INSURANCE & INSTRUCTIONS TO INSURER - Page 2

DESIGNATION OF
LIFE INSURANCE BENEFICIARY

TR-27 © LawForms

Effective Date:	County and State of Transaction:
Insurer (Name, Address & Zip Code):	Policy Owner (Name, Address & Zip Code):

Policy Number:	Face Amount:	Life Insured (Name of Policy Owner):

New Beneficiaries (Name, Relation [if any] and Address):

   Primary:

   1st Contingent:

   2nd Contingent:

INSTRUCTIONS: UNLESS OTHERWISE PROVIDED, surviving beneficiaries in the same class will share equally. Terms like "share and share alike" are not necessary. It is not necessary to name beneficiaries in each class above.

1. Revocation and Change. All previous beneficiary designations under each policy numbered above are revoked. All proceeds shall be paid to the "new beneficiaries".
2. Effect On Policy. The other provisions of the policy shall remain in full force and effect. Any ownership or assignments of the policy previously transferred or held are not to be affected. Unless otherwise provided, the right to change beneficiaries or to transfer or assign ownership is reserved to the policy owner.
3. More Than One Policy. If more than one policy number is listed above, the changes effected shall apply to all such policies.
4. Endorsement Of Change. If the policy requires endorsement of change of beneficiary, I/we request that the Insurer waive all such requirements.
5. Effective Date. This revocation and change of beneficiary, upon being filed with the Insurer, will take effect as of the date of the notice, except as to any payment made by the Insurer before the notice is received by the Insurer.
6. Additional Procedures. One copy of this document has been attached to my copy of the policy. I/We request that you attach this to your copy and otherwise record this change. The Insurer is requested to notify the policy owner immediately if additional procedures or documents are needed to effect this change.

....
Signature of Witness
Name: _____

....
Signature of Policy Owner

Address:

STATE OF	**Acknowledgement of Policy Owner.** On this date, before me, a Notary Public, personally appeared:	Signature of Notary Public:
COUNTY OF	_____, known to me or satisfactorily proven to be the person whose name is subscribed to this instrument and acknowledged that he executed the same. If this person's name is subscribed in a representative capacity, it is for the principal indicated.	
Date of Acknowledgement:		Notary Expiration Date:

EMPLOYEE'S DESIGNATION OF BENEFICIARIES

TR-28 © LawForms

Name of Corporation (Employer):	Name of Retirement Plan Trust:
Employee (Name, Address & Zip Code):	Primary Beneficiary (Name, Address & Zip Code): Relationship to Employee:

Contingent Beneficiaries (Names, Addresses, Zip Codes and Relationship to Employee):

1st Contingent:

2nd Contingent:

---

1. **Primary Beneficiary.** I designate the above name Primary Beneficiary to receive the death benefits to which I am entitled under the above named Retirement Plan Trust.

2. **Contingent Beneficiaries.** In the event the Primary Beneficiary should predecease me, or in the event that our deaths should occur simultaneously, or in a common disaster or calamity, then, I designate the above named Contingent Beneficiaries to receive the amount to which I am entitled under the Trust. If more than one Contingent Beneficiary is named, they shall benefit equally, if no designation is given to the contrary. Should a Contingent Beneficiary not survive me, then the share of such person shall be distributed as follows:

☐ Per Capita, in its entirety, to the surviving Contingent Beneficiary, if there be only one; in equal shares to the surviving Contingent Beneficiaries, if there be more than one.

☐ Per Stirpes, equally by right of representation, to the living descendants of the deceased Contingent Beneficiary; but if there are none, then equally to the remaining Contingent Beneficiaries, if any, or if any be deceased, then equally by right of representation to the living descendants of the other deceased Contingent Beneficiaries.

3. **No Beneficiary Surviving Employee.** If, at the time of my death, none of the above name beneficiaries survive me, then my trust share shall be distributed as provided in the Trust.

4. **Right To Revoke Or Change Beneficiary.** I reserve the right to revoke or change the designation of any beneficiary, but such revocation or change shall be in writing to the Advisory Committee, and no such revocation or change shall be effective unless, and until, received by the Advisory Committee prior to my death.

5. **Effect Of Marriage Or Divorce.** I understand that my marriage or divorce after the effective date of this document shall be deemed to revoke the above designations, if written notice of such marriage or divorce is received by the Advisory committee before payment of the amount to which I am entitled under the Trust is made in accordance with such designations. I understand that I should file a new Designation of Beneficiaries following such marriage or divorce.

6. **Affidavits And Other Evidence.** The Advisory Committee may require an affidavit or other evidence, in form satisfactory to the committee, from any Primary or Contingent Beneficiary as proof of such beneficiary's right to receive benefits from the Trust. Payments made by the Trustee, upon directive of the Advisory Committee, in good faith reliance upon such affidavit or other evidence, shall relieve the Trustee and Advisory Committee from further liability.

(Continued on Reverse Side)

7. Rights Subject To The Trust. Rights of the designated beneficiaries shall be subject to the terms and conditions of the Trust and all rules and regulations formulated thereunder.

8. Release And Discharge. Payment of any credits or funds in my Trust Account to any beneficiary designated above shall be a full and complete release and discharge of the Trustee, the Advisory Committee and the Employer to the extent of such payment.

9. Revocation Of Prior Designations. I hereby revoke all prior designations of beneficiaries made by me before the effective date of this document.

....
Employee's Signature   Spouse's Signature

....
Signature of Witness   Signature of Witness

Name: _____   Name: _____

Address: Address:

Acceptance Of Designation. The above Designation of Beneficiaries is hereby accepted this date:_____

THE ADVISORY COMMITTEE

By ....

Title:

STATE OF COUNTY OF Date of Acknowledgement:	**Acknowledgement of Employee.** On this date, before me, a Notary Public, personally appeared: _____, known to me or satisfactorily proven to be the person whose name is subscribed to this instrument and acknowledged that he executed the same. If this person's name is subscribed in a representative capacity, it is for the principal named and in the capacity indicated.	Signature of Notary Public: Notary Expiration Date:
STATE OF COUNTY OF Date of Acknowledgement:	**Acknowledgement of Spouse.** On this date, before me, a Notary Public, personally appeared: _____, known to me or satisfactorily proven to be the person whose name is subscribed to this instrument and acknowledged that he executed the same. If this person's name is subscribed in a representative capacity, it is for the principal indicated.	Signature of Notary Public: Notary Expiration Date:

CERTIFICATE OF TRUE COPY

TR-29 © LawForms 6-90

1. I, _____ , the undersigned Notary Public, hereby certify that the attached is a true, complete and correct copy of that certain document titled:
_____ .

2. The above named document is dated: _____ .

3. The above named document is by and between _____ as _____ ,
and _____ as _____ .

4. An original of the above named document is on file at: _____ .

5. I am a notary of the State of _____ , and the county of _____ .
IN WITNESS WHEREOF, I have hereunto set my hand and seal this date: _____ .

Notary Expiration Date: _____   ....
                                                        Signature of Notary Public

10. How To Terminate Your Living Trust 35
   10.a. Before Grantors Die 35
   10.b. After Grantors Die 35

11. How To Safeguard Your Living Trust Documents 37
12. General Instructions for Filling Out Blank Forms 38
13. How To Process Blank Forms For Implementing Your Living Trust 39
14. Documents For Your Living Trust 40
   14.a. Living Trust (Declaration of Trust) 40
   14.b. Certificate of Trustees' Powers and Abstract of Trust 54
   14.c. Schedule of Assets Transferred to Trust 60
   14.d. Affidavit of Succession of Trustee for Trust 62
   14.e. Amendment of Trust 64
   14.f. Statement of Wishes 68
   14.g. Affidavit Terminating the Revocable Living Trust 70
   14.h. Special Warranty Deed 72
   14.i. Bill of Sale to Trust of Household Good and Effects 76
   14.j. Bill of Sale to Trust (General) 78
   14.k. Deed, Bill of Sale and Assignment (Omnibus) 80
   14.l. Letter of Instruction 84
   14.m. Affidavit of Trustee for Transfer of Motor Vehicle 86
   14.n. Stock Power and Assignment Apart from Certificate 88
   14.o. Bond Power and Assignment Apart from Certificate 90
   14.p. Assignment of Partnership Interest to Trust 92
   14.q. Assignment and Bill of Sale of Sole Proprietorship Property 96
   14.r. Assignment and Assumption of Lease 100
   14.s. Assignment of Promissory Note / Receivable to Trust 102
   14.t. Assignment of Mortgage to Trust 104
   14.u. Deed and Assignment of Interest in Deed of Trust to Trust 106
   14.v. Deed and Assignment of Interest in Realty Agreement for
         Sale of Real Property to Trust 110
   14.w. Deed and Assignment of Interest in Realty Trust to Trust 114
   14.x. Change to Financing Statement 118
   14.y. Affidavit of Revocable Living Trust Disclosure 120
   14.z. Assignment of Ownership of Life Insurance and Instructions to Insurer 124
   14.aa. Designation of Life Insurance Beneficiary 128
   14.bb. Employee's Designation of Beneficiaries for Retirement Plan Trust 130
   14.cc. Certificate of True Copy 134

15. Appendix A -- Examples of Sample Paragraphs
    of Final Distribution of Principal to Children. 136

16. Appendix B -- Examples of Sample Paragraphs
    of Final Distribution of Principal to Grandchildren 138

17. Appendix C -- Examples of Sample Paragraphs
    of Designation of Principal to Grandchildren 140

18. Glossary 142

Preface To The Living Trust Kit

Why has LawForms waited so long to write a Revocable Living Trust Kit? For a long time LawForms refused to prepare a Revocable Trust Kit. For over 10 years the LawForms company specialized in providing legal forms for attorneys only. After being requested by the Courts, the Bar Association and various governmental agencies, we finally began distributing law forms to the general public -- the non lawyers. But we still refused to create a Living Trust Kit. We perceived that Trusts were too complicated for the general public. These were documents that only lawyers could prepare!

However, in recent years, the public has been exposed to more and more books and seminars on Revocable Trusts. "Living Trust" has become a commonplace household word. More and more people want to "avoid probate", "centralize management of their assets", "avoid unnecessary taxes", and "avoid will contests and creditors". We saw a trend developing -- Living Trust Kits have been created by various legal form companies around the country. We have come to the realization that the general public is now educated enough to be able to implement the complex documents in a Living Trust when given careful guidance by experienced attorneys.

The legal practice of our firm, Goodson and Manley, Ltd, has concentrated on doing Trusts and other estate planning procedures for large and complex families. Usually large family owned businesses have varied business interests. Families of this nature need a much more complex trust than what is needed by families with estates of $600,000 or less. We have used our research and experience from this complex client work to structure special trusts for smaller estates.

We looked at some of the so called "Living Trust" kits on the market and found that they were incomplete. These kits often had serious mistakes which would cause problems after death of a Grantor, or when the Trustees or Successor Trustees tried to sell real property and convey a clear title. We felt compelled by the poor legal quality of these kits, to take the expertise we had from drafting intricate trusts for complex estates and to fit these ideas into a simplified but complete trust for families owning less than $600,000 worth of assets. In this kit we have included most of the transfer of asset forms and the other forms needed with a Living Trust. We feel that it is safe to say that LawForms has produced the most complete Living Trust Kit in America today.

In creating the Living Trust Kit we realized that the customer may conveniently use the LawForms Last Will and Testament Kit or preferably the LawForms Basic Estate Planning Documents for Families and Individuals Kit for a small family as the foundation for the Living Trust. LawForms, working with the Preventive Law Resource Center, strives to give the family complete legal protection. We strongly recommend that every individual with an estate with a net worth of $30,000 - $600,000 use the LawForms Basic Estate Planning Documents for Families and Individuals Kit with the Pour Over Wills, Living Wills, Durable General Powers of Attorney; Durable Powers of Attorney for Health Care, together with a Funded Living Trust. Funding the trust means that you will transfer all your assets to the trust.

Even though we have made the Living Trust Kit as understandable and simple as possible, we recommend that (1) you fill out all the legal documents in the Basic Estate Planning for Families and Individuals Kit or the Last Will and Testament Kit, (2) you have an attorney review your filled in documents, and (3) an attorney safeguard the original documents until they are needed.

We are struggling in today's world to economically survive the "goods and services" competition from Europe and Asia. We can no longer afford the losses in time, money, and emotions, when we don't have protective legal documents for our families.

We want the average American to enjoy the benefits of Preventive Law.

Sincerely,

John F. Goodson
President -- LawForms

1. Introduction To Your Living Trust

1.a. Background

The author of this LawForms Living Trust Kit, John F. Goodson is the President of LawForms, and a Lawyer who has practiced Estate Planning for more than 28 years. He has handled the estates of some of the largest families in his state, and has families come to him from other states for structuring of their estates and their family businesses.

Goodson gives lectures on Estate Planning at Law Schools, Colleges, State Bar Associations, National Conventions and other groups all over the United States. He is one of the few attorneys asked to speak two years in a row to the Million Dollar Roundtable, a national convention of the top Life Insurance Agents in the United States. He was acclaimed to have given the finest Estate Planning presentation ever given at the Million Dollar Roundtable.

In talking to these groups he saw an interesting phenomenon. When asking for a show of hands from these prestigious groups of Lawyers, Financial Planners, Life Insurance Agents, Certified Public Accountants, Business Executives, Undertakers, and Doctors, he found that less than 5% had more than two of the basic protective documents which every adult in the United States should have for their legal protection.

These intelligent, sophisticated, educated adults, most of them with legal advisors did not have Wills, Living Wills, Durable Powers of Attorney, Durable Powers of Attorney for Medical Care, Medical Authorization for their minor children and Living Trusts. As the founder of the Preventive Law Resource Center, this appalled Mr. Goodson.

It was like a medical doctor asking an audience of Parents; "How many of you have vaccinated your children against Polio, Diphtheria, Small Pox, Tetanus/Lockjaw, or Measles," and find that less than 5% of the audience had given their children this preventive medical care.

This LawForms Living Trust Kit and the Basic Estate Planning Documents for Families and Individuals Kit is dedicated toward educating the American public in Preventive Law. They provide our citizens and their families with understandable and affordable preventive law, with legal forms as good as those used by the practicing lawyers.

Because protecting an individual and/or family is very complicated, we urge all our readers, and form users, to have a "family lawyer" review the documents prepared in this Trust. It is important to see if anything has been forgotten, if mistakes have been made when filling out the documents, if additional documents are needed, if special circumstances require specialized "legal surgery", and to safeguard the originals in a fire proof safe. Your "family attorney" will do all the above including placing the documents in a safe in his/her law office so that the documents will always be available in the event of multiple catastrophes in the family. The lawyer will also be available immediately to help the family with emergencies.

1.b. When this Booklet can be Used

This LawForms Living Trust Kit is designed for families and/or individuals with a net worth of $30,000 - $600,000 who want to avoid probate court proceedings and give themselves the other advantages and protection offered by the Living Trust. Net worth is the total of the face value of all your assets, including the fair market value of your Life Insurance, minus your debts. If you arrive at numbers between $30,000 - $600,000, then you are a candidate for a Living Trust.

If you estate net worth is more than $600,000, or likely to rise above $600,000 soon, then the Trust in this Kit is not for you. You need the services of a Lawyer specializing in Estate Planning and an accountant knowledgeable of estate and tax planning.

If you own Life Insurance, it will be valued at its "face value" for purposes of valuing your estate.

The reason why going over the $600,000 will cause a problem is that the estate tax exemption stops at $600,000. Now you begin to run into tax problems which will require a new trust or an amendment to the trust to include special sub trusts known as Survivors Trusts (A Trusts), "Credit Shelter

Trusts" (B Trusts), "Marital Trusts" (Q or C Trusts), and Disclaimer Trusts (D Trusts).

Sounds complicated. It is, in fact it takes a great deal of skill to explain this simple Basic Living Trust. If you are an individual with an estate valued over $ 600,000, you are also a candidate for a Charitable Remainder Unitrust or a Charitable Annuity Trust.

When families have estates with net worth over $ 1,200,000 and individuals over $ 600,000, they must consider making a tax free gift to friends and relatives or charitable gifts: by making such gifts they will bleed away assets that will be taxed later with estate taxes.

If these legal moves are not timely made in large estates, the families and individuals will lose 37-60% of their estate assets to estate taxes when they die.

If you use this LawForms Living Trust Kit as directed your family will have many advantages, which we will discuss later in this explanatory booklet, avoid all probate costs, and not pay any Federal Estate Taxes.

This kit is ideal for retired people, wage earners, middle class families, small farmers, government workers, members of the Armed Services, teachers, and the small business person -- the people who do the work and pay the taxes in this country. They deserve the same legal protection that the very rich can afford!

The LawForms Living Trust Kit can help you even if you have an estate over $ 600,000. The only major benefit an estate over $ 600,000 will miss is estate tax protection. If you are slightly over the $ 600,000 figure you may still use the kit to avoid estate taxes if each year you give to charity, or to your family, gifts of assets to keep the value of your estate at a level of $ 600,000 and no more.

With this kit a husband and wife with an estate of over $ 600,000 can avoid estate taxes on the death of the first spouse to die if all assets are distributed to the surviving spouse. Here you will enjoy the famous "Unlimited Marital Deduction" which our beneficent government has given us to favor marriages. This has been given to discourage divorces in later life and keep families together. In this situation, however, when the second spouse dies you will be hit with estate taxes on the value of all combined assets over $ 600,000.

If, in the provisions of this trust, you gift, before or at the time of death, to your children, family, friends, or charity, everything over the $ 600,000 that you give to your spouse, you may still use this kit and avoid estate taxes on the death of each spouse. With this pattern you will have enjoyed the estate tax exemption belonging to both spouses. Simply stated it works like this; you die and, through the trust, gift $ 600,000 to your children. You use your $ 600,000 estate tax exemption. This leaves less than $ 600,000 in the trust for your spouse to transfer, at his or her death, with his or her exemption of $ 600,000.

If you fit into any of these patterns, then this Law-Forms Living Trust kit will provide the legal and tax exemptions you need.

1.c. Use of an Attorney

Of course, it would be best for you to use an attorney to do your Living Trust and your Basic Estate Planning documents. If you do, make sure your attorney is an estate planning specialist. Believe me, the run of the mill, non-specialist, attorney has less knowledge on estate planning than we provide in the LawForms Living Trust kit.

LawForms has received not one complaint from any attorney who has read our kits. Most of the forms used in these kits -- the LawForms Basic Estate Planning Documents for Families and Individuals Kit and the LawForms Living Trust Kit -- are better than those used by 90% or more of the attorneys. Our forms have been designed by estate planning attorney specialists.

An estate planning specialist has a unique pair of "legal glasses" which allows him/her to find special problems and tailor your documents to your own family business situation. The difference between this kit and what an estate planning specialist can do for you could be compared to the difference between a well constructed tract home and custom home.

In any event, we urge you to have an attorney review the documents after you have filled them out. The attorney can hold the original documents in a fire proof safe so that you are assured of having legal advice and protection if you have multiple family tragedies. The lawyer holding custody of the documents will also give you advice on how and when to update documents. He/she will also alert you when the laws change.

The cost of having an attorney review the documents as compared to drafting the documents is radically different. It will cost you between $ 50 - $ 200 to have a trained attorney review and approve the documents. It would cost you between $1,000 - $5,000 to have an attorney draw up and process your trust and do the property transfer documents.

We urge you to have an attorney review any documents relating to the transfer of real property assets -- land, buildings, farms, mortgages, deeds of trust. If you would rather not have an attorney review the documents, you should at least take them to a title company for review to make sure you haven't made a mistake which "clouds your title". Be certain to ask advice from an attorney if you have any exotic, complicated, or unusual property which you plan to transfer to the trust.

Remember, everybody in the United States wants to have a friendly family attorney who is available to help with every family emergency. Are you close enough to an Attorney that you know he/she will come to the jail in the middle of the night and bail you out? This is the test of your family lawyer relationship!

Your LawForms Legal documents however are still valid and enforceable even if you don't want to have an attorney review them if you followed the instructions correctly in this kit.

1.d. How to use this Booklet

This booklet contains all the legal forms necessary in full-sized samples, with numbered instructions for each page, for your living trust. This has proven to be the fastest, most accurate, and easiest way to complete the forms. You should read this booklet completely before filling out any forms to prepare the Trust or the Transfer documents for Funding the Trust.

The Living Trust Kit must be used in conjunction with the LawForms Will Kit or the LawForms Basic Estate Planning Documents for a Families and Individuals Kit which contains a LawForms Last Will and Testament. **You must have a Pour Over Will** with the Living Trust for full protection. The LawForms Will provides language to put assets into the trust which you may have inadvertently missed when you die. Imagine loading the Trust truck with baggage and driving away. You want someone there to pick up any baggage you leave and take them to the Trust truck when you die. All your baggage (property) should be in the truck (Trust) when you die for easy administration. If it is not your "pour over" Will pick up the rest and toss them into the truck using the pour over provisions of the Will.

2. Other Estate Planning Documents That You May Need

The LawForms Living Trust kit is not like the laundry soap DUZ, that does everything. The Living Trust fits in with other legal documents which every family and individual needs for preventive law protection. If you have a house, you still need a yard. If you have a car you want a garage to park it in.

Along with the living trust, the family, or individual, needs the basic documents contained in the LawForm's Basic Estate Planning Documents for Families and Individuals Kit. These documents are also included in the individual kits below:

- LawForm's Last Will and Testament Kit
- LawForm's Living Will Kit
- LawForm's General Power of Attorney Kit
- LawForm's Medical Protection for Minor Children Kit
- LawForm's Integrity Agreement - Protection from Lawsuits and Legal Hassles Kit

The legal documents for all the above kits and more, are included in the LawForm's Basic Estate Planning Documents for Families and Individuals Kit.

Most families and individuals without these documents have created a situation where a disaster is waiting to happen. Studies by the State Bar in California have shown that over 80% of the population has no legal protection whatsoever -- no protection from death, disability, brain damage, lawsuits or injuries to their minor children. The legislature in California was so concerned about this, they designed a Last Will and Testament form to circulate to the citizens of the state.

The following are the bare-bones, basic legal protection which everyone in the United States needs.

(1) **For protection on death**, everyone needs a Last Will and Testament. If you do not have a Will, you will have extra legal costs, confusion, delays in court, and possibly unnecessary family fights or/and psychological damage.

(2) **For protection from brain damage**, everyone needs a Living Will which is sometimes called a "Die with Dignity Will". The lack of a Living Will can subject you and your family to unnecessary medical costs and emotional damage. The Living Will gives direction and protection to those who have the courage to carry out your Living Will.

(3) **For protection when disabled**, every person must have a pre-signed Durable General Power of Attorney. Not having the Durable General Power of Attorney results in having to go to court, paying attorneys fees, and paying medical and other expenses necessary to have guardians and conservators appointed to act for you. Your personal and financial affairs tend to be complicated and delayed by these court proceedings.

(4) **Everyone needs protection against unnecessary lawsuits.** Not having the lawsuit avoidance form signed in advance will expose you to the blackmail and exorbitant costs of lawsuits and lawsuit threats. This form also allows you to settle discomforts with other people without losing their friendship and respect.

(5) **Everyone needs protection when needing medical care.** You are in the hospital - unconscious or delirious. You are not mentally able to give consent for medical treatment, and the doctors are afraid to operate. Must you go through a court proceeding at this time to have a special guardianship appointed while you are lying there in pain with gangrene festering? A Durable Power of Attorney for Medical Care will allow family and friends to take care of you immediately. It allows a trusted person to give consent for medical treatment for you, when you are unable to act for yourself.

(6) **For protection for minor children (age 17 or younger)**, everyone must have the temporary custody forms filled out in advance to provide medical care and discipline for your children while you are away.

(7) **For life, medical and disability, property and liability insurance needs,** we have designed "agent-of-record" contracts. Every family should sign these contracts with their insurance agent. This contract will make your insurance agent responsible for comprehensive plans of insurance. The agent-of-record

forms spell out the duties and responsibilities for you and your insurance agent. You will work together to establish the necessary protection.

Every mountain climber carries a backpack of emergency equipment. Every car owner has tools and jacks. We also should carry with us Preventive Law First Aid Kits.

One might say that you are derelict in your duty to your family, yourself, and to those you leave behind, or to those who must care for you, if you do not have these basic documents which are now readily available and affordable through LawForms.

Your next task today is not to buy toys for your children, trim the hedge, or plan your weekend. The most important task you have is to spend less than $60 and three hours of time to buy the legal forms that you need to protect yourselves and your family, fill them out, and review them with your family attorney.

3. Advantages Of A Living Trust

Reading this information will benefit you. We want you to be knowledgeable of all the advantages and benefits you will have when you read this booklet and complete, and process, the forms in this kit.

Revocable living trusts became a subject of living room conversation in 1967 when the book *How to Avoid Probate* was at the top of the best seller lists. Trusts were number one on the author's list of devices for avoiding probate. Now, more and more attention is being given to the revocable living trust as a tax-saving, probate-avoiding, and otherwise useful device for managing family estates.

While trusts of this type may take many different forms and variations, essentially they will provide income to you for life, may be amended or completely revoked during your life, and will manage and distribute the principal remaining after your death to your beneficiaries.

The Advantages of a Revocable Living Trust are:

3.a. Management of Assets

The trustee is responsible for management, including investment decisions, safeguarding of assets, and record keeping. The trustee's knowledge, experience, and access to information, particularly when a professional fiduciary is used, can often be helpful in increasing both income and principal.

3.b. Protection During Illness, Incompetency or Absence

The trust continues to operate while you are unable to attend to your affairs. If you like to travel, you can do so, secure in the knowledge that your interests will be fully protected. The trust, in conjunction with a Durable General Power of Attorney, will allow you to avoid the legal expenses of guardianships and conservatorships.

3.c. Continuity

Upon your death, the trust continues to operate uninterrupted by probate proceedings. If the trust provides income to be paid to your spouse, distribution will be according to plan. Usually, there is a delay when a Will is probated while assets are collected by the personal representative.

3.d. Probate Avoidance

In a continuing trust, assets do not go through the probate process. This saves attorney fees and expenses that would otherwise be incurred. However, this advantage should be weighed against the possible need for the trustee to render a formal accounting which entails some expenses as well. Taking property through probate results in expenses as high as ten percent of the value of the property. Whenever people own real property in more than one state, it is advisable to place that property in a living trust. If you do so before death of the Grantor, you will avoid multiple probates in each state where real property is located. When a trustee or beneficiary dies, the trust does not die, but continues to own the property. If a probate appears to be advantageous for any reason, a probate could be created using the optimum asset through a pour back clause in the trust.

3.e. Privacy

A trust generally provides more privacy than a Will, which becomes a matter of public record.

3.f. Choice of Law

You may create the trust in a state other than the one in which you are domiciled. Your home state may have undesirable laws regarding investments, accountings, and other matters. To take advantage of the laws that would best suit you, you should talk to a good estate attorney. Furthermore, you may want to name a trustee who might not qualify as such under the laws of your home state.

3.g. Less Easily Challenged than a Will

Disappointed relatives often try to upset a Will on the grounds of undue influence or mental incompetence. This is much more difficult to prove when a trust existed during the creator's life which was operated under his observation and was subject to his power to revoke.

3.h. Coordinated Estate Plan

The revocable living trust, when used in conjunction with a properly drafted Will and properly designated life insurance, pension plan, and profit sharing plan beneficiaries, places all assets into the trust for centralized control and distribution. Without the trust, the estate may be distributed piecemeal, resulting in delays and unintended inequities.

3.i. Qualification of Trustee

Competent family members or friends who live out of state might not qualify to serve as your personal representative in probate. However, with the revocable living trust, you can designate and qualify any person as the trustee without regard to out-of-state residency. You may want two trustees -- a money-wise trustee (the disinterested co-trustee) and a people-wise trustee (the family co-trustee).

3.j. Estate Tax Savings

With the LawForms Living Trust Kit you will avoid all estate tax if the net worth of your estate is less than $ 600,000 total -- adding up your assets at fair market value with the face value (what you get when you die) of your life insurance and deducting your debts:

Assets at Fair Market Value	$ 700,000
Face value of Life Insurance of Husband and Wife	$ 200,000
Less Debts	$ (300,000)
Net Worth	$ 600,000

You are safe from estate taxes as an individual or a family if your net worth, as calculated above, is $ 600,000 or less.

If a married couple gives all of their assets in their trust to the surviving spouse, they will avoid all estate taxes on the death of the first spouse. They will pay the estate taxes when the surviving spouse dies years later, if they don't spend or gift away enough assets or dollars to leave a net worth in the trust of less than $ 600,000 when the surviving spouse dies.

Here we recommend "Riotous living" and "extravagant gifting" for the surviving spouse to avoid estate taxes on the second death. This could be great fun for the survivor.

You can avoid most estate taxes on the death of the first Grantor if you give special distributions to your children, friends, or charities, with the LawForms Living Trust up to $ 600,000 and leave the rest to your spouse.

Of course, with the LawForms living trust you can avoid all estate taxes if you give to charity all your assets over $ 600,000 when you both die. You can also gift it away to children and friends before you die, in tax free gifts of $ 10,000 per donee person per year.

With the living trust and an annual gifting program by each spouse, you can avoid all estate taxes. You can gift away all your assets above the $ 600,000 net worth mark before you die in tax free annual gifts to each child and grandchild. To do this you are allowed to give $ 10,000 to each person -- this is $ 20,000 in gifts by the married couple to each child, grandchild, or other tax free gift donee.

3.k. Declaration of Trust

Most people desire to be the trustees of their trusts as long as they are living, and then, upon death or disability (and occasionally on retirement), to relinquish management of the trust to successor trustees. This type of instrument is called a declaration of trust. A declaration of trust will be created when a family places all assets into a living trust with the husband and wife as co-trustees. The survivor and a trusted financial adviser may serve as successor co-trustees upon the death or disability of either spouse. The family assets would then be managed in one centralized entity, similar to a family investment company. Should tragedy strike the family at any time, management of the trust continues without interruption under the direction of the successor trustees.

A declaration of trust is not only an excellent vehicle for estate planning on death or disability, but also a professional way to centralize management of the family investments and other assets with one financial statement and set of accounting records.

3.l. Saves Capital Gains in Community Property States

In community property states, property that would otherwise have been joint tenancy property (the usual way to avoid probate for small estates) may be placed advantageously in the trust. In this way it may be designated as community property belonging to the grantor husband and wife. If the property is in joint tenancy, on the death of one spouse, only the deceased spouse's share of the property (representing a one-half interest in each parcel of property) receives a new carry-over basis at death. This value is based upon the appraisals used for the estate tax return and the complicated formulas relating to establishing the new carry-over basis. However, if the assets are owned as community property, not only does the decedent's share of the property receive the new and higher tax basis, but also the survivor's share. This means the survivor's share, to the extent that the tax basis on that share has been raised, will avoid capital gains tax on that share when the property is eventually sold. What the preceding language is saying is that you can save tax dollars at the time of the death of the first spouse because you avoid some of the capital gains tax, when the surviving spouse sells the property.

3.m. Flexibility and Mobility

The living trust may be moved from one state to another without having to be licensed. There are very few recordation requirements when moving a trust. Compared with corporations and partnerships, which carry fees and recordation requirements, a trust can change location with relative ease.

Super trust provisions can be placed in a living trust to permit movement instantaneously from one state or one nation to another. Countries operating under English common law recognize trusts and permit trusts to move to and from their jurisdictions with minimum control.

Unfortunately, countries such as France, Germany, Spain, and Italy, which operate under Napoleonic Code, do not recognize the legal entity of trusts. Therefore, a trust document must be worded in such a way as to permit a trustee-beneficiary relationship to be defined as an analogous civil law relationship, if it is contemplated that the trust will be moved to a non-common law country. Imagine a trust document which provides that the moment Fidel Castro's invasion ships land on the shores of an island where the trust is situated, the trust automatically transfers its situs to Canada! The reason such a provision is necessary is because a trust must follow the laws of it's situs (the place where it is located and administered). If Fidel makes the operation of a Revocable Living Trust illegal and you lack this provision, a serious legal problem is created. Trust provisions which allow this are called Protector Provisions.

3.n. Spare Your Loved Ones the Hassles of Probate

Having a Living Trust gives a family or individual the feeling of security, They know that their estate has been taken care of and that the family will be spared the hassles of Probate. All decisions will be made in advance without burdening someone with being the executor of an estate, or heirs trying to second-guess the intent.

3.o. Speedy Transfer of Property to Heirs

With the Living Trust, the settlement of the estate is a quick, painless and delay-free matter handled according to your wishes. Since the transfer of property is done by your family instead of the legal system, the transfer can take place in almost no time at all.

3.p. Good Feelings

All of these advantages translate into the savings of money, time, emotions, court proceedings, legal fees, and peace of mind for you.

4. What Is Probate -- Why It Is To Be Avoided

4.a. Definition of Probate

Probate is the process of "proving" the Last Will and Testament, and making sure the title of the property is "clear". Probate is not necessary for all estates, but it is necessary to establish ownership of the property if the value of the estate is $ 30-60,000, or if real estate is included in the estate.

The title to a car or house must be proven to a buyer, so too must the title to assets in an estate be proven.

No court will direct the holder of a Will to go through probate -- the purpose of probate is to establish clear title to the property of the estate. If your spouse dies, and you don't plan to ever sell any of the property, you don't have to go through probate. However, if you ever wish to sell your home, car, or other assets that were held by you and your former spouse, you would have to have clear title, and this "clear title" is established by probate.

It is the responsibility of the Executor to oversee the probate. Probate is a complicated and time consuming process involving time in court, money and time spent with attorneys, and a good measure of frustration. The complexity of probate grows with the size of the estate. The steps required for a simple estate will go something like this:

The Executor of the estate must:
- Safeguard all the Assets;
- Petition the Court for Probate of the Will;
- Assemble and Inventory all the Assets;
- Get Appraisals of all Assets;
- Administer the estate according to the wishes expressed in the Will;
- Prepare and File final Tax Returns;
- Settle all Claims by Creditors and Family Members;
- Publish Notice to Creditors in the Newspaper;
- Distribute the Property of the Estate;
- Obtain Final Discharge from the Court.

As you can see from this abbreviated list probate can be a complicated, expensive, and time-consuming process. Problems will multiply if one of the parties challenges the Will at any point in time.

Most probates take at least two years to complete. Many Wills are challenged. If one of the heirs or family members can demonstrate that the intent of the writer of the Will changed after the Will was written, the court can rule against the Will. If the Will is challenged it must go through probate. For example, if a disinherited son claims that the deceased father would have given him part of the estate if the Will was written later, that son may gain some of the estate - even if the Will expressly left him out!

20% of Wills are successfully challenged in court! That means that out of every 10 Wills that are challanged in court, because someone thinks that they are wrong, 2 will be thrown out by the court. In other words, the Will that you wrote may be challanged and changed by a court after you are dead.

4.b. Costs of Probate

There are at least four different costs that can be found in a probate:

(1) **Legal Costs**. Probate normally costs from 5 to 10% of the estate. This cost includes lawyer's fees, court costs, and costs of witnesses and publishing.

(2) **Family Costs**. Probate also causes friction between family members. The longer a probate drags on, the more family members and other people involved with the estate are likely to disagree and have tension.

(3) **Publicity**. Probate requires publishing information about the estate. The property involved, and who will receive the property must be published in the newspaper for all to see.

(4) **Complexity**. You may have to do more than one probate. If the person making the Will had real property in more than one state, probate must be conducted in each of those states.

As you can see, probate can be a long, expensive hassle that hurts the family at the worst possible time. The good news is that it is entirely possible to avoid probate completely.

4.c. Ways to Avoid Probate

There are ways to partially or completely avoid probate. If done properly, even a Will can help the probate proceedings. The following examples are ways to avoid or help a probate proceeding:

(1) Last Will. A Last Will and Testament <u>will not</u> avoid probate. Most people think that a Will can be used to avoid probate. A Will can make probate easier and faster, but will not prevent probate proceedings.

(2) Joint Tenancy. Owning your property in Joint Tenancy will avoid probate on that property <u>on the death of the first spouse only</u>. Probate will still be necessary upon the death of the second spouse. Also, any property not owned as Joint Tenants will have to be probated.

(3) An Estate of Small Value. If the value of the estate is less than the minimum required for probate under State Law, no probate is required. The minimum amount varies from $30,000-$60,000. Usually, if any real property is owned, there must be a probate to prove title.

Keep in mind that this minimum value will be at the time of death, not when the Will is written. If the assets in the Will have increased in value because of inflation into the $30,000-$60,000 range, probate will be necessary.

(4) Living Trust. This is the best way to avoid probate. The estate will be settled in less than one hour, in private, with the property going exactly where it was intended to go. As we will see, a Living Trust is almost immune to legal challenges. It is fast and efficient, and also has tax advantages.

5. Other Information On Living Trusts

5.a. Definitions

To help you understand the terms used in this booklet, you may want to review the definitions below:

(1) Beneficiaries. These are the people who will receive money from the trust. Beneficiaries can be the Grantors, Trustees, friends, family, or charities which the Grantor has decided to name as beneficiaries in the trust.

(2) Estate. The estate is all the property that you have in your possession at any point in time. This includes real, personal, and intangible property. When you die this property will be taxed by the state with what are called estate taxes. You can avoid these taxes through the use of a Living Trust.

(3) Probate. This is a court procedure which is used to retitle property after someone dies. A probate action determines who has the title to what property after you die. Probate is very costly, and is to be avoided if possible. You can avoid probate by using a Living Trust.

(4) Real Property. This is land. Property is defined in three ways: 1) real property, which is the land and buildings located on the land; 2) personal property, which is the property that you have in your house such as the couches, beds, furniture and other items that you can see and touch; 3) intangible property, which is that property which cannot be seen, or held. This property is the stocks and bonds that you own, bank accounts, and insurance coverages.

(5) Trust. This is the document which you will be preparing to avoid estate taxes and probate. It has possession of your property, and a system for caring for the property, both before and after your death.

(6) Trustor. This person is also called the Grantor. It is this person that puts his/her property into the trust to avoid estate taxes and probate.

(7) Trustee. This is the person who will administer the trust. Generally this will also be the Grantor before the Grantor's death.

(8) Executor. This is the person who will distribute your money and property after you die, in the event you do not have a Living Trust.

5.b. The Difference Between a Last Will, a Living Trust, a Will, and a Living Will

Many people are not entirely clear about the differences between these three separate, distinct documents.

A Last Will is a Statement outlining who gets what property, who will receive no property, and detailing other wishes of the deceased. There are two basic types of Wills and a category for those who die without a Will:

(1) Holographic Will. This most basic type of Will is simply written by the property owner in his/her own handwriting on a plain piece of paper. As long as the Will is hand written and signed, it does not need to be witnessed. These Wills can cause problems later on if they do not have witnesses. Imagine how your children would react if they found out after you died that you had cut them off from any of your property. They would probably contest the Will, and they might just win.

(2) Attested Will. This is a more formal Will that is signed by three or four witnesses. It is either a pre-printed legal form, or a typewritten document prepared by the individual, or by an attorney.

(3) Intestate. When a person dies without any Will at all he/she has died Intestate. If this happens, the state will make a Will for that person automatically. Normally, all the property will be given to the surviving spouse, or to the children (states have different laws about who gets what property). This process takes a very long time to complete and must be avoided.

All property must be distributed out of the estate, as there is nobody named to hold title to the property (unlike a Trust, which lives on after you). If a person dies without a Will, they will not be able to make special gifts to friends and charities There is a much higher chance of family disagreements about who gets what property. Every adult in the United States must at least have a Last Will to avoid family and legal problems upon their death. It is important to understand that some family members may have rights to property even though they were left out of, or not mentioned in, the Will.

It is definitely better for a person to have a Will than to leave their estate to the mercy of the courts. But for most people, a Living Trust provides even greater advantages when added to a Last Will.

Don't confuse the Living Trust with the "Living Will". The Living Will is a special kind of Will used for giving legally enforceable instructions to terminate your life using passive means ("pull the plug") when you are hopelessly dying.

5.c. Living Trust

A Living Trust is a formal, binding contract upheld by the courts which separates the property from the family. The family still has the use and control of the property, but it is not considered part of their estate.

The major difference between a Last Will and a Living Trust is in the ownership of the property. With a Last Will, you and your family own the property of your estate, and the court and executor you name will oversee the distribution according to your wishes. The Probate process will prove the ownership is valid.

With a Living Trust all your property is owned by your Trust. Since you have no property, there is nothing to Probate. Upon the death of a spouse, the property is simply divided according to the terms of the Trust just like a private contract.

You control the property in the Trust. Even though your Trust owns your property -- you control the property. You may sell, assign, lease, or trade the property just as you do now. You may add new property to the trust and change the way it is divided on your death -- without having to re-write the Trust.

5.d. A Trust is a Contract and is Run Similar to a Corporation

A Living Trust is a legal contract that sets up a legal entity to handle your property under the guidance of a Trustee. The Trust actually owns your property which it directs the Trustee in handling. Of course, you will most likely appoint yourself and/or your wife as Trustee, so that you can continue to handle the property just as you have been.

The legal entity of the Trust is similar to a Corporation in that the Trust can own property and do other things for you and your family. Like a Corporation, the Trust exists independently of you and the other people involved. The Trust does not die when you die, but lives on to fulfill the wishes of you and your family as long as the Trust is necessary.

In this contract, you make agreements with family members and other people you choose to involve in the Trust. These agreements specify such things as: what will be done with the property upon the death of a family member, who will take care of minor children, how taxes will be paid (with some limitations), and other actions.

Because these agreements are made in advance, there is generally no reason to involve the court system. Privacy and the avoidance of legal hassles, are the biggest advantages of a Living Trust. A Trust creates peace of mind. You know that all your affairs are in order and that your family is taken care of.

5.e. Limited Liability

"Liability", as used regarding estates, is someone's exposure to a possible lawsuit. If a person does something that may bring a suit against him or her, that person has liability.

A Trustee who is buying or selling the property of a Trust could be worried about liability. He or she might worry that a creditor, the IRS, or some family member might file a lawsuit if they act according to the Trust. For example, a banker might worry that if he transfers an account from a deceased husband to the wife, the son may file a lawsuit.

To relieve these concerns, a good Trust (like the one in this kit) has a clause that expressly limits the liability of people acting according to the Trust.

Remember that the Trust is basically a contract. One of the things stated in the contract is that nobody involved will sue these people. That gets them "off the hook". The Trustee is further protected by the "LawForms Integrity Agreement".

5.f. Property Transfer Documents

No Trust is valid without transferring property into the Trust. Any Trust document without the required Property Transfer Documents is worthless.

These Transfer Documents simply take the property out of your name and put it in the name of the Trust. No need to be nervous, remember that you will still control the property.

5.g. "Pour Over" Will

It is generally not possible to include everything you own in the Trust. Most humans forget some piece of property. All your small personal items would take some time to transfer, and you will gain and lose many personal items over the years. The "pour over" Will will take care of all these miscellaneous items that you forget.

Even though this "pour over" Will is a Last Will and Testament, it is still possible to write it so you avoid probate. Each state has a minimum estate value required for probate. By keeping the value of the property passing under the "pour over" Will below this minimum, you will avoid probate with the "pour over" Will.

5.h. Economic Recovery Act of 1981

Congress gave some relief to taxpayers by passing the Economic Recovery Act of 1981. This law effectively exempts estates of $600,000 or less from any estate taxes.

This exemption is called the "Unified Credit". It is available to all estates, whether the estate is protected by a Will or Living Trust. If your estate is smaller than $600,000 at the time of your death, your estate will be exempt from Federal Estate Taxes, although you may still have to pay State Estate or Inheritance Taxes, depending on your state laws. This exemption has two types of deductions which may be used:

(1) Unlimited Marital Deduction. If you are married, the tax laws allow you to pass your property or estate to your spouse free of gift or estate taxes. However, this passing of property under the act must be specifically stated in your Will or Trust or it cannot be used. If your Will was made before 1981 it should be redone to insure that you get the unlimited marital deduction.

(2) Combined Exemption for Married Couples. The major tax advantage of the Living Trust in this kit is that it allows each married person the $600,000 exemption. In other words, the husband gets his $600,000 exemption and the wife gets her $600,000 for a combined total exemption of $1.2 million. By using the Living Trust included in this kit (or some other properly drawn Will or Trust) and follow the instructions you avoid estate tax up to $1.2 million!

5.i. Stepped-Up Valuation

The person receiving the property as an inheritance will have it valued at the market price -- at the time of death or six months after death. Increasing the value of the property to adjust for appreciation and inflation is stepped-up valuation. This gives a tax advantage to the person receiving the property under a Will or Trust.

5.j. How the Living Trust Works

The Living Trust is created when the forms in this kit are completed and properly processed as shown in the instructions that follow. Under law, there must be certain conditions present to create a Trust:

(1) Actual and Constructive Expression. Actual and constructive expression either by words or by conduct that the Trustor intends to establish a Trust in respect to some particular property;

(2) Identifiable Designation of Property. Identifiable designation of property to be owned by the Trust;

(3) Actual Designation of Parties to the Trust;

(4) Valid Trust Purpose. Valid trust purpose such as providing for one's children, and family -- it is not legal to create a trust to hide property from creditors;

(5) Effective, Immediate and Present Transfer of Property to the Trust. Once the Trust has been created, it must be funded by transferring property into the Trust. This kit includes transfer documents that will accomplish this purpose.

You must appoint the following people to manage and administer the Trust:

(1) Trustor/Grantor. This is the person who will transfer the property into the trust; **(2) Trustee.** This is the person who will administer the Trust, and make sure it serves its purpose correctly -- you can be both Trustor and Trustee; (3) **Successor Trustees.** This is a backup Trustee in case the primary trustee is unable to fulfill the responsibilities as Trustee for any reason; (4) **Beneficiaries.** The persons who will benefit from the Trust. In most cases, this will be you and your children.

5.k. Dower Law States

Dower Laws apply only to the following states. In these states the surviving wife is entitled to the use of 1/3 or more of the departed husband's real property as long as she lives. This applies even if the property was sold to a third party without the wife's signature on the deed.

- Alabama
- Delaware
- Florida
- Hawaii
- Kentucky
- Massachusetts
- Michigan
- Montana
- New Jersey
- Ohio
- Rhode Island
- South Carolina
- Tennessee
- Vermont
- Virginia
- West Virginia
- Wisconsin

The wife needs to sign off on the documents transferring property to avoid creating a cloud on the title of the property after the husband dies. If she does not, it will be hard to sell the property out of the trust later.

5.l. Curtesy Law States

This is very similar to the Dower Law. The states listed below have Curtesy laws which give the surviving husband the use of at least 1/3 of the real property as long as he lives. This law only holds for the states listed below:

- Delaware
- Hawaii
- Kentucky
- Massachusetts
- Ohio
- Rhode Island
- Tennessee
- Vermont
- Virginia
- Washington D.C.
- West Virginia
- Wisconsin

The husband needs to sign off on the documents transferring property to avoid creating a cloud on the title of the property after the wife dies. If he does not, it will be hard to sell the property out of the trust later.

5.m. What the Trust Does Upon Your Death

Upon the death of one of the spouses, it is not necessary to inform the probate court of the existence of the Living Trust. The Trustee can then carry on with the wishes of the deceased Grantor as quickly as desired, in privacy.

It may be necessary to show a copy of the Living Trust to persons who hold property owned by the Trust such as bank officers, stock brokers, etc. We recommend that you keep a Certificate of True Copy (LawForm TR-29, see section 14.b) and an attached Certification of Trustees' Powers and Abstract of Trust (LawForm TR-2, see section 14.cc) that the trustee can use in this situation.

6. Steps For Implementing Your Living Trust

You took the most important step. You purchased this kit... and you have begun to read it. WAY TO GO!! Now what are the steps for you to have all the benefits of the Living Trust?

Step One -- Read the Booklet

Read the instructional booklet. It is important for you to read through the booklet to get a general idea of what you need to know about living trusts. By creating a living trust on your own, you are saving $ 600 - $ 3,000 which you would have paid to an attorney to do this work for you.

You will probably learn more about living trusts after you read this booklet than the lawyer could or would have told you, while his meter was running at $ 100 - $ 200 an hour.

The material is important to you and your family. You may want to read it out loud to one another and talk about it as you go through it.

Step Two -- Charge Up Your Determination.

Determine if you are willing, ready and able to make the commitment. When you read the material it will sound complicated. You will have doubts as to whether you can do all this yourself.

You probably will save your family more than one years salary by having the living trust to avoid probate, taxes and other complications. You know you will save $ 600 - $ 3,000 on attorneys fees by doing the kit yourself. Best of all, you will know and understand what you have done with the living trust. You are less dependent on others. You are providing for your family yourself -- in the pioneer American spirit.

You should read the booklet a second time if you don't understand it completely. Actually you will find it easy to fill out the forms, and set up your trust, once you are started. You have examples and instructions. You will see how the example forms and instructions fit in with what you read in the instruction book. You will feel the logic and common sense of what you are doing.

If you have read to this point you are ready, willing and able to finish all that is necessary for you and your family to enjoy the advantages of a living trust. If you still have any doubts read Section 3 -- Advantages of Your Living Trust -- and count the dollars, time and aggravation you and your family will save by having a living trust.

Step Three -- Make Sure You Have Your Basic Documents in Order

Your family needs other protective legal documents besides the living trust. You will need the LawForms Last Will and Testament contained in the LawForm Will Kit and in the LawForms Basic Estate Planning Documents for Families and Individuals Kit. The LawForms Last Will and Testament has in it a "pour over" clause which combines your living trust with the other documents of your estate.

You will also need a Durable General Power of Attorney contained in the LawForms' General Power of Attorney Kit, and in the LawForms' Basic Estate Planning Documents for Families and Individuals Kit. The Durable General Power of Attorney will authorize your family members to transfer assets you may have missed, and to clean up any mistakes when you are incapacitated before your death.

These basic documents are all discussed in Section 2 (Other Estate Planning Documents That You May Need). If you don't have the basic documents in place your Wills, Living Wills, Durable General Power of Attorney, Durable Power of Attorney for Health Care, your family may suffer something even worse than having your property being complicated with court involvement, extra taxes, delays, and aggravation from not having a living trust.

The Living Trust does not fix all your estate problems. You need the other basic estate planning documents listed even more than the living trust.

Step Four -- Think Through and Fill In the Living Trust Forms

Go for it! Next you should begin filling out the Living Trust. Before you actually start writing, you will want to talk to your family about important decisions you need to make when filling out the trust.

- Who do we want to be the major beneficiary of our estate? (Paragraph 1.2 of Trust)
- Who do we want to be the successor trustees when we die? (Paragraph 1.3 of Trust)
- Do we want to discourage addictions in our children and beneficiaries? (Paragraph 1.15 of Trust)
- Do we want to distribute special gifts when one of us dies, and if so, to whom? (Paragraph 2.5.b of Trust)
- Do we want to distribute special gifts when both of us die, and if so, to whom? (Paragraph 2.5.b of Trust)
- How do we want to divide our estate among our children, relatives, and friends? (Paragraph 2.6.a and 2.6.b of Trust).
- When our children or other primary beneficiaries die, how do we want to take care of their children? (Paragraph 2.7.c of Trust).
- Do we want to provide money to any churches, synagogues or charities? (Paragraph 2.9.a of Trust)
- Do we want to provide any disincentives if our loved ones do things we don't approve of? (Part 12 of Trust)

These are some of the points you will want to discuss among yourselves and with your family before filling in the Living Trust form.

Now you're ready. Use a **red pen** and write in the inserts you want for your Trust in the space provided in the booklet where the example is given. You may compare your inserts with the example inserts.

You will find in Appendix A sample inserts for various provisions, previously used by our clients, for successor trustees and principal distribution clauses.

If you want to remove any provision of the trust which you don't like, cross it out with a "Z" pattern and initial the top and bottom of the "Z" as illustrated in Section 12 (How to Fill Out Your Blank Forms).

After you've thought through the decisions required in the Living Trust, discussed it with your family, and drafted inserts in red ink in the example spaces in the booklet, you are ready to type up the Living Trust.

Step Five -- Fill In the Certificate of Trustees' Powers and Abstract of Trust

No Problem! You merely take the corresponding provisions from the Living Trust which you have filled in and transpose them into your Abstract. The Abstract is an abbreviation of the trust which you will show to the general public when you deal with them as a Trustee.

Step Six -- Document Your Property

We have provided you with a "Schedule of Assets Transferred to the Trust" (LawForm TR-3, see section 14.c) for listing all your property. Think of everything you own of value and list it on that form using a "nickname" for each property. The nickname clearly identifies the property for you and your accountant. Examples of nicknames are:
- "Our Residence"
- "The 12th Street Rental"
- "Fennedy Corporation Stock"

You may want to put approximate values of the assets on this form. We suggest you write it in red ink on the sample form, then transfer it to the blank form.

Step Seven -- Transfer Assets to the Trust

Now comes the heavy work. You will want to prepare transfer documents for every asset on your Schedule of Assets. Write what you want to fill in on each transfer form example in red ink then copy it onto the forms themselves. If you need more transfer forms, call LawForms at 1-602-254-0424.

With complicated assets such as real estate ownership interests you may want to talk to a real estate attorney or a title company before executing and recording the documents. You don't want to make a mistake which creates a problem on the title to your property!

If you have any complicated interests in business corporations such as restricted stock, S-Corporation stock, professional corporate stock, you may want to talk to the attorney for the corporation, your attorney, or your accountant to be sure that your transfer does not cause tax or legal problems.

You have finished step 7 when you have a transfer document, or a letter of instructions filled out for every asset on your schedule of assets.

Step Eight -- Execute the Documents

You will want to bring in or visit a notary public and execute all of the documents and have them notarized. You will also need to have the three witnesses sign the documents, on documents where three witnesses are required, at the same time.

If you are planning to have your documents reviewed by the estate planning attorney, this would be the best time -- right before you execute the documents.

The attorney may catch a mistake you couldn't see, or see a good idea that wasn't apparent to you. Our firm charges $ 100 for a review of this type. This includes the notary public services and the storage of the original documents in a fire proof safe. An attorney review is like buying an insurance policy to protect something you may have overlooked.

Step Nine -- Make Copies and Process

When the documents are executed you will want to make extra copies from the originals for Co-Trustees, family members, your family attorney, and your family accountant. Some of the copies you will want certified. We recommend that you have in your possession at all times, one certified copy of the Living Trust (LawForm TR-1, see section 14.a), and 3 certified copies of the Certificate of Trustees' Powers and Abstract of Trust (LawForm TR-2, see section 14.b). As you use these, ask the person who looks at the Certificate of Trustees' Powers and Abstract of Trust to make a copy for their files so that you may use the Certified Copy of the Certificate of Trustees' Powers and Abstract of Trust again.

You will want to record Certified Copies of your Certificate of Trustees Power and Abstract of Trust with your county recorder, and with the county recorder in every county where you own real estate.

Do this before you record and process your transfer documents. You will want to take the recording information and write it into each of your transfer documents so that the trust information will be available for all who deal with those transfers.

Follow the instructions for processing each form that is contained with the instructions. We have included A Certificates of True Copy (LawForm TR-29, see section 14.cc) for you to use in processing your documents.

The original documents you should place in the document envelope to safeguard them as we have suggested in Section 11 (How to Safeguard Your Living Trust Documents).

If you need more than one form for multiple properties, LawForms has consented that you photocopy up to five copies of each form without violating our copyrights -- or you may want to phone LawForms at 1-602-254-0424 to request additional forms.

Step Ten -- Review Your Documents

We suggest your review your estate and trust each year at the same time each year, right after the year end when you do your income tax.

Re-read all your Basic Estate Planning Documents, and your trust, to remind yourself of what you have. If you think of better ideas or have discomfort, you can easily amend the documents as described in Section 8 (How to Amend Your Living Trust). You may want to review the documents with your family attorney and your accountant.

It is helpful to have recent information on the tax returns and a new year end financial statement when you do your review. You will want to be sure that every asset on your financial statement is in your trust.

If a Trustee dies, documents will be processed to replace the Trustee as outlined in Section 9 (How to Change Trustees of Your Living Trust). If on your review you are fed up with the trust or there are reasons to terminate it, refer to Section 10 (How to Terminate Your Living Trust).

Each year before or after your review you may want to re-read the instruction book to refresh your memory on the Living Trust (Section 3 -- Advantages of Your Living Trust, and Section 7 -- How to Operate Your Living Trust).

After doing all this, you will have a feeling of pride, confidence, and security -- you have protected your family and your property with your Living Trust and other Basic Estate Planning documents.

7. How To Operate Your Living Trust

A Living Trust is a legal vehicle -- just like a car. When you buy one you will want to know how to operate it.

A financial planning colleague explained a Living Trust to a client as being "like a toy box in which you put all your toys to safeguard them". The Trustees are the persons in charge of the toy box. If one dies, another supervises the toy box. The toy box keeps toys from getting lost. The toy box supervisor makes sure the toys are kept in good order. If you take them out of the box, you make sure you put them back. Before you go to bed you want to make sure all your toys are picked up and in the box. The toys are always there for the kids to play with.

So also is it with trusts. When you are the Grantor, you put all your assets (toys) in the trust. Then the Trustees make sure the assets are maintained, and that the money and assets in the trust are available for the beneficiaries to play with -- all in accordance with the instructions in the trust document.

As soon as you, the Grantor, put the assets into the Revocable Living Trust (The Toy Box), you become the primary Trustee responsible for the toy box. When you die, become disabled or incompetent, someone else, whom you have designated in the Trust, will be the successor Trustee.

All Trustees need to know how to manage a Living Trust. This is important because the Trustees will be the persons responsible to make sure that there are enough toys left for the next generation of children to be happy. The next generation will not be happy if there are not enough toys to play with.

People have various reasons for creating revocable living trusts. The most common are:

- To avoid probate administration upon death or in the event of lifetime disability
- To obtain favorable estate tax consequences
- To provide for the management of assets
- To provide for the distribution of assets during the administration of the trust and at its termination

The terms of the trust instrument can help reduce or eliminate estate taxes. If probate avoidance is the goal, it can be accomplished by the transfer of assets to the Trustee upon the creation of the trust. To avoid probate additional assets, acquired after the creation of the trust, should be placed in the trust by the Grantor (the person funding the trust).

Both Trustee and Grantor will need to understand the process of transferring assets, since, as noted above, this is essential if probate is to be avoided. In effect, the Grantor of a trust is transferring property, while he is capable of doing so, rather than leaving assets in his name to be cleared through a probate administration at his death. Under most state probate procedures, the living person can transfer his or her own property more easily than a personal representative can on that persons death. A living person has freedom to act with his own property. A personal representative is limited by a Will (if any), by statute, by court procedures, and by the taxing authorities. The advantage of a trust is that the property is transferred out of the name of the grantor before he dies and into a vehicle which will remain "alive" even after he dies, making the transfer of assets to his children easy. For a trust to work best it must be funded. Toys must be placed in a toy box.

These guidelines are designed to explain the transfer process and to assist the individual Trustee in administering a trust.

7.a. Funding the Trust

Funding the trust is crucial. The Trustee can only work with the assets which have been transferred to the trust. In addition, probate administration can be avoided if assets are in the Trustee's name at the Grantor's death, or in the event of a disability which would otherwise require a Probate Court supervised guardianship. Any assets in the Grantor's name which are overlooked and are not transferred to the Trustee prior to the Grantor's death or disability, will be subject to a probate administration at his death. The Grantor's attorney often handles most of the initial asset transfers. This kit provides all the transfer documents needed and the information to make the transfers to the trust. Both the Grantor and Trustee should be familiar with the transfer process. Assets acquired after the trust is created must be transferred into the trust in order to become part of the body of the trust.

(1) How to Transfer Registered Securities - Stock Certificates and Bond Certificates

Where all the active Trustees are individuals (not bank officers) the most common method of funding the trust with registered securities (stocks and bonds) is to place them in the name of the Trustee of the specific trust. An example of this situation is to register the securities as follows: "John K. Fennedy, Trustee of the Fennedy Family Trust, dated January 1, 1990." Take the shares to your stock broker, or transfer agent, and ask him/her to place them in the name of the trust.

Registration or re-registration of securities in this manner is not difficult. There may be some delay upon transfer of a security so registered while the requirements of the stock transfer agent are satisfied. Securities registered in this manner are not expected to be registered securities held which will be traded actively.

While steps are being taken nationally to ease transfer requirements where Trustees are involved, transfer agents still proceed with caution. Although generally not required, it may be necessary to provide the transfer agent with a copy of the trust agreement. However, the Certificate of Trustee's Powers and Abstract of the Trust, referred to in the section 7.a.(4) below on real estate, will serve as substitute for a copy of the entire trust agreement.

The forms used for transferring securities are the Stock Power (LawForm TR-14, see section 14.n) and the Bond Power (LawForm TR-15, see section 14.o). If you have a stock broker, you may want to have him or her transfer certificates for you. In this case you will provide the stock broker with information on the trust using the Letter to Securities Broker (LawForm TR-12b, see section 14.l).

(2) How to Transfer Unregistered Securities

Securities in bearer form present no particular transfer problems, and there are no registration problems. A Bond Power (LawForms TR-15, see section 14.o) from the Grantor to the Trustee of the specific trust should be executed. The assignment should describe the property with enough clarity to prove the Grantor's intent that the security be considered a trust asset. Stapled or otherwise attach the Bearer Bond to the Bond Power.

(3) How to Transfer Street Name Accounts - Holding Securities

A convenient method of holding securities is in a broker's street name account. This device is available only when the trust maintains sufficient trading activity from the broker's viewpoint to justify the street name account.

For transferring the Street Name Account you will use the Letter to Securities Broker.

(4) How to Transfer Real Estate Interest

For transferring interests in real estate you will use: the Special Warranty Deed (LawForms TR-8, see section 14.h).

Conveying real estate to a Trustee with a Special Warranty Deed may lead to the same problems encountered as with transferring securities. The trust agreement can define limits on the Trustee's power to deal with real estate. A prudent purchaser, lessee, etc. may demand proof of the Trustee's powers. Proof will be established by recording with the county recorder, a copy of the Certificate of Trustee's Powers and Abstract of Trust, and referring the recording information in that transfer document.

The Certificate of Trustee's Powers and Abstract of Trust is signed by the Grantor and Trustee. The Abstract contains pertinent excerpts from the trust agreement, including: the Trustee(s); a description of the mechanism by which a designated successor Trustee becomes active; a statement of the trust's revocability; a listing of powers given the Trustee, particularly the power to sell, mortgage, make improvements, and enter into leases with respect to real estate; and, finally, a recitation of any provisions in the trust agreement designed to protect purchasers of trust assets.

Recording costs for a Certificate of Trustees' Powers and Abstract of Trust are nominal. If privacy is an issue you do not have to state the assets which are in the trust. When someone looks at the Certificate they will find out the powers of the Trustee but are not allowed to find out how much money has been left to the beneficiaries.

When the Certificate of Trustees' Powers and Abstract of Trust has been recorded, the Grantor will refer to the docket and page of the recording in the space provided in the deed.

This makes reference to the place of recording the Certificate of Trustee's Powers and Abstract of Trust. This approach should be completely satisfactory for identifying the trust and trustees' powers.

Out-of-state real estate poses a special problem. In many cases a corporate (i.e., bank) trustee, or successor Trustee, from the state of the Grantor's residence will not be empowered to act as trustee when property of the trust is located out of state. This may preclude a conveyance to a bank trustee if you have designated a bank trustee in your trust. If out-of-state real estate is acquired subsequent to the creation of the trust, an attorney should be consulted regarding how title to the real property will be transferred if you have a bank as one of your trustees.

Any less than absolute ownership in real estate, such as a land contract, seller's or buyer's interest, or a tenant's interest, should also be assigned to the Trustee. If recordation is not involved, no reference need be made to the Certificate of Trustees' Powers and Abstract of Trust reflecting the trust's existence and the Trustee's authority. The terms of the land contract, lease or other relevant document should, of course, be reviewed to assure that assignment is permitted.

If your real estate is encumbered by Deeds of Trust, or other mortgage documents, we recommend that you consult with the financial institution which holds the Deed of Trust mortgage or other encumbrance, to make absolutely certain that the transfer of the property to your trust will not cause any acceleration of your mortgage. This is usually not a problem because your Living Trust is a REVOCABLE trust which means that you are still the 100% beneficial owner of the property. However, we recommend that you make absolutely certain that there will be no problems or future questions. You should have the financial institution give you a letter indicating that they consent to the transfer.

Whenever you acquire a new piece of property, you may ask the escrow company to title the asset in the name of your Living Trust.

(5) How to Transfer Tangible Personal Property

Since tangible personal property such as household furniture and furnishings, jewelry, etc., is without any recognized documentation of title, transferring this property to the trust is made by a bill of sale from the Grantor to the Trustee. However, since this property changes constantly, the initial bill of sale should cover any and all tangible personal property now owned or hereafter acquired. A bill of sale of this type should be sufficient evidence of the Grantor's intent to achieve the desired probate avoidance, especially when the assignment is coupled with a Pour Over Will leaving everything to the trust.

This kit has forms for transfer of all types of Tangible Personal Property into the trust; Bill of Sale - Household Goods (LawForms TR-9, see section 14.i), and the Bill of Sale (General) (LawForms TR-10, see section 14.j).

(6) How to Transfer Bank Accounts

The best approach to transferring bank accounts to a trust is registration in the name of the Trustee of the specific trust, e.g., "John K. Fennedy, Trustee of the Fennedy Family Trust, dated January 1, 1990". Trust registration need only be on the signature card held by the financial institution. You are not required to put the name of the trust on passbooks, checkbooks, or checks. The signature card for the savings or checking account may provide that one signature is sufficient, so that each Trustee can transact business in the absence of other Trustees. The Certificate of Trustees' Powers and Abstract of Trust referred to in connection with the funding of real estate can be used to supply basic information about the trust. This way it is possible to avoid giving the financial institution in which the account is located, a copy of the entire trust agreement with the financial institution.

You will also want to change your safety deposit box into the name of the trust. If anything happens to you, a Trustee can get into the safety deposit box.

We have provided a Letter to Bank (LawForm TR-12c, see section 14.l) to educate the banker on the trust and how to change over the accounts and the safety deposit box.

(7) How to Transfer Life Insurance

The trust should be the beneficiary and owner of life insurance policies on the Grantor's life. However, if the Grantor is the owner of insurance on his or her spouse's life, ownership of the policy must be transferred to the Trustee as well. This could constitute a probate asset in the Grantor's estate if the Grantor predeceases the insured spouse if the ownership of the life insurance is not transferred to the trust.

The forms transferring the ownership and beneficial interest in the life insurance to the living trust are; Assignment and Ownership of Life Insurance (LawForm TR-26, see section 14.aa), and Designation of Beneficiary of Life Insurance (LawForm TR-27, see section 14.bb).

Watch Life Insurance closely. If your Life Insurance face values throw the value of your estate over $600,000, you will want to confer with an attorney on how to get the Life insurance out of your estate.

(8) How to Transfer Series E Government Bonds

If a Grantor has Series E government bonds and desires to retain them, an application made to the Bureau of Public Debt (or Federal Reserve Bank) on the Bureau's Form PD 1851 will reissue each bond in the name of the Trustee. The same ownership designation used for bank accounts may be used here. The original issue date is given on each new bond and no income tax consequences result.

(9) How to Transfer Retirement Benefits

The guaranteed portion of any retirement benefits, as opposed to benefits terminating at the Grantor's death, should be discussed with an attorney familiar with retirement plans before designating the trust as beneficiary. The proceeds from a retirement plan made payable directly to the surviving spouse may be rolled over into an individual retirement account. When the surviving spouse withdraws the funds from the individual retirement account, he or she can transfer these funds into the trust. The benefit to the surviving spouse will avoid probate on these funds on the death of the first spouse. On the death of the surviving spouse, the funds will be held for and distributed through the trust to the secondary beneficiaries (usually the Grantor's children) in accordance with the terms of the trust.

We recommend that you use a Designation of Beneficiary of Retirement Plan form (LawForm TR-28, see section 14.cc) to assign Retirement Plan assests to the Living Trust.

For tax reasons we suggest the first beneficiary should be the "surviving spouse" so that she/he may "roll over" the proceeds tax free into a tax sheltered I.R.A. until the surviving spouse is 70 1/2 years old. The secondary beneficiary will be the Living Trust. We set this type of plan up for most of our clients who have Pension Plans, Profit Sharing Plans, Employee Stock Option Trusts, Keogh Plans or I.R.A.s (Individual Retirement Account).

(10) How to Transfer Promissory Notes and Other Accounts Receivable

The right to receive money, evidenced by documents such as a Promissory Note, is an asset that must to be transferred to a Living Trust, like every other asset. Promissory notes and accounts receivable indicate that you are owed money, but there is no security guaranteeing repayment. You create these rights when you loan money to your children, friends, or business associates. If you are owed money for work that you have done for someone in the past that they still owe money on, and have promised to pay, this also is a right to money which may be legally protected by a promissory note. All documents which indicate that you are owed money for any reason should be transferred to the trust. If you do not transfer these rights they will have to be probated like any other asset that is not transferred to the trust.

You can use the Assignment of Promissory Note (LawForm TR-19, see section 14.s).

If your Promissory is secured by a Real Estate Mortgage, Deed of Trust or other lien on real estate you will want to follow the instructions in the next section 7a(11) (How to Transfer Receivables Connected With Real Property).

If your Promissory Note is secured by a lien (collateral), on personal property such as a Chattel Mortgage Security Agreement or a Pledge Security Agreement -- or a lien on intangible property, such as a Collateral Assignment of Accounts Receivable, a Collateral Assignment of Partnership Interests, then you will want to assign and transfer that collateral with a Promissory Note to the trust using the Change to Financing Statement (LawForms #F-UCC-2, see section 14.x). Where there is security for the promissory note of this type, the secured party will usually have filed a Uniform Commercial Code Financing Statement with the Secretary of State. The

Change to Financing Statement will reflect the transfer of that security on the public record so as to continue the protection of the security against other creditors or the bankruptcy of the maker of the Promissory Note.

If you transfer receivables other than the Promissory Note, you will also want to use the Assignment of Promissory Note/Receivable to Trust form.

(11) How to Transfer Receivables Connected With Real Property

Many assets owned by families and individuals are in the form of monies owed to them which are secured by real property. This area of trust transfers may seem very complicated, especially if you do not own much in land or buildings. If this is the case, and all you own is a house, you can transfer it to the trust with a Special Warranty Deed (LawForm TR-8, see section 14.h)

If you own a Mortgage or a Deed of Trust (Lien) on a piece of property, you may transfer all your interests in the property to the trust with two documents. An Assignment of Promissory Note (LawForm TR-19, see section 14.s) transfers the promise to make the payments to the trust. A Deed and Assignment of Deed of Trust (LawForm TR-21, see section 14.u) will transfer your right to control the real property to the trust. Both these documents must be executed to transfer the entire asset. If one of the two documents is not executed, that part of the interest in the property will have to go through probate.

Unfortunately, there are many different ways to own an interest in real property. Sometimes these interests are very complicated. The following is a list of different real property ownerships. Don't panic if you don't understand these different real estate ownerships where you own the right to receive money from the property but not to possess it.

There are five basic real property interests where the property is encumbered with debt, they are:
- Mortgagee's (the person receiving the money) interest in Real Property Mortgage;
- Beneficiarys' (the person receiving the money) interest in Deeds of Trust;
- First Beneficiarys' (the person receiving the money) Interest in Real Estate Trusts;
- Seller's (the person receiving the money) Interest in Real Estate Agreement for Sale;
- Lessor's (the person receiving the rent) Interest in Real Estate Leases.

What is interesting about these interests in real estate receivables is that the Grantors may also be involved in the other side of these interests where you have the right to possess but owe money on it, for example the:
- Mortgagor is the person owing money on the Real Estate Mortgage but has the right to live on, and possess the property;
- Trustor is the person owing money in the Deed of Trust but has the right to live on, and possess the property;
- Second Beneficiary is the person owing money in a Real Estate Trust but has the right to live on, and possess the property;
- Buyer is the person who will owe money in the Real Estate Agreement for Sale but will have the right to live on, and possess the property;
- Lessee is the person owing the rent but has the right to live on, and possess the property.

Whether you, as Grantors of the trust, are receiving or paying the money in these transactions you will want to transfer the interests to the trust using the following forms:

- Assignment of Promissory Note / Receivable (LawForm TR-19, see section 14.s);
- Deed and Assignment of Beneficial Interest in Deed of Trust (LawForm TR-21, see section 14.u);
- Deed and Assignment of Mortgage (LawForm TR-20, see section 14.t);

- Deed and Assignment of Realty Interest in Agreement for Sale (LawForm TR-22, see section 14.v);
- Deed and Assignment of Real Estate Trust (LawForm TR-23, see section 14.w);
- Assignment and Assumption of Real Estate Lease (TR-24, see section 14.x).

Except for the real estate mortgage, each of these transfers will allow you to select which side of the transaction you, as Grantor -- represent with a simple "X" in the box in the form -- either Trustor/Beneficiary; 1st Beneficiary/2nd Beneficiary; Seller/Buyer; Lessor/Lessee.

With Real Estate mortgages the mortgagee's interest (the right to receive payment) is transferred with the Assignment of Real Estate Mortgage. The Mortgagor who owes the payments, will transfer his interest with a Special Warranty Deed (LawForm TR-8, see section 14.h) which is subject to an assumption of the Real Estate Mortgage or is subject to a lease.

Most of these real estate related transfers require the assignment of a Promissory Note. A Promissory Note accompanies the mortgage agreement. A Promissory Note accompanies a Deed of Trust. The Real Estate Agreement for Sale sometimes has a Promissory Note as part of the Agreement. A Real Estate Trust involves a Prommissory Note. In these four situations you must prepare two documents to complete the transfer -- an assignment of the promissory note and a transfer of the real estate interest associated with it.

When you transfer the Real Estate Lease for the lessor -- the owner or landlord -- you must also transfer the ownership of the real property itself with the Special Warranty Deed (subject to the Real Estate Lease) which is described in the Deed, as well as an Assignment and Assumption of Lease.

If you have any questions about your interests in real property, you can ask an attorney what your property interests are and how to transfer them.

(12) How to Transfer a Sole Proprietorship Business

Sometimes the Grantor owns a business that is not incorporated into a corporation or partnership, this is called a Sole Proprietorship -- should we transfer the business to the trust, and if so how is this done?

A business has both tangible assets -- property you can touch and feel like furniture and equipment, and other such assets which you can see, touch or carry in your hands. It also has intangible assets -- paper assets -- trade names, trade marks, accounts receivables production files, customer goodwill and similar "intangible" assets which you cannot touch or carry in your hands.

We have designed a form to transfer these usual tangible and intangible assets of the sole proprietorship -- the Bill of Sale and Assignment of Sole Proprietorship Assets (LawForm TR-17, see section 14.q).

If the sole proprietorship owns real estate, promissory notes, motor vehicles and other assets discussed in this kit, you will use the forms described in other sections of this book to transfer these assets. In the "legal description" on the transfer document you must indicate that these assets are "Used by Sole Proprietorship".

(13) How to Transfer Motor Vehicles, Motorcycles, Motor Homes, Trailers, Boats and Airplanes

Some attorneys have said that you don't have to transfer motor vehicles to the Living Trust. We disagree. Why be half safe? It is best to have all of the assets in the Living Trust -- the big ones and the little ones. It doesn't cost any more to go first class! If we are wrong you lose ten minutes preparing the transfer document and perhaps less than $10 filing it, if we are right and you do not transfer these assets, you may lose hundreds of dollars in probate fees.

We have provided you with a Letter of Instructions Regarding Motor Vehicles (LawForm TR-12a, see section 14.l) and an Affidavit of Trustee for Transfer of Motor Vehicle into Trust (LawForm TR-13, see section 14.m). It gives instructions to the office in your state which processes vehicle title documents. You should use this document to transfer motor vehicles to the trust. Generally, you fill out the special forms provided by each state for the transfer of motor vehicles into the name of the trust. You may contact the department of motor vehicles in your state, to find out where to transfer title of your vehicle.

Boats, motorcycles, motor homes, and trailers are usually transferred in the same way as motor vehicles. In most cases, the state has an office which registers and transfers the boats, motorcycles, motor homes and trailers. Call your state office and use the same instruction letter that you used for motor vehicles.

Airplanes are transferred under federal laws and regulations. Get the government forms from the Federal Aviation Administration (FAA). You will find a phone number for this government office in the government section of the phone book listed under "F". Once you get the forms, fill them out and show the federal clerk your Letter of Instructions For Motor Vehicles. This will prevent you from having trouble with clerks who do not know whether it is possible to transfer airplanes to a family trust.

The various transferring agencies may ask to see a copy of your Certificate of Trustees' Powers and Abstract of Trust.

Bicycles, wagons, and smaller forms of transportation, are transferred like any other tangible personal property discussed elsewhere in this booklet (see section 7.a.(5) - How to Transfer Personal Property). If no state office is set up to transfer these items or any other moving asset, you may use the Bill of Sale (General) (LawForm TR-10, see section 14.j).

(14) How to Transfer Partnerships

Partnership transfers are easy. They are accomplished by using an Assignment of Partnership Interest (LawForm TR-16, see section 14.p). The same assignment form is used when your transfer either a general, or limited partnership interest.

You need the approval of all the general partners for each assignment in order to fully transfer the partnership units or percentage. If you don't have the general partners approval, then the trust will not have full ownership. It will only own what is called an "Assignee of Partnership Interest". Such interest allows the assignee to receive the income accruals and distributions but no voting rights.

(15) How to Transfer Corporation Business Interests

Ownership of a corporation is represented by voting stock and non-voting stock. These stock certificates will be transferred like any other stock certificates, as described in section 7.a(1)(How to Transfer Registered Securities), 7.a(2)(How to Transfer Unregistered Securities), and 7.a(3)(How to Transfer Street Name Accounts -- Holding Securities) using Stock Powers. The forms are illustrated at section 14.n.

Some stocks require great caution when they are transferred: (1) Privately issued or "restricted" stock; "S" Corporation stock, closely held stock, professional corporation stock; "ESOT" stock or incentive stock options. It is best to check with the corporation issuing the stock, your attorney, or your accountant, to ascertain any restrictions or adverse tax consequences prior to transferring these stocks. When the transfer is complete, the issuing corporation will provide you with new stock certificates in the name of the Living Trust. When these certificates are issued, the old certificates are returned to the corporation with the stock power.

(16) How to Transfer Mutual Funds

You may call your stock broker or the Mutual Fund company to ask what they will want to transfer your account to the living trust. The Mutual Fund is a pool of stocks or bonds which is managed by a paid advisor for the benefit of persons who buy into the Fund.

You may use your Letter to Security Broker to assist with these transfers (LawForm TR-12b, See section 14.l).

(17) How to Transfer Miscellaneous

We have included an all purpose transfer document which we suggest you execute and hold in your file with your original trust document. The form is called "The Omnibus Transfer. It is a combination Deed, Bill of Sale and Assignment (Lawform TR-11, see section 14.k). This transfer evidences Grantor's intent to have all assets belonging to the Grantors transferred to the trust.

Should you accidently forget to transfer some property to the trust before you die, this document may be used to transfer the asset to the trust. There have been instances when a person has inherited something right before they die and fail to transfer it to the trust. Here's where the Omnibus Transfer comes in handy. By using this document you can avoid probate on those properties which you forgot, or did not have time to transfer, when you transferred your assets to the trust. IT IS BEST TO USE THE PROPER DOCUMENT WHEN TRANSFERRING ITEMS TO THE TRUST. This "Omnibus

Transfer" is a "back up". Even though the Omnibus Transfer is not as effective as the specified transfer document, we have found that it will be honored by most persons. It works as a good bluff. We have successfully used it in several situations to avoid costly probate of assets.

7.b. Acquiring Assets in the Living Trust After You have Established the Living Trust

After you have transferred all assets into the Living Trust, then you will want to be careful to place all new assets in the trust. If you are buying an asset, ask the seller to show on the Deed, Bill of Sale, Assignment, or other document of transfer, that the transferee is the "Fennedy Family Trust dated January 1, 1990". If someone is planning to give you money or property, ask them to give it directly to your trust.

7.c. Identifying the Trust for Taxes

Although a revocable living trust is a separate entity, a federal tax identification number is not required for income tax purposes. The social security number of Grantor is the tax number of the trust and must be given to banks, corporations and others who pay interest or dividend income to the trust.

7.d. Protecting Trust Assets

Once the trust agreement has been signed, and assets have been transferred to the trust, the trust agreement is fully operative as to those assets. At this point, there are certain basic moves which the Trustee should make.

(1) Insuring the Trust Assets

Any assets which have been transferred to the trust should be covered and protected by insurance. If an asset is already covered, the insurance policy should be revised to add the trust as a named insured on the policy. This can usually be done by your property and casualty insurance agent at no additional cost. If personal property, a residence, or an automobile have been transferred to the trust, the trust should make certain that these assets are covered by insurance and that the Trustee is the named insured.

Send a copy of your Schedule of Assets Transferred to the Trust to your insurance agent.

(2) Placing Trust Assets in a Safe Location

Assets such as stocks and bonds, which you have transferred to the trust, should be placed in a safe location, such as a safe deposit box. If the safe deposit box holds only trust assets, and is in the name of the trust, you will have no problem in identifying bearer bonds or unregistered securities as trust assets. You will have a problem if the box is taken out in your name alone. If you successfully transfer all your assets to your trust, you will have no probate of those assets. As a result you will not need a "personal representative" on your death or disability to deal with a safety deposit box. Your successor trustee has immediate authority to enter the safe deposit box.

7.e. Administering the Trust

The Trustee is the legal owner of the trust assets. If more than one Trustee is acting, Trustees' own the trust assets with survivorship rights similar to those of joint tenants. Property held in the names of Trustees will pass to the surviving Trustee and any successor Trustee at the death of a Trustee. If more than one Trustee is acting, they must act together unless expressly provided to the contrary in the trust agreement. The Trustee is not acting as the agent of the beneficiaries of the trust; his actions are his own, and he is responsible for them.

Of critical importance in the creation of a trust, is the trust agreement. This instrument instructs the Trustee how to manage, administer and dispose of the assets transferred to the trust. These guidelines are directed predominantly at the revocable trust situation, where the trust was created by the Grantor primarily to avoid probate; the Grantor is the Trustee or a Co-Trustee with his/her spouse; and the Grantor is also the primary beneficiary during his or her lifetime. In this type of trust, the Grantor has as much freedom in dealing with his/her assets after they are transferred to the trust, as he/she had before such transfer. As the Grantor and Trustee of this type of trust, the Grantor's wishes will control the management and disposition of the trust assets during his/her lifetime.

These guidelines are also relevant, to the irrevocable trust situation after one of the Grantors dies, where the trust was created to minimize income or estate tax consequences. After one of the Grantors of a Revocable Living Trust dies, the trust becomes an Irrevocable Trust. There are certain basic obligations of a Trustee which apply under all conditions, such as the duties to keep records, segregate trust property, and file any required tax returns. The exercise of these functions reflects the fact that the Grantor intends the assets to be a part of a trust arrangement under which other parties have interests.

7.f. Record-Keeping

After the death of one of the Grantors all transactions involving trust assets should be carefully documented -- this is similar to how you would act if you were operating a business through the trust. You may want to ask an accountant for advice on how to keep records. You will need good records on:
- Income received;
- Income paid out;
- Additions to principal;
- Deductions from principal;
- Principal on hand; and
- Changes in trust investments.

When the trust books are originally set up, the value of each asset transferred to the trust should be determined. It's much easier to obtain this information while the Grantor is alive, and his records readily available, than to try to track down the information when the assets are sold, or otherwise disposed of, or after the Grantor's death. In addition to satisfying the Trustee's legal responsibilities, accurate books and records will make the successor Trustee's job much easier. A Trustee should not feel burdened by accounting responsibilities he/she is unable to handle, a professional accountant should be retained when required, or the Grantor might consider using the services of a bank as "custodian" of the assets, the bank will keep the accounting records for the trust.

7.g. Segregation of Trust Property

The Trustee has an obligation to segregate the trust property from the Trustee's own property. If trust property is commingled (mixed together) with his/her own property, the Trustee will have to prove what property is his. Any doubt will be resolved in favor of the trust. For Community Property States, the Trustees will want to keep records of the wife's separate property (which her husband does not own), separate property of the husband, and community property.

In our Schedule of Assets (LawForm TR-3, see section 14.c) we have provided spaces to segregate and identify the separate and joint ownership of property.

7.h. Tax Returns

While all Grantors of the trust are alive, the Trustee of a Revocable Living Trust has no obligation to file a fiduciary income tax return on federal Form 1041 and all income will be taxed to the Grantor. The Grantor should insert the total amount of each type of income (such as dividends, interest, rents) received by the trust in the appropriate schedule of his federal Form 1040.

Some states do not require that a fiduciary income tax return be filed for a living trust. You should contact a CPA, he will be able to tell you whether your state requires a fiduciary tax return. Whatever the case, all income received by the trust should be reported in the appropriate schedules of the Grantor's individual state tax form.

7.i. Common Mistakes With a Living Trust

We have seen many mistakes in revocable trusts. We have included some of the most important ones for your information.

(1) It is important that all revocable trusts are funded. You must transfer the ownership of the assets to the trust. If you do not fund the trust you get the worst of all worlds. You pay for the trust and later you pay to probate the assets as they go into the trust after the Grantor dies. Probate usually costs 5% of the estate in attorney's fees. It costs more if you have property in several states. By funding the trust with all your property, you will avoid all probate proceedings.

(2) Your revocable trust must have multiple successor Trustees so that there is always a set of responsible Trustees. The king is dead -- long live the queen! Most times, the husband and wife are Co-Trustees. If one spouse dies, the surviving Trustee is Co-Trustee with the children or one of the close trusted relatives.

consider a bank Trustee. We find it best that you never have a bank act as successor Trustee without also having an individual Trustee -- there is too much danger of a "run away" Trustee situation. It is better to have a family member Co-Trustee with a disinterested, financially competent (such as a bank or responsible professional) Trustee. One can focus on the family needs, the other can focus on the financial matters -- both keep each other in check from getting too far out of control.

Summary

You have purchased a sophisticated estate plan. A great deal of thought and effort was devoted to the creation and funding of your trust. If, at this point, the trust is simply forgotten, many benefits which it otherwise provides, will be lost. A trust does not require much continued attention. If you familiarize yourself with the requirements and guidelines suggested in this section, you will enjoy the full effectiveness and advantages of the trust with minimum effort.

8. How To Amend Your Living Trust

While all Grantors are living the trust may be amended at any time using the Amendment of Trust Form (LawForm TR-5, see section 14.e).

The Amendment of Trust Form contains a space where you may;
  a. Add a paragraph.
  b. Delete a paragraph.
  c. Change the wording of a paragraph.

Here's how you do it:

8.a. Adding a Paragraph

When you add a paragraph give it a number -- the next number available in the part where you believe it fits. For instance, if you have a paragraph to add concerning distribution of property, you would add it to Part Two (the Fennedy Family Trust) the last numbered paragraph in that part is "2.4". Your additional paragraph will then read:

"2.5 *Care of Cats. Other provisions of this part notwithstanding, we want to declare to the world our love for our two intelligent, talking cats, and direct that Trustees, on the death of Grantors, find someone who will take care of them. Trustee shall give that person $500 a month as long as either cat is alive -- to make certain our beloved cats have the finest cat food and vetinary care available -- including imported oriental squid and Norwegian sardines harvested at least two years after the Russian atomic plant explosion.*"

When adding paragraphs you may clearly override other provisions of the trust which conflict with your amended paragraph by using words like;

"other provisions notwithstanding..."

"contrary to paragraph 2.2a..."

"*This paragraph shall supersede and override all other provisions.*"

The mere fact that the amended paragraph is later than earlier paragraphs will infer your intent to supersede the earlier paragraphs.

8.b. Deleting Paragraphs

When you delete a paragraph you need only write into the Amendment of Trust form the words -- *"Delete all of paragraphs 2.2b, 3.1 and 6.5."*

This was easy. Right?

8.c. Changing the Wording of a Paragraph

When you change the wording of a paragraph, we suggest you do it as follows;

"Delete paragraph #3.1 and substitute this new paragraph #3.1..."

If the amendment changes one of the paragraphs contained in the Certificate of Trustees' Powers and Abstract of Trust, then you will want to record the Amendment of Trust in all the governmental offices where the original Certificate of Trustees' Power and Abstract of Trust was recorded. If you have amendments that are very personal to the family, and some which change paragraphs in the Certificate of Trustees' Power and Abstract of Trust, then we suggest you prepare two Amendments of Trust -- one containing the personal paragraphs which you don't want the rest of the world to see, and another with the paragraphs which change the paragraphs of the Certificate of Trustees' Powers and Abstract of Trust, and record only the latter.

8.d. Other Considerations When Making an Amendment

Be sure that all amendments are physically attached by staple to the front of the original trust so that they will be seen whenever anyone reads the original trust or who makes certified copies of the trust. Also send courtesy copies to all living Grantors and all Trustees who have copies of the original trust.

Be sure to designate each amendment by date and by numerical designation "First, Second, Third, etc.", to easily identify them and prevent later confusion. If you make multiple amendments over a long period of time, you may want to amend the trust in its entirety completely restating the entire trust with all the amendments. If you do so, use the words "Complete Amendment and Restatement of Trust".

9. How To Change Trustees Of Your Living Trust

While Grantors of the Living Trust are alive they may change the Trustees, and successor Trustees, by an Amendment (see section 6 "How to Amend Your Living Trust"). If Grantors change a Trustee they must record the Amendment with the County Records of every county where the original Certificate of Trustee's Powers and Abstract of Trust was recorded.

When one Grantor dies, the living trust becomes irrevocable. If you want to change a Trustee after a Grantor has died you must use the Affidavit of Succession of Trustee (LawForm TR-4, see section 14.d). This form may be used:

(1) When a Trustee Dies. In this situation you will fill out the Affidavit of Succession of Trustee and attach a death certificate.

(2) When A Trustee Is Incapacitated. In this situation you will fill out the Affidavit of Succession of Trustee and attach the statements of three doctors confirming Trustee's incapacity.

(3) When A Trustee Resigns. In this situation you will fill out the Affidavit of Succession of Trustee and attach a notarized letter of resignation. This letter may be very informal stating Trustees intent to resign, directed to the successor Trustee. In the letter, the resigning Trustee must make arrangements with the successor Trustee to provide the new Trustee with the books and records of the trust, an accounting, and arrange for time to brief and train the successor Trustee.

(4) When An Incapacitated Trustee Recovers. In the situation where an incapacitated Trustee has recovered, he or she will fill out the Affidavit of Succession of Trustee and attach the certificate of three doctors affirming that the incapacitated former Trustee is now recovered enough to resume the position of Trustee. In this situation, we recommend that the incapacitated former Trustee talk to the then acting Co-Trustees and beneficiaries to reassure them of the recovery, and to obtain their consent to act again as Trustee. A "sticky situation" is created if the former Trustee presses to reacquire his/her position when the co-Trustees, or beneficiaries, doubt that the complete recovery has taken place, even though 3 or more doctors affirm his/her competence. (I'm from Missouri -- show me!).

The Affidavit of Succession of Trustee cross references the docket and page where the original Certificate of Trustees' Powers and Abstract of Trust (LawForm TR-2, see section 14.b) was recorded, and when it is recorded. It will be recorded in every county where the Certificate Of Trustee's Power and Abstract of Trust was recorded. This will show the world -- the banks, stock brokers and title companies who rely on public records -- that a new Trustee or co-Trustee has been qualified.

One original of the Affidavit of Succession of Trustee should be affixed by staples to the front of the original trust -- like an Amendment of Trust (LawForm TR-5, see section 14.e) to inform all who deal with the trust, and anyone placing reliance on certified copies of the trust, that the Trustee has been changed.

Copies of the Affidavit of Succession shall also be mailed to all living Grantors, Co-Trustees, and beneficiaries, and the guardians of minor beneficiaries.

The King is Dead. Long live the Queen! The Trustee is dead, disabled, or has resigned -- Long live the new Trustee.

10. How To Terminate Your Living Trust

10.a. Before Grantors Die

Terminating your trust before one of the grantors die is easy. If you changed your mind about having a trust after you accomplished all the steps to form it and fund it with your property you need only do the following:

(1) Fill out the Affidavit Terminating Trust (LawForm TR-7, see section 14.g) and record it at all governmental offices where you recorded your Certificate of Trustee's Powers and Abstract of Trust.

(2) Contact LawForms and obtain extra copies of the legal forms you used to transfer property into the trust. Then transfer the property back using the same form and procedure for each asset that you put into the trust. The trust will be the "Grantor", "Assignor", "Seller", the person at the left top of each transfer document, and the Grantors will be the "Grantee", "Assignee", "Buyer". The transfer process is the exact reverse of what you did when you created the trust. The documents you prepare will be processed in the same manner as when you transferred the properties to the trust.

Don't voluntarily terminate your revocable living trust without careful consideration. We suggest that you consult an attorney before you terminate your trust. At this time, it is hard for me to imagine a situation for terminating the trust during the lifetime of the Grantors.

10.b. After Grantors Die

Once one of the Grantors has died, the trust is legally irrevocable. The surviving Grantor does not have the legal power to terminate the trust.

When the trust is irrevocable there are only two ways to terminate it:

(1) **Transfer all the property out of the trust.** If a trust does not own property, it automatically terminates. A trust without property has no legal existence. We always put $10 into the trusts for each new trust when we form it. We hold the $10 in a trust bank account so that the trust will not inadvertently terminate if at any moment all the assets except the $10 were transferred out.

All trusts have provisions which indicate how and when money and assets will be transferred out of the trust. When Trustees comply with those provisions and distribute all assets to the beneficiaries following the terms of the trust, nothing is left in the trust. At that point the trust ceases to exist.

Even though the trust has legally terminated as a matter of law when all assets of the trust are distributed, we still recommend that the Affidavit Terminating Trust be recorded in all places where the Certificate of Trustee Power and Abstract of Trust has been recorded.

(2) **If you can obtain consent of all person's concerned with the trust and obtain court approval for termination, the trust can be terminated.** Sometimes the reason for the trust is no longer logical because of changing laws, changing facts, or changing family conditions. Examples of reasons for terminating the trust might be:

- Tax laws change and severely tax the trust;
- Children mature and no longer need the protection of a Trustee;
- The costs of operating the trust are too great when compared to the small income of the trust;
- Too much unresolvable dissention between the Trustees and beneficiaries is present;
- The Trustees have become oppressive.

In these, and similar instances all parties, or the aggrieved parties, may apply to the local probate court with a written petition and ask the judge to terminate the trust. Most times when all Trustees, all living Grantors, all adult beneficiaries, all persons representing the minor and contingent beneficiaries, are before the court and have agreed in writing that they want the trust terminated, the Judge of the probate court has the power to terminate the trust. The application (Petition) to the court must state the reasons for terminating the trust, why termination does not frustrate the intentions of the Grantor, why termination is in the best interests of all parties, and why termination will save money, taxes, delays, or problems.

Even though all persons concerned with the trust -- the surviving Grantors, Trustees, Beneficiaries -- desire that the trust be terminated, the Judge may disagree if he/she believes it frustrates the original purpose of all the Grantors when the trust was established.

When the order terminating the trust is signed by the Judge of the Probate Court, it will be attached to the Affidavit Terminating the Trust and recorded wherever the Certificate of Trustee's Power and Abstract of Trust has been recorded.

In all terminations, we recommend that copies of the Affidavit Terminating Trust be sent to all living Grantors, Trustees, Beneficiaries -- current and contingent -- and to the guardian of minor beneficiaries when the trust is terminated.

We have provided in the Affidavit Terminating Trusts easy to understand "boxes" and "blanks" to fill in the necessary information you will need.

When you record the Affidavit Terminating Trust you will want to indicate the docket and page number where the Certificate of Trustee's Powers and Abstract of Trust was recorded. This will facilitate the cross reference of all documents related to the trust.

11. How To Safeguard Your Living Trust Documents

We have provided a "Documents Envelope" in which you may place the originals of your "Certificate of Trustee's Powers and Abstract of Trust", "Living Trust", "Schedule of Assets", and other originals when they are completely processed and recorded.

Our experience has been that the best place to put originals is in the safe deposit box, or fire proof safe of your family attorney. He is then able to advise you on emergencies when they occur, and to make certified copies of any document you may need.

We have provided you with a Certificate of True Copy (LawForms TR-29, see section 14.cc) forms for making certified copies of your documents. Be sure the Notary imprints their seal on all pages to prevent anyone from questioning whether pages have been substituted.

We suggest you make up a certified copy of the Certificate of Trustee's Power and Abstract of Trust, the Living Trust, and the Schedule of Assets for each Co-Trustee.

The Grantors will want to keep a desk copy at home to use for easy reference.

If you have a family accountant and/or family attorney, you will want to give to them copies of all the documents you prepared.

You should put the originals of your trust documents with the originals of your other estate planning documents -- your Last Will and Testament, Living Will, Durable Powers of Attorney, and your Durable Power of Attorney for Medical Care.

Advise members of your family where your important documents are located by filling out and giving them a copy of your "Records Location Worksheet" (LawForm #W-44k). Also carry around with you your "Wallet Information Card" (LawForm #W-6). These are some of the forms contained in the LawForms Basic Estate Planning Documents for Families and Individuals Kit.

LawForms has a Safe Deposit Inventory Form (LawForm #W-66) which you may use to inventory your original documents in your safety deposit box, or fire proof safe. This form is included in the Basic Estate Planning Documents for Families and Individuals Kit.

12. General Instructions for Filling Out Legal Forms

12.a. Reckon With Each Blank

Most blank forms have either blanks, blocks or lines with an indication of some "fill in" needed. Do not skip over any blank, block or line. If you fail to complete an insert, the reader is left in doubt. Did you forget to fill in the blank? Did you leave the blank empty for some reason? Did you intend someone else to fill in the blank?

If you have nothing special to write in each blank, then indicate to the reader that you dealt with the blank by either putting "N/A" for "not applicable," the word "None" if this is appropriate or simply putting a dashed line "- - -."

Not only does leaving empty blanks create confusion in the mind of the reader, but it is also dangerous. Unscrupulous people can fill in harmful information on a form that you have undersigned and notarized thus jeopardizing your property and rights.

12.b. Carry "Spillovers" to Addendum Page

If a form does not have enough space for your answer, type as much as will fit in the blank, leaving just enough space to write in parenthesis "(Continued on Page - -) ." On that addendum page write "tie-in" information indicating (1) the title of the document, (2) the title of the blank and (3) the page number from which the information was carried over.

12.c. Practice Makes Perfect

You may avoid making unsightly mistakes on the actual forms if you first fill in the sample forms in this book, and then transfer the information onto the actual blank forms.

12.d. One Quality Original

Do all your typing and correcting on one original and then use that original as a "master" for making copies.

If someone else types the forms, you may want to write your information in the instruction book and give the blank forms to the typist. Anyone will be able to fill in your legal forms with this information.

12.e. Deleting Paragraphs

When you find a paragraph you do not wish included on the Living Trust (LawForm #T-1, see section 14.a) or Certificate of Trustees' Powers and Abstract of Trust (LawForm #T-2, see section 14.b) you can remove it by making a "Z" pattern through the paragraph and initialing both ends of the "Z".

13. How To Process Blank Forms For Implementing Your Living Trust

We are providing you the same forms used by competent, practicing Estate Planning attorneys.

We have modified them slightly to make them easier to use. Ironically, as we restructured the forms to make them understandable to the non-lawyer, we found at least 25 new ideas for processing complex trusts for our clients with large estates.

We have given you examples of the filled in forms which came from real life experience with our clients -- which have been used. In many cases clients have died and the trust continues to exist. No theoretical ideas -- no lawbook abstractions -- only real world, practical applications.

We wrote the instructions as we would verbally give them to a new lawyer, associate, law clerk, legal assistant or legal secretary, when we ask them to type up the forms for one of our clients.

As our readers write in questions and comments we will be adding to these instructions to make them more clear and complete. We want to hear from you with your ideas for further improvements.

We have included one copy of each form. LawForms has consented to your making five copies of each transfer form where you have multiple pieces of property, without violating the LawForms copyright. If you need more copies of any form, you may call LawForms at 1-602-254-0424 to order more forms if they are needed for multiple property situations.

Where you need additional copies of the forms you fill out -- for instance to send copies of the Affidavit of Succession to multiple beneficiaries -- you may photocopy the filled in form. You are not in violation of U.S. copyright laws when you copy a filled in form.

You do violate the copyright laws when you photocopy more than 5 blank forms before they are filled out. Stealing someone's idea without paying for it is as bad as stealing someone's car.

Be sure to write us if you have any questions while filling out the forms, or if you have any suggestions for improving the forms.

Living Trust (Declaration of Trust)

Purpose of this Form: The purpose of executing and using the Revocable Trust is to have a binding legal instrument which will take care of your property during your lifetime, while you are disabled, and when you die without involving expensive court processes and attorneys fees. The advantages of the revocable trust are discussed in detail in section 3 "Advantages of a Living Trust".

1. **Name of Trust**. Most times the Trust is named after the family with the family name "The Fennedy Trust" or "The Fennedy Family Trust". Persons with a penchant for efficiency will use initials or acronyms such as "JJF Trust" or "JOHJAQ Trust". Do not use long names "John annd Jacolyn Fennedy Family Trust" -- too much to write each time. Don't put the word "revocable" in the title because when one spouse dies, the trust is no longer revocable. Be imaginative. Perhaps you have a word with zing "The Pizzazz Trust". If you use a name other than the family name you will have more privacy with your financial and property matters.

(1)

The Fennedy Family
TRUST

DATED: 1 January 1990

2. Effective Date. Use the first of a month. Reason: the date of a trust is used whenever you identify a trust. Make it easy on yourself -- date back to the first of this month or the first of the next month. Having the trust start on the first of a month also facilitates accounting. Ideally you would want to start the trust at the beginning of the year -- Jan 1, 1990, that is usually also the beginning of the fiscal year to almost all trusts.

3. Effective County and State of Execution. The place a legal document is signed is usually the location which determines the laws applying to that trust unless it is otherwise agreed in writing in the trust. Write the county and state in the blank. Usually the county recorder of that county is the place designated as the place where the abstract is first filed and where amendments, terminations, affidavits of succession, and other documents are recorded, which tell the world of the status of the trust.

4. Name of Grantor. Write the full legal name of the persons who are forming the trust. This trust is designed to have a sole grantor, a husband and wife as grantor or two or more unmarried family members -- mother and daughter, brother and sister, write in the mailing address which all grantors want to use as the official address of the trust. Usually this will be in the effective county or state.

5. Name of Primary Trustee. In a declaration of trust usually these are the same persons as the grantor -- the individual himself/herself, the husband and wife, or the grantor family members. These persons control the trust and the property in it. If the grantors are old and feeble at the time the trust is prepared, they may want to name other persons as the primary Trustees; a trusted family member, child, grandchild, brother, sister, niece, nephew, etc. And as Co-Trustee, a so called "disinterested trustee" someone outside the family who is financially responsible and objective, or a bank or trust company. It is good to have 2 trustees in this situation so as to have "checks and balances" and to take the "heat" off of just one person. Human beings are accustomed to having a ruling pair -- a mother and father, a husband and wife, a king and queen, a king and prime minister.

6. Identification of Beneficiaries. List all beneficiaries of the trust receiving $1 or more. Instead of listing the addresses, you list their relationship to the grantor; children, grandchildren, brother, sister, niece, nephew, friend. You have the option here of treating a brother, sister, niece, nephew, or friend as if they were your child by writing after their name, "treated like a child". This means wherever you give to a child, the person treated as a child will receive the same distributions as all other children - and if that person dies before trust distribution his/her children will receive distributions through the grandchildren's subtrust - like natural grandchildren.

Here also you have the option of placing the words "per capita", meaning that you want distributions to go to that person only if they live. If they die before the distribution all rights vanish.

If you put "per stirpes" beside the named beneficiary, that person's children, grandchildren receive their share splitting it up among them equally.

Be sure the list of beneficiaries here matches the list in the Certificate of Trustees' Power and Authority and Abstract of Trust. Be sure that you have every loved one mentioned.

If you plan to disinherit family members, list them as a beneficiary - "per capita" and give them a special distribution of $1 elsewhere in the trust. Explain why you only gave them $1 so that they will not have a psychological trauma the rest of their lives wondering why you didn't like them ("What did I do to deserve such shabby treatment").

Creation and Intention of Trust and Identification of Parties

Effective Date: 1 January 1990 ②	County and State Where Trust is Located: Maricopa, Arizona ③
Grantor (Name, Address, and Zip Code): John K. Fennedy & Jacolyn O. Fennedy 1956 Massachusetts St. Scottsdale, AZ 85100 ④	Primary Trustee (Name, Address, and Zip Code): John K. Fennedy & Jacolyn O. Fennedy, 1956 Massachusetts St. Scottsdale, AZ 85100 ⑤

Part One

1.1 **Trust Property.** Concurrently with the execution of this trust, Grantor has conveyed and delivered to Trustee the property described in a schedule of trust assets, and Trustee hereby acknowledges receipt of that property and agrees to hold and dispose of that property and all additions thereto and income therefrom IN TRUST upon the terms and conditions hereinafter set forth. Additional property from time to time may be transferred to Trustee with Trustee's consent by Grantor or by any other person, estate or trust. Any such additional property shall become a part of the trust property and shall be held, managed, invested, reinvested and disposed of on the same terms and conditions as hereinafter provided.

1.2 **Identification of Beneficiaries.** The names of beneficiaries of this trust, other than the Grantors who have lifetime rights, are: ⑥

Name of Beneficiary	Relationship	Per Stirpes or Per Capita
a. John K. Fennedy	Husband & Grantor	Per Stirpes
b. Jacolyn O. Fennedy	Wife of Grantor	Per Stirpes
c. John K. Fennedy, Jr.	Son of Grantor	Per Stirpes
d. Carolyn Fennedy	Daughter of Grantor	Per Stirpes
e.		
f.		

   Per Stirpes indicates that Grantor intends that the Beneficiaries' children and other issue receive the Beneficiaries' share on death. Per Capita indicattes that Grantor intends that No One except the named beneficiary receive that share on beneficiaries' death.
   Where Grantor has indicated a Beneficiary is "Treated like a child", that beneficiary shall receive all distributions, benefits, and considerations that are designated for a child in this trust.

7. Designation of Successor Trustees. In a declaration of trust usually these are the same persons as the grantor -- the individual himself/herself, the husband and wife, or the grantor family members. These persons control the trust and the property in it. If the grantors are old and feeble at the time the trust is prepared, they may want to name other persons as the primary Trustees; a trusted family member, child, grandchild, brother, sister, niece, nephew, etc. And as Co-Trustee, a so called "disinterested trustee" someone outside the family who is financially responsible and objective, or a bank or trust company. It is good to have 2 trustees in this situation so as to have "checks and balances" and to take the "heat" off of just one person. Human beings are accustomed to have a ruling pair --like a mother and father. See Appendix C for sample paragraphs.

8. Governmental Office. This is usually the county recorder's office in the effective county and state where the trust was executed, or the governmental office where deeds are recorded. This becomes the "bullitin board" for the trust where amendments, terminations, and successions may be recorded. It provides a place where banks, title companies, stock brokerage firms may look to verify that the trust has not been terminated or radically changed, and to verify who is the official trustee. This is sometimes called the place for "constructive notice to the world".

9. Special Distributions on Death of All Grantors. We recommend that you remember as many of your friends and relatives in this section as possible -- giving all of them some gift even if it is small as a demonstration of your love and affection. These gifts at death have a special significance. They will encourage those you leave behind to be loving and generous by your example. Bravo! Tell them why you liked or loved them so much or the actions you appreciated.

If you want to disinherit a child do it lovingly also giving them $1 or a small gift and explaining why they didn't get more. Express your love, concern for that child or grandchild in writing and describe the "actions" that provoked you to disinherit them. This will prevent psychological damage in the person disinherited, and is likely to prevent civil wars in the family when the disinherited person thinks another child might have poisoned your mind. I have seen tragedies in families who have failed to clarify the reasons for disinheritance.

If you have carefully listed all beneficiaries on the first page of the trust and indicated "per stirpes" or "per capita", you may merely insert the words "see page one."

If you want another person to receive a certain gift on the death of the first named donee, then write in "to Averill Harriman -- my hideout home in West Virginia per capita, if he predeceases the distribution, then to Harry Hopkins per capita, if he predeceases then to Martin Luther King per stirpes".

Do not list here specific items of household goods (furniture), personal effects (gold watch) or other personal property. These should be designated in the "Tangible Personal Property Inventory" (LawForm # W-4) which is part of this Kit or some other personal property distribution list authorized by Grantor's will. This Revocable Trust incorporates the Will and the Tangible Personal Property form without having to rewrite this list for the trust. It is in this Tangible Personal Property inventory that you will want to give items of household goods, personal effects and keepsakes to good friends. We suggest you make a list for all your family members and good friends whom you would want to come to your funeral and give at least some keepsake or symbolic trinket of yours to them in the tangible personal property list that is incorporated into your LawForm Will and this trust.

Use the special distributions section of this Revocable Trust for gifts you intend at the time of your death - in money, real property, stocks, bonds, business interests and other major "chunks" or "collections" of property -- don't use it for household goods, personal effects, keepsakes, paraphernalia or other pieces of personal property you own.

1.3 **Designation of Successor Trustees.** The successor trustees are as follows:

1.3.a Designation of Single Successor Trustee. References in the trust instrument to Trustee shall be deemed to include not only the original Trustee but also any additional or successor Trustee or Co-Trustee, and all the powers and discretions vested in Trustee shall be exercisable by any such additional or successor Trustee or Co-Trustee. If the primary Trustees dies or otherwise ceases to function as Trustee, the following persons shall serve as Successor Trustees in the order of priority hereafter set forth:

1.3.a(1) Successor Co-Trustees.
a. John K. Fennedy, Jr., 1956 Massachusetts St., Scottsdale, Az. 85100
b. Carolyn Fennedy, 1956 Massachusetts St., Scottsdale, Az. 85100
c. Steve Austene, 6 Million Dollar Avenue, Majors, WI, 73490

1.3.b Upon the death, resignation, disqualification, or removal of all but the last one designated Successor Trustee, the last remaining Successor Trustee shall select a replacement in the event that he or she ceases to be a Trustee, so that the trust will always have one Trustee.

1.3.c(2) Selection Procedure. Selection shall be made by a written Affidavit of Succession mailed to the (a) then serving Co-Trustee, (b) to all beneficiaries or their representatives, and (c) recording a duplicate original where the trust has its situs.

1.13 **Place of Constructive Notice of Trust Revocation, Amendment or Trustee Succession.** The parties to this trust designate this government document recording office: _Maricopa County Recorders Office_, as the location where title companies and others may check to ascertain if this trust has been revoked or amended in any material respect to change the Trustees or Successor Trustees or the powers originally granted to the Trustees. A signed Certificate of Trustees' Powers and Abstract of Trust contains certain terms of this trust shall be filed or recorded with that public office as notice of the existence of this trust, its Grantor, Trustees, beneficiaries, powers of the Trustees, and other relevant terms. All parties dealing with this trust may rely on the abstract, amended abstracts, and other documents filed or recorded with that public office in ascertaining the status of this trust and may assume, if there are no official filings or recordings to the contrary, that no material changes have been made to the trust since the last filing or recording.

2.5 **Death of Grantor.** After all Grantor's death, the trust shall be administered and distributed as follows:

2.5.b <u>Special Distributions on Death of All Grantors</u>. If any residence and/or personal property described in the Last Will and Testament of Grantor have been transferred to the trust, then it is the Grantor's intent and the Trustee is instructed to distribute the residence and/or personal property as set forth in the Will or in any codicils to that Will in the LawForms Tangible Personal Property List included with the Will, or in other documents that are incorporated by reference. Further, the following special distributions shall be made on the death of Grantors.

Name of Beneficiary	Money or Property Distributed and Quantity	Per Stirpes o Per Capita
a. Charles E. Jones	$500.00	Per Capita
b. Scottsdale Lutheran	Property on Scottsdale & Lincoln	Per Capita
c. Carolyn Fennedy	$1.00	Per Capita
d.		

Carolyn, we love you very much, but we feel that you do not need our money as you are marrying the Bankers

10. Percentage of Children's Shares. If you want each of your children to share the principal of your trust equally, mark the first box. If you want to make unequal distributions of your trust principal, mark the second box. Remember to include people you have designated "treated like a child". If you mark the second box and are giving unequal shares, list each child or person "treated like a child" and indicate the percentage of the principal they will receive.

11. Final Distribution of Principal to Children. Here is where you will want to do some careful thinking. What is best for your children and the persons you love designated to be "treated as children". Will early distributions of money or property spoil them, if so, delay the distribution. Are inlaws or creditors likely to grab the property that is distributed, if so, restrict the distributions further. Are the children old enough to manage their money and property, set the distribution dates at the times when they are mature to handle matters. You may want to keep the trust as a "family bank" not distributing principal to anyone for two generations. This will insure that your family will "never be poor". They will always have monthly income from the trust and a place where they may borrow money when they have emergencies.

See Appendix A for common alternative distribution methods.

Alternative a. Four distributions every specified number of years. This has been our more popular method for normal children of a normal family. The children don't get everything at once. You distribute in "small doses" to allow them to absorb and learn from each infusion of property and money into their lives: We fill in the periods of time usually at 3 or 5 year intervals.

Alternative b. Four distributions at different ages. Sometimes if the children are maturing slowly we designate distributions at specific ages usually five years apart.

Alternative c. On a specific date after death. Some persons want a simple distribution -- one time -- all. They are not concerned about their children's maturity, spoiling them, creditors, inlaws -- they believe their heirs are able to handle what they receive now. Most times we will delay the distribution until at least one year after death of the last Grantor, giving the trustees time to organize the property, pay bills, pay taxes, and make the special distributions.

Alternative d. Cradle to Grave. Some families want to take care of their children for their lifetime and give them money for retirement.

Alternative e. Fixed age of each beneficiary. Sometimes a family will want each beneficiary to receive benefits at a fixed age.

Alternative f. This one is called the "Dynasty Provision". This alternative will protect the children from creditors, inlaws, and estate taxes for their life. It will also protect the grandchildren from creditors and inlaws. However, during the period that the property and money is in trust the beneficiaries receive income and may borrow extra money -- like borrowing from a "family bank". We always suggest to trustees that any loans be fully secured.

12. Final Distribution of Principal to Grandchildren. You will want to select from the same alternative principal distribution provisions that you selected for the children. Only one may not be used: the lifetime benefits only provision. Here are your choices. (Refer to "Alternative Provisions For Distributing" text examples).

Alternative a. Distribution every specified number of years.

Alternative b. Four distributions at different ages.

Alternative c. On a specified date after death.

Alternative d. Cradle to grave. Use this one if you want to continue the Dynasty Trust provisions from Alternative f of the childrens' distribution provisions.

Alternative e. Fixed age of each beneficiary.

Children's Trusts

2.6 **Division of Trust.** Trustee shall divide the remaining trust estate into as many equal shares as may be necessary to apportion one share for each child of Grantor then living, and one share for the then living descendants collectively of each deceased child of Grantor. Trustee shall obtain a separate tax identification number for each trust share and, except as provided elsewhere in this trust document, treat each trust share as a separate tax entity in accordance with proper accounting rules and procedures.

2.6.a <u>Childrens' Shares</u>. The shares for children or persons treated as children shall be: ☐ Equal ☒ As follows:

```
90% to John K. Fennedy Jr.- grantor's son.
5% to Roger Smith - grantor's friend to be treated like a child.
5% to Kathy Jones - grantor's friend to be treated like a child.
```
(10)

2.6.c <u>Final Distribution of Principal to the Children</u>. Principal shall be distributed to the children as follows:

(11)

```
The Principal of each separate Trust established for each child shall be held in trust for the benefit
of each child for life.  The child shall receive all net income and additional amounts in the sole
discretion of the Trustee for the child's care, maintenance, support and  education as long as the
beneficiary shall live and secured loans to assist the child with professional and business oppor-
tunities and establishment of a comfortable, safe home.  On the death of the child, the remaining
principal shall be distributed as provided for in paragraph 2.6d. (Distribution on Death of Child).
```

2.6.d <u>Distribution on Death of Child</u>. Each share apportioned in accordance with paragraph 2.6 (Division of Trust) to a child of Grantor shall on the death of that child be distributed to the living descendants of the deceased child of Grantor and shall be held or distributed in accordance with paragraph 2.7 (Distribution for Grandchildren).

2.6.e <u>No Special Power of Appointment to Children Beneficiaries</u>. No child of Grantor, from and after the date of Grantor's death, shall have the power to appoint by deed or by will the whole or any part of the principal of the trust.

Grandchildren Trusts

2.7 **Distribution for Grandchildren.** Upon the death of Grantor and upon the disclaimer or death of a child of Grantor, the portion that such child would have received but for his or her death or disclaimer shall be held, administered and distributed by Trustee as follows:

2.7.c <u>Final Distribution of Principal to Grandchildren</u>. Principal shall be distributed to the grandchildren as follows:

(12)

```
All or any portion of the principal of each separate trust share established for a grandchild of Grantor
may be distributed at any time after the beneficiary has reached the age of 65 years. Payment shall be
made without question upon the grandchild's written request.  The right of withdrawal shall be a
privilege which may be exercised only voluntarily and shall not include an involuntary exercise. In the
event that any principal is not distributed, the beneficiary shall retain a life estate in such property.
On the death of such grandchild, the property shall be distributed as provided in provision 2.7d.
(Distribution on Death of Grandchild).
```

13. Contingent Distribution. This provision applies if you have no children, or grandchildren, and no one designated as a beneficiary "Treated Like a Child" living at the time of the distribution. You have to select one of these choices:

Alternative a. Use the laws of successions of the state of your choice. If you have no specific knowledge of the succession laws that apply when no spouses, no children, no grandchildren or other issue survive use the effective state where the trust is executed. Usually the laws of succession will follow common sense patterns of fairness dividing the state among survivor parents, grandparents, brothers, sisters, aunts, uncles, nieces and nephews all relatives of a common grandfather.

Alternative b. You may exercise your own common sense judgment to designate who gets your money and property, and in what percentage when everybody in your immediate family is already gone. We have included a proration clause among the rest where a named person is not there when the distribution is made. YOU CANNOT X BOTH OF THESE BOXES FOR BOTH ALTERNATIVES.

14. Contingent Charities. The worst has happened -- an atomic disaster -- no one you have named as a beneficiary has survived. When this happens in most states, your money and property revert to the state where the trust property is located. The state may not be your favorite charity! Therefore in order not to have "built in obsolescense" we urge you to set forth your favorite charities, setting forth the charity, its address if you know it (if you don't know the address, don't worry -- your trustees can easily find it), and the percentage to each charity.

If you want to "make points" with the charity, you may call them to say that you are putting them in your trust as a beneficiary, and you want to know their address.

Contingent Distribution

2.8 **Contingent Distribution.** If all descendants of Grantor predecease the termination of this trust, so that no beneficiary remains to take under the foregoing provisions, then, upon the death of the last surviving beneficiary, the trust shall terminate and be distributed to:

| - | The heirs at law of Grantor in accordance with the laws of succession of the State of N/A as they exist at the time of executing this trust.

| x | To the following named contingent distributees, in the percentages indicated (13)

	Name of Beneficiary	Mailing Address	Percent
a.	Theodore Fennedy	1944 Boston Ave., NY, NY 10011	50
b.	Robert Fennedy	1968 California St., Boston, MA 11100	50
c.			
d.			
e.			

If one of the above named contingent distributees or their issue predeceases, then that distributee's share shall be allocated to the others pro rata.

2.9.a **Contingent Charities.** However, in the event there are no descendants of Grantor closer in consanguinity than the issue of a common grandparent, or no other contingent distributees remain alive to receive distributions, and in the further event there are state laws applicable to this trust in any state which provide that the property of the trust will escheat to the state because of there being heirs at law of insufficient closeness to qualify for succession, then, if both these conditions occur at the time of distribution, Grantor directs that the remaining assets of the trust be given to the following charities:

(14)

Name of Beneficiary	Mailing Address (if known)	%
Watergate Foundation	11 E. Washington St., NY, NY 10011	50
Teapot Dome Committee	12 E. Harding Ave., NY, NY 10011	30
Democrats Forever	118 S. Jackson Rd., Salem, OR 97114	20

15. Optional Provisions. Here you have some optional provisions you may choose to add frills and personalize your trust. We have included paragraphs that have been used successfully in many of the trusts which we have done for wealthy people.

Option a. Education of all Children. This equalizes distribution to children, where older children have already been educated and the younger haven't. This provision results in taking enough "off the top" for the education of children who have not been educated, before dividing the trust equally.

Option b. Wedding Expenses. This provision also equalizes distribution among children where older children have already had their wedding paid for by the family. This provision allocates "off the top" extra to those who have not yet been married so they have a reasonable sum for their marriages before the distribution.

Option c. Use of Family Residence by children of Grantor. This provision advises the trustee of your direction to let your children use the family residence.

Option d. Use of Family Residence by Guardian. When you die and turn your minor children over to a Guardian, the Guardian may need a larger home. You may also want your children to grow up in the home to which they are accustomed.

Option e. Incentives to Children or Grandchildren. These are like the management incentives that you use in a business to spur your employees to greater heights. We have had clients awarding their children earlier distribution, or special distributions, for actions which exemplify excellence. Some examples are releasing to a child when they run their first marathon; graduate from high school, college, medical school; read certain books, visit the parents home in Yugoslavia, lose weight, or stop smoking. Start thinking imaginatively, help your family move in the direction which your experience indicates the best probabilities of success and survival for your family.

Option f. Disincentives to Children or Grandchildren. Already in this trust we have several incentives and disincentive set forth in provision 1.8 (Statement of Wishes) and 1.15 (Protection Against the Dissipation of Trust). Read these provisions again. Some of them may already take care of your concerns. Human experience has indicated that firm, direct punishment can help children, grandchildren (AND ADULTS ALSO) to be disciplined -- you've heard it -- tough love. Had we been more determined and strict with certain family members and employees about smoking they may not be dying in the hospital with lung cancer. Here's where at last you can put your money where your philosophy of life is. Some examples of these disincentives follow:

If my children or grandchildren eat meat they will lose all inheritances.

Whenever my children or grandchildren are overweight more than 5 lbs. above the weight established as the highest safe weight by the American Heart Institute, their distributions shall be withheld until they have a doctor's certificate stating that their weight is again within the safe parameter.

If any of the children no longer work in the family business -- Widgets Incorporated -- their income distributions from the trust shall be reduced 50% and given to the "Widget Family Foundation" instead.

Every Sunday that a child fails to attend church $100 shall be taken from the principal of their share of the trust and given to the "Holy Valley Church". This assessment shall be verified annually by an attendance record signed by the pastor of the church.

If a child or grandchild drops out of high school and college and fails to return and complete their studies within 5 years 20% of their share of principal of the trust shall be transferred to the National Teachers Association.

Can you think of some other ideas to keep your family on the right track?

Option g. Other Additional Provisions. You may have some other provisions you want. Be sure that you don't contradict provisions already in the trust.

If you want to change a provision in the trust, cross it out and initial the crossed-out lines and write, "See provision 12.y for the amended provisions".

Don't put in mere directions which you don't want to be mandatory and controlling unless you write the words "Statement of Wishes" in front of the provisions. This means the provisions is an "I'd like you to" but not a "must".

12.1 **Optional Provisions.** Grantor adopts the following additional provision which are "X'd". (Dash out those you don't want to apply "--" so as to make clear the ones you do not want to apply.)

⑮

12.1.a [-] Education of All Children. If, upon the death of Grantor, there are any children of Grantor who have not completed a college education, then, before the trust is divided into shares in accordance with provision 2.6 (Division of Trust), Trustee shall set aside a special fund, in an amount to be determined by Trustee, for the education of each child who qualifies for this benefit. The purpose of this provision is to achieve fairness among the children by providing each child with a college education or its equivalent plus an equal division of the remaining trust assets. If a child for whom an education fund was set aside elects to attend an alternate educational training program other than college, this shall be treated as equivalent to a college education for purposes of funding hereunder. The Grantor considers an apprenticeship program for a non-white collar trade to be the equivalent of college within the meaning of this provision, it being the Grantor's intention not to discriminate against children who would prefer and be better qualified for an honest "blue collar" profession. In order to have adequate funds, if principal is inadequate to educate all the children through the youngest, Trustee is authorized to withhold income payments to the children who have completed college educations and accumulate income to be used to educate the younger children through four years of college. The remaining income and principal shall be divided equally among all the children.

12.1.b [-] Wedding Expenses. If, at the time of Grantor's death, there are children of Grantor who have not yet married, then Trustee shall set aside sufficient funds to pay for a wedding and reception in a reasonable amount to be determined by Trustee for the first wedding only of each unmarried child. Such amount may not only be used for the wedding ceremony, reception, and other wedding festivities, but may also be used for a dowry, curtesy, a honeymoon, presents, and all other costs of a lawful marriage. It is Grantor's intent to encourage the children of Grantor to marry and have families comparable to or better than Grantor's family. This additional amount shall augment the trust share of such qualifying child and be administered the same as other assets in that child's trust share until the assets are distributed or reallocated.

12.1.c [x] Use of Family Residence by Children of Grantor. If any child of Grantor is under the age of 21 years after the death of Grantor, Trustee shall permit the residence property of Grantor to be used by the child, and no disposition of the residence property shall be made until such time as there are no children of Grantor under the age of 21 years.

12.1.d [-] Use of Family Residence by Guardian. If Grantor dies leaving a child or children under the age of 18, then, in that event, Grantor specifically directs that the guardian of Grantor's minor child or children be allowed to reside in Grantor's home rent-free for as long as the guardian serves in this capacity.

12.1.e [-] Incentives to Children or Grandchildren. Grantors give the following special or earlier distributions to Grantors' children or grandchildren if they perform the following acts or satisfy the following conditions:

12.1.f [-] Disincentives to Children or Grandchildren. Grantors limit, take away or penalize children or grandchildren if they do the following acts or fail to satisfy the following conditions:

12.1.g [x] Other Additional Provisions as Follows:

Any child or grandchild shall be considered deceased for the purposes of this trust if they marry a republican.

16. Signature of Grantor. Grantors sign their full name here in front of notary publics.

17. Signature of Trustee. Trustees sign their full name here in front of notary publics.

18. Witnesses. You will need adult witnesses, who are not mentioned in the trust in any capacity.

Since these persons will validate your trust you want persons of high character and reputation where possible. We have the trust executed with the same formality as a Will so that it is less likely to be attacked in any other jurisdiction.

19. Notary Public. This will be filled in by the notary public.

Steps to Process

A. Complete the numbered instructions.

B. Place this document in the file where you keep copies of all your trust documents.

IN WITNESS WHEREOF, the parties execute this legal instrument intending that it be effective on the Effective Date and at the Effective Place of Execution.

..........*John K. Kennedy*.......... (16)   ....*John K. Kennedy*.......... (17)
..........*Jacolyn O. Kennedy*..........   ....*Jacolyn O. Kennedy*..........
Signature of Grantor   Signature of Trustee

The foregoing trust was at the date thereof by the named Grantor signed, sealed, published and declared to be a trust which incorporates the Last Will and Testament of the Grantor and serves as a receptacle to receive the pour over of assets. This trust was signed in the presence of us who, at the request and in the presence of Grantor and in the presence of each other, have signed the same as witnesses thereto.

..........*Pandy Pandy*..........   (18)   ....*11530 W. Zoo St. Scottsdale*..........
Signature of Witness   Address of Witness

..........*Walter Moss*..........   ....*6707 W. Neon Dr. Scottsdale*..........
Signature of Witness   Address of Witness

..........*Ruth Wells*..........   ....*1480 N 67th St, Scottsdale*..........
Signature of Witness   Address of Witness

STATE OF ___*Arizona*___   )
) ss.   (19)
County of ___*Maricopa*___   )

On this day, ___*December 31, 1989*___, before me, the undersigned Notary Public, personally appeared the above-subscribed Grantor, Trustee and witnesses, respectively, known to me or satisfactorily proven to be the persons whose names are subscribed to the foregoing instrument, who being first duly sworn, did hereby declare to the undersigned Notary Public that the Grantor and Trustee signed and executed theinstrument with the formality of a Last Will and that Grantor and Trustee executed it as their free and voluntary act for the purposes therein expressed, and that each of the witnesses, in the presence of the Grantor and Trustee, signed the trust as witnesses and that to the best of their knowledge, the Grantor and Trustee were at the time 18 or more years of age, of sound mind, and under no constraint or undue influence; and this trust was subscribed, sworn to and acknowledged before me on the date hereinabove written.

_____*May 1, 1992*_____   ....*Carolyn Toledo*..........
Notary Expiration Date   Signature of Notary

53

Certificate of Trustees' Powers and Abstract of Trust

Purpose of This Form. The Certificate of Trustees' Powers and Abstract of Trust is an abbreviation of your trust informing all the rest of the world of certain facts about your trust. You record the Certificate Of Trustee's Powers with the governmental office where deeds are recorded as notice to the world of the trust, who the trustees and successor trustees are, the trustees' powers, and a few other provisions which title companies, banks, stock brokerage firms, governmental offices, and other persons dealing with the trustees are likely to require for legal transactions. By using the Certificate of Trustees' Powers and Abstract of Trust instead of the whole trust itself to prove its existence, you do not disclose confidential family provisions in the trust. You do disclose the names and the addresses of the beneficiaries so as to comply with the Blind Trust Disclosure statutes of some states, but not who gets what, when, which information should be revealed.

1. Name. Put the name and address of the person who is allowed to request this document from the recording agency. The person named is generally one of the trustees.

2. Office Space. Do not write in this space, it is for official use only.

3. Name of Trust. Most times the Trust is named after the family with the family name "The Fennedy Trust" or "The Fennedy Family Trust". Persons with a penchant for efficiency will use initials or acronyms such as "JJF Trust" or "JOHJAQ Trust". Do not use long names "John and Jacqueline Fennedy Family Trust" -- too much to write each time. Don't put the word "revocable" in the title because when one spouse dies, the trust is no longer revocable. Be imaginative. Perhaps you have a word with zing "The Pizzazz Trust". If you use a name other than the family name you will have more privacy with your financial and property matters.

4. Effective Date. Use the first of a month. Reason: the date of a trust is used whenever you identify a trust. Make it easy on yourself -- date back to the first of this month or the first of the next month. Having the trust start on the first of a month also facilitates accounting. Ideally you would want to start the trust at the beginning of the year -- Jan 1, 1990, that is usually also the beginning of the fiscal year to almost all trusts.

5. Effective County and State of Execution. The place a legal document is signed is usually the location which determines the laws applying to that trust unless it is otherwise agreed in writing in the trust. Write the county and state in the blank. Usually the county recorder of that county is the place designated as the place where the abstract is first filed and where amendments, terminations, affidavits of succession, and other documents are recorded, which tell the world of the status of the trust.

6. Grantor. Write the full legal name of the persons who are forming the trust. This trust is designed to have a sole grantor, a husband and wife as grantor or two or more unmarried family members -- mother and daughter, brother and sister. Write in the mailing address which all grantors want to use as the official address of the trust. Usually this will be in the effective county or state.

7. Primary Trustees. In a declaration of trust usually these are the same persons as the grantor -- the individual himself/herself, the husband and wife, or the grantor family members. These persons control the trust and the property in it. If the grantors are old and feeble at the time the trust is prepared, they may want to name other persons as the primary Trustees; a trusted family member, child, grandchild, brother, sister, niece, nephew, etc. And as Co-Trustee, a so called "disinterested trustee" someone outside the family who is financially responsible and objective, or a bank or trust company. It is good to have 2 trustees in this situation so as to have "checks and balances" and to take the "heat" off of just one person. Human beings are accustomed to have a ruling pair -- a mother and father, a husband and wife, a king and queen, a king and prime minister.

This instrument was recorded at request of:

John K. Fennedy
1956 Massachusetts St.
Scottsdale, AZ 85100

①

②

The recording official is directed to return this instrument or a copy to the above person.

Space Reserved For Recording Information

Certificate of Trustee's Power and Abstract of Trust of the

③

Fennedy Family Trust

TR-2 © LawForms 6-90

Effective Date: 1 January 1990 ④	County and State where Trust is Located: Maricopa, Arizona ⑤
Grantor (Name, Address and Zip Code): John K. Fennedy & Jacolyn O. Fennedy 1956 Massachusetts St. Scottsdale, AZ 85100 ⑥	Primary Trustee (Name, Address and Zip Code): John K. Fennedy & Jacolyn O. Fennedy as trustees for the Fennedy Family Trust, dated 1 January 1990 1956 Massachusetts St. ⑦ Scottsdale, AZ 85100

The following provisions are found in that certain trust agreement named and described above, by and between the above-designated Grantor and Trustee, and may be relied upon as a full statement of the matters covered by such provisions by anyone dealing with Trustee or any successor Trustee. However, in the unlikely event there is a clerical error causing a discrepancy between the original trust and this certificate and abstract of the trust, the original trust document will control the interpretation and administration of the trust.

Names and Addresses of Beneficiaries. In compliance with applicable state and federal statutes, we disclose only the names and addresses of the beneficiaries of this trust, other than the Grantors, who have a lifetime beneficial interest, as follows:

	Name of Beneficiary	**Mailing Address and Zip Code**
a.	John K. Fennedy	1956 Massachusetts St. Scottsdale, AZ 85100
b.	Jacolyn O. Fennedy	1956 Massachusetts St. Scottsdale, AZ 85100
c.	John K. Fennedy	1956 Massachusetts St. Scottsdale, AZ 85100
d.	Carolyn Fennedy	1956 Massachusetts St. Scottsdale, AZ 85100
e.	⑧	
f.		
g.		
h.		
i.		
j.		

8. Names and Addresses of Beneficiaries. Here is an easy fill in! Look through the trust to get the names of everyone who receives any distributions from the trust, $1 to all of it, and list their names and addresses. If you intend to disinherit someone, give them a special distribution of $1 and list them here. No one will know that you had given them only $1 from reading the recorded abstract. It is not necessary to list persons who receive "contingent distributions" after someone else dies such as grandchildren who receive distributions when their parent dies unless you want to make them feel good should they read the recorded abstract. The naming of beneficiaries of a trust is required in some states with laws prohibiting "blind trust" -- trusts with secret beneficiaries. By naming the beneficiaries in the Certificate of Trustees' Power and Abstract of Trust, recording the Certificate of Trustees' Power and Abstract of Trust and then writing on every deed involving the trust the "docket and page" where the Certificate of Trustees' Power and Abstract of Trust is located, you comply with the statute without "garbaging up" your deeds with the names and addresses of the beneficiaries of the trust.

By listing all the beneficiaries here by name and address, even those getting nominal distributions, you make it difficult for anyone to know who received what. Friends chancing upon the Certificate of Trustees' Powers and Abstract of Trust before your death will see their name on the list of beneficiaries -- not knowing how much you're giving them -- and feel good toward you.

9. Designation of Successor Trustees. This insert will take some deep thought by all the grantors. You may want to have:

a. a sole successor trustee;

b. two consisting of a family co-trustee -- a family member and a "disinterested trustee", a competent and objective person or a bank or trust company; or

c. a board of trustees -- all your children, a group of close and trusted friends -- like a board of directors of a corporation.

First decide whether you want the successor trustees to qualify on the death of (1)one or (2)all of the primary trustees. Since this trust is used for estates with a net worth of $600,000 or less, most families will want the surviving trustee to continue along and not get successor trustees involved. However in circumstances where the successor primary trustee is infirm, unskilled in business and finance or subject to influence you may want to require that the successor trustees qualify to assist.

Here are some alternative successor trustee provisions which you may want to consider: (These are illustrated in Appendix C).

Option a. Single Successor Trustee. This is the one we least prefer because it does not have built in "checks and balances". Upon the death, resignation, disqualification, or removal of all but the last one designated Successor Trustees, the last one remaining Successor Trustee shall select a replacement in the event of his or her death.

Option b. Family And Disinterested Successor Trustee. This is the most preferred selection.

Option c. Board of Trustees as Successor Trustee. This is used when you have a harmonious family of children of equal abilities or when you have no close family members, but have a group of close and trusted friends or business associates. (This insert will be the same as 1.3 of the Trust --- they correspond).

10. Governmental Office. This is usually the county recorder's office in the effective county and state where the trust was executed, or the governmental office where deeds are recorded. This becomes the "bulletin board" for the trust where amendments, terminations, and successions may be recorded. It provides a place where banks, title companies, stock brokerage firms may look to verify that the trust has not been terminated or radically changed, and to verify who is the official trustee. This is sometimes called the place for "constructive notice to the world".

1.1 **Trust Property.** Concurrently with the execution of this trust, Grantor has conveyed and delivered to Trustee the property described in a schedule of trust assets, and Trustee hereby acknowledges receipt of that property and agrees to hold and dispose of that property and all additions thereto and income therefrom IN TRUST upon the terms and conditions hereinafter set forth. Additional property from time to time may be transferred to Trustee with Trustee's consent by Grantor or by any other person, estate or trust. Any such additional property shall become a part of the trust property and shall be held, managed, invested, reinvested and disposed of on the same terms and conditions as hereinafter provided.

1.3 **Designation of Successor Trustees.** The successor trustees are as follows: ⑨

1.3.a Designation of Single Successor Trustee. References in the trust instrument to Trustee shall be deemed to include not only the original Trustee but also any additional or successor Trustee or Co-Trustee, and all the powers and discretions vested in Trustee shall be exercisable by any such additional or successor Trustee or Co-Trustee. If the primary Trustees dies or otherwise ceases to function as Trustee, the following persons shall serve as Successor Trustees in the order of priority hereafter set forth:
1.3.a(1) Successor Co-Trustees.
a. John K. Fennedy, Jr., 1956 Massachusetts St., Scottsdale, Az. 85100
b. Carolyn Fennedy, 1956 Massachusetts St., Scottsdale, Az. 85100
c. Steve Austene, 6 Million Dollar Avenue, Majors, WI, 73490

1.3.b Upon the death, resignation, disqualification, or removal of all but the last one designated Successor Trustee, the last remaining Successor Trustee shall select a replacement in the event that he or she ceases to be a Trustee, so that the trust will always have one Trustee .

1.3.C(2) Selection Procedure. Selection shall be made by a written Affidavit of Succession mailed to the (a) then serving Co-Trustee, (b) to all beneficiaries or their representatives, and (c) recording a duplicate original where the trust has its situs.

1.13 **Place of Constructive Notice of Trust Revocation, Amendment or Trustee Succession.** The parties to this trust designate this governmental office: _____Maricopa County Recorder's Office_____ ⑩ , as the location where title companies and others may check to ascertain if this trust has been revoked or amended in any material respect to change the Trustees or Successor Trustees or the powers originally granted to the Trustees. A signed abstract of certain terms of this trust shall be filed or recorded with that public office as notice of the existence of this trust, its Grantor, Trustee, beneficiaries, powers of the Trustee, and other relevant terms. All parties dealing with this trust may rely on the abstract, amended abstracts, and other documents filed or recorded with that public office in ascertaining the status of this trust and may assume, if there are no official filings or recordings to the contrary, that no material changes have been made to the trust since the last filing or recording.

4.19 **Trustee.** References in this instrument to Trustee shall be deemed to include not only the original Trustee or Co-Trustees but also any additional or Successor Trustee or Co-Trustees, and all the powers and discretions vested in Trustee shall be vested and exercisable by any such additional or Successor Trustee or Co-Trustees.

5.2 **Trustee Powers.** In the investment, administration, and distribution of the trust estate and the several shares thereof, the Trustee (subject only to the duty to apply the proceeds and avails of the trust property to the purposes therein specified) may perform every act in the management of the trust estate which individuals may perform in the management of like property owned by them free of trust, and it may exercise every power with respect to each item of property in the trust estate, real or personal, which individual owners of like property can exercise, including, by way of illustration but not by way of limitation, the following powers:

****** **THIS FORM IS ONLY A SAMPLE -- MAIN BODY DELETED** ******

11. Signatures of Grantor. Grantors sign their full name here in front of notary publics.

12. Signatures of Trustees. Trustees sign their full name here in front of notary publics.

13. Notarization. This notarization form will be filled in by the notary.

Reproductions of this executed original (with reproduced signatures) shall be deemed to be original counterparts of this Certificate and Abstract.

IN WITNESS WHEREOF, the parties execute this legal instrument intending that it be effective on the Effective Date and at the Effective Place of Execution.

..........John K Fennedy.......... ....John K Fennedy..........
..........Jacolyn O Fennedy.......... ....Jacolyn O Fennedy..........
Signature of Grantor Signature of Trustee

(13)

STATE OF ___Arizona___)
                            ss.)   ACKNOWLEDGEMENT OF GRANTOR
County Of ___Maricopa___)

On this date, ___December 31, 1989___, before me, the undersigned Notary Public, personally appeared ___John K. Fennedy and Jacolyn O. Fennedy___, who acknowledged himself/herself/themselves to be the person named herein and executed the within instrument for the purposes contained therein.

___May 1, 1993___   ....Marilyn A. Hurdo..........
Notary Expiration Date   Notary Public

IN WITNESS WHEREOF, I hereunto set my hand and official seal.

STATE OF ___Arizona___)
                            ss.)   ACKNOWLEDGEMENT OF TRUSTEE
County of ___Maricopa___)

This instrument was acknowledged before me this date, ___December 31, 1989___, by, ___Jacolyn O. Fennedy and John K. Fennedy___ who acknowledged himself/herself/themselves to be the acting Trustee, being authorized to so do, executed the within instrument for the purposes therein contained by signing for that trust as such Trustee.

___May 1, 1993___   ....Marilyn A. Hurdo..........
Notary Expiration Date   Notary Public

SCHEDULE OF ASSETS TRANSFERRED TO TRUST

Purpose of this Form: This form is a listing of assets which have been transferred from the Grantors to the trust. It can be used for easy reference whenever there is a question of what items are owned by the trust. The form also states the approximate values of items in the trust, and the form of ownership at the time of transfer. New entries are made each time items are transferred to the trust.

1. Name of Grantor. Insert the name(s) of the Grantor(s) which have granted the properties listed in instruction 5, to the trust.

2. Name and Date of Trust. Put the name of the trust here as it is stated in the trust title. Following the name of the trust, state the date when the trust was created.

3. Item Number. Number each item in the order by which it was granted to the trust.

4. Date of Transfer. Put the date when each item listed in number 5 was transferred.

5. Assets Transferred. State the name of each item which is transferred to the trust. This is usually a common name that can distinguish it from any other item that would be transferred to the trust. The name is agreed upon by the trustee and accountants who may work with the trust, so that all will know the "nickname" of each asset.

6. Form of Ownership. There are four basic forms of ownership which you may indicate here, CP, TC, WSP, HSP. CP is the community property form of ownership. If an item is owned by the couple as community property indicate the form of ownership by inserting CP. If you own property as tenants in common, insert TC here. If the property was the husband's personal property before marriage or by gift or inheritance, and the wife has not gained any interest, then insert HSP. If the wife had personal property before marriage or by gift or inheritance in which the husband has not gained any interest, insert WSP.

7. Tax Base at Time of Transfer. If you have an accountant working with you at the time of the formation of your trust, he or she will indicate what the tax base of the asset is, at the time of transfer. If you don't have an accountant, and don't know the tax base, either leave this space blank or insert "N/A". Generally this represents the money you spent for the property.

8. Fair Market Value. Put the value of the property transferred to the trust here if it is known at the time you transfer the property to the trust.

9. Date. Put the date that you sign this form on the line.

10. Signature. Sign your name on the dotted line.

Steps to Process

A. Fill out the form. Since this form is updated periodically when you transfer assets, it may never be completed.

B. Put the form in your safe file with your other trust documents.

C. Send copy to your property and casualty insurance agent and your accountant.

SCHEDULE OF ASSETS TRANSFERRED TO TRUST

TR-3 © LawForms 5-15, 6-90

Name of Grantors of Trust:	Name of Trust and Date of Formation:
John K. Fennedy and Jacolyn O. Fennedy ①	Fennedy Family Trust, 1 January 1990 ②

No.	Date of Transfer	Assets Transferred (For Real Property use Common Name or Address)	Form of Ownership	Tax Base at Time of Transfer (If Known)	Fair Market Value on Date of Transfer (If Known)
1	1 Jan 90	Residency	CP		250,000.00
2	2 Jan 90	Flagstaff Summer Home	CP		115,000.00
3	2 Jan 90	Mercedes 450 SEL (1988)	HSP		50,000.00
4	4 Jan 90	Life Insurance Policy (John)	CP		100,000.00
5	4 Jan 90	Deed of Trust (Tucson Property)	WSP		80,000.00
③	④	⑤	⑥	⑦	⑧

The undersigned Grantors have reviewed the Schedule of Assets and approve the form of partnership of property as set forth above this date: __1 January 1990__ ⑨ .

John K. Fennedy ⑩   *Jacolyn O. Fennedy*
Signature of Grantor   Signature of Grantor

AFFIDAVIT OF SUCCESSION OF TRUSTEE FOR TRUST

Purpose of this Form: This form acts to change the trustee(s) of your trust if a trustee: dies, becomes incompetent, resigns, or recovers from incompetency.

1. Effective Date. Put the date of the change in trustees in this space. Generally this is the date that you sign the document.

2. Name of Trust. Put the name of your trust here. Be sure to include the date when the trust became effective.

3. Amendment Number. If the trust has been amended, put the number of each amendment here.

4. Effective Date of Amendment. Put the effective date of each amendment in the space across from the amendment number.

5. Original Grantors. List the names of the original Grantors.

6. Original Primary Trustees. Lists the names of the original primary trustees.

7. Locations of Recorded Abstract. Indicate all places where the Certificate of Trustees' Powers and Abstract of Trust (LawForm #TR-2, see section 14.b) has been recorded here.

8. Location of Original Trust and Amendments. Put the location where you keep all your trust documents here.

9. Replaced Trustee. Put the name of the Trustee who is to be replaced here.

10. Circumstances Warranting Succession. Mark the box which indicates the reason that the Trustee named in instruction 9 is to be replaced.

11. Signature of Successor Trustee. The Trustee who is replacing the Trustee named in instruction 9 signs this form here.

12. Notary. A notary must witness the signature of the Successor Trustee. Have the Successor Trustee sign in front of the notary. The notary will fill out this part of the form.

Steps to Process

A. Complete the numbered instructions.
B. Have this form signed by the Successor Trustee in front of a notary public.
C. Record the Affidavit of Succession of Trustee for Trust in each county where the Certificate of Trustees' Powers and Abstract of Trust (LawForm #TR-2, see section 14.b) has been recorded.
D. Put a copy of this document in the safe file where you keep copies of all your trust documents.

AFFIDAVIT OF SUCCESSION OF TRUSTEE FOR TRUST
TR-4 © LawForms 6-90

Effective Date of Trust:	Name of Trust:
1 January 1990	Fennedy Family Trust, dated 1 January 1990

Amendments to Trust and Effective Dates of Amendments		Names of Original Grantors:
Amendment Number	Effective Date of Amendment	
1	31 Oct 1991	John K. Fennedy
2	10 Aug 1992	Jacolyn O. Fennedy
-	-	**Names of Original Primary Trustees:**
-	-	John K. Fennedy
-	-	Jacolyn O. Fennedy

Public Places Where Trust or Abstract of Trust Has Been Filed or Recorded:	Places Where Originals of Trust and Amendments Are Located:
Maricopa County Recorders Office	Office safe in John K. Fennedy's Study

1. **Circumstances Warranting Succession of Trustees.** Trustee: _____Jacolyn O. Fennedy_____ has:
- [ ] Died as evidenced by death certificate attached.
- [ ] Become disabled as evidenced by statements of 3 physicians attached.
- [x] Resigned as evidenced by written resignation attached.
- [ ] Recovered as a former disabled Trustee as evidenced by statements of 3 physicians attached.

2. **Affirmation of Successor Trustee.** The undersigned Successor Trustee affirms that the above facts are true and the documents are genuine. And that Successor Trustee is designated in the trust document as the next Successor Trustee. Successor Trustee is willing to assume the responsibilities of Successor Trustee.

3. **Public Notice of Succession.** Executed copies of this Affidavit will be recorded in the County where the former Primary Trustee resides and in all counties where real property belonging to the trust is situated, as indicated above.

4. **Notice to Persons Concerned With the Trust.** A copy of this Affidavit shall be mailed or delivered to all beneficiaries of the trust, to all persons known to have copies of the trust, and, as soon as these are ascertained, to all persons known to have business relationships with the trust.

5. **Verification.** We have read the foregoing and know, of our own knowledge, that the facts stated therein are true and correct, and execute this Affidavit for the purpose set forth herein.

6. THIS AFFIDAVIT IS MADE TO NOTIFY ALL PERSONS concerned with the trust that the undersigned is, as of this date, a Successor Trustee of this trust.

_____John K. Fennedy, Jr._____
Signature of Successor Trustee

_____
Signature of Successor Trustee

STATE OF Arizona
COUNTY OF Maricopa

Date of Verification:
October 30, 1991

Verification of Successor Trustee. On this date, before me, a Notary Public, personally appeared: _____John K. Fennedy, Jr._____ who, being duly sworn upon oath, stated that he had read this document and knows of his own knowledge that the facts stated within are true and correct, except for those matters based on information which he believes to be true.

Signature of Notary Public:
Marilyn A Aurdo

Notary Expiration Date:
May 1, 1992

AMENDMENT OF TRUST

Purpose of this Form: This form will amend your Revocable Trust document. With this document you may add or remove beneficiaries, change the percentage of trust funds that will go to any single beneficiary, or change any provision in the trust.

1. Name of Trust. If you have not amended the trust prior to this document, this will be the First Amendment. If you have amended the trust before, this will be numbered accordingly (i.e. Second, Third, Fourth Amendment).

2. Number of amendment. Put the title of the original trust on the line.

3. Effective Date of Original Trust. Put the date on which the original trust was created here.

4. Effective Date of the Amendment. Put the date that this amended trust will go into effect in this box.

5. Effective Place of Execution. Insert the county and state where you want your amendment to trust to be located. This will be the county and state where the trust will be administered.

6. Grantors. Write or type the full names of each Grantor, and their relationship, along with an address in the space provided.

7. Primary Trustees. Insert the full name and address of each primary Trustee. Generally, the names used will be the same as the Grantors.

8. Detailed Changes. You must fill this out carefully. If you are making an addition to the trust write or type "addition:" followed by the specific wording which you want added to the trust. If you wish to substitute a provision in the trust start with "Substitute" (add the provision you are taking out) then say "for" (state the specific language that you want to use in place of the old language). If you want to delete any provision start with "Delete:" followed by the specific wording that you want deleted. Always give the paragraph number of all provisional language.

THE __Second__ AMENDMENT
__Fennedy Family Trust__ TRUST

TR-5 © LawForms 5-90

Effective Date of Trust:	Amendment Effective Date:	Effective Place of Execution:
1 January 1990	10 Aug 1991	Maricopa County, Arizona

Grantors:

John K. Fennedy and
Jacolyn O. Fennedy,
husband and wife,
1956 Massachusetts St.
Scottsdale, AZ 85100

(Hereinafter referred to as Grantors)

Primary Trustees:

John K. Fennedy and
Jacolyn O. Fennedy
as Trustees of the Fennedy Family Trust
1956 Massachusetts St.
Scottsdale, AZ 85100

(Hereinafter referred to as Trustees)

The above-described trust, by and between the above-named Grantors and Trustees, is amended by substituting provisions, adding provisions, or deleting provisions as follows:

Delete paragraph: 1.4.a.

Add paragraph: 1.16 Trust for Cats. The Grantor's desire that their cats be given $500 each month for cat food and other necessary feline accessories.

Substitute this paragraph: "1.5 __Trust Objectives__. Grantor intends the following:" in place of paragraph 1.5.

9. Signature of Grantor. Have the Grantors sign their names on the dotted line.

10. Signature of Trustee. Have the Trustees sign their names on the dotted line.

11. Signature of Witness. The witnesses of the Trustee(s)' and Grantor(s)' signatures will sign here.

12. Address of Witnesses. Put the address of each witness across from where he or she signed.

13. Notary. A notary must witness the signature(s) of the Grantor(s) and Trustee(s). Have both the Grantor(s) and Trustee(s) sign in front of the witnesses and a notary. The notary will fill out this part of the form.

Steps to Process.

A. Complete document, filling out all the numbered instructions stated above.

B. Have the form signed by the Grantor(s) and Trustee(s) in front of witnesses and a notary.

C. Record this document at all places where you recorded the Certificate of Trustees' Powers and Abstract of Trust (LawForm TR-2, see section 14.b).

D. Put a copy of this document in the safe file where you keep copies of all your trust documents.

THE Second AMENDMENT
Fennedy Family TRUST

TR-5 © LawForms 5-90

(Continued)

All provisions of the above-named trust are incorporated by reference herein with the exception of the provisions expressly changed by this Amendment.

IN WITNESS WHEREOF, the parties hereto have duly executed this Amendment to the trust, to be effective on the Amendment Effective Date above written.

John K. Fennedy
Jacolyn O. Fennedy
Signature of Grantor

John K. Fennedy
Jacolyn O. Fennedy
Signature of Trustee

The foregoing amendment was at the date thereof by the named Grantors signed, sealed, published and declared to be an amendment to a trust which incorporates the Last Wills and Testaments of the Grantors and serves as a receptacle to receive the pour over of assets. This trust amendment was signed in the presence of us who, at the request and in the presence of Grantors and in the presence of each other, have signed the same as witnesses thereto.

Peter N Storm
Cindy Johnson
Jane Wilson
Signature of Witnesses

1321 N. 2nd, Scottsdale, AZ 85111

1231 W. Northern, Phoenix, AZ 85021

21 West Eastern Ave, Duluth, MN 25322
Address of Witnesses

STATE OF Arizona COUNTY OF Maricopa Date of Acknowledgement: August 9, 1991	**Acknowledgement of Grantor.** On this date, before me, a Notary Public, personally appeared: *John K. Fennedy*, known to me or satisfactorily proven to be the person whose name is subscribed to this instrument and acknowledged that he executed the same. If this person's name is subscribed in a representative capacity, it is for the principal named and in the capacity indicated.	Signature of Notary Public: *Marilyn A. Aurdo* Notary Expiration Date: May 1, 1992
STATE OF Arizona COUNTY OF Maricopa Date of Acknowledgement: August 9, 1991	**Acknowledgement of Trustee.** On this date, before me, a Notary Public, personally appeared: *John K. Fennedy*, known to me or satisfactorily proven to be the person whose name is subscribed to this instrument and acknowledged that he executed the same. If this person's name is subscribed in a representative capacity, it is for the principal indicated.	Signature of Notary Public: *Marilyn A. Aurdo* Notary Expiration Date: May 1, 1992

STATEMENT OF WISHES

Purpose of this Form: This form is a letter which tells the beneficiaries of the trust what your wishes are and how you would like the trust funds to be used. The form is not legally binding on the trustees, it gives them guidance.

1. Name. State your full legal name in the area provided.

2. Wishes. Write or type anything that you wish to tell those who you have included in the trust. This is basically a letter indicating your thought and desires concerning the trust. This letter is not a requirement of the trust and has no legal authority. In the letter you can let people know that you are not giving trust money in amounts which indicate how much or little you love or like a particular person.

3. Date. Put the date that you sign this form on the line.

4. Signature. Sign your name on the dotted line.

Steps to process

A. Complete the numbered instructions.

B. Attach the original to your trust document and place it in the safe file where you keep copies of all your trust documents.

STATEMENT OF WISHES
AS A SUPPLEMENT TO WILLS AND TRUSTS

TR-6 © LawForms 2-81, 4-81, 6-90

I, __John Fennedy__ ①, having previously executed certain wills, trusts or other documents, set forth hereafter this statement of wishes to guide my designated personal representatives, trustees, conservators and/or guardians in carrying out my wishes.

I intend this statement of wishes as advisory only and not mandatory. It is written to assist, but not control my fiduciaries.

My wishes are that:

②

All my children and grandchildren benefit from this trust. I particularly wish for Carolyn to use trust funds in pursuing her Law degree. Furthermore, I desire that John Jr. follow my footsteps in politics and that he will use trust funds towards that end.

I am leaving a smaller share of the trust to Carolyn as she is engaged to Donald Strump. It is my belief that she has little need for financial aid at this point.

I want it clearly stated that the amounts of the trust are not based in proportion to my love and affection. I have given by way of this trust where I see need. No one should feel less loved because of a small percentage of the trust.

SIGNED this date:__1 January 1990__ ③   _John K. ④ Fennedy_
                                        Signature

AFFIDAVIT TERMINATING THE REVOCABLE LIVING TRUST

Purpose of this Form: This form will terminate your Revocable Living Trust. If, for any reason you decide to terminate your trust, you can use this form.

1. Name of Trust. Indicate the name of the trust that you are terminating here.

2. Date of Trust. Give the effective date of your trust here.

3. Name of Grantor. Put the names of the Grantors here.

4. Name of Trustees. Put the names of the Trustees here.

5. Beneficiaries. Indicate the names and addresses of all the primary beneficiaries listed in paragraph 1.2 of the trust document.

6. Basis for Revocation. "X" the box which is applicable. Use the top box if both Grantors are still alive. Use the middle box if all assets have been distributed out of the trust. Use the bottom box if the trust is terminated by court order.

7. Recording Information. Put the recording information on your trust (where the Certificate of Trustees' Powers and Abstract of Trust is recorded for this property) here. This generally includes the name of the recording agency, the docket number and the pages of the docket where the Certificate is recorded. Be sure to include the date that the Certificate was recorded.

8. Counties of Recordation. Insert the names of all counties where you have recorded your Certificate of Trustees' Powers and Abstract of Trust.

9. Signature of Grantor. Have the Grantor sign this form in front of the notary public.

10. Notary. A notary must witness the signatures of the Grantor. Have the Grantor sign in front of the notary. The notary will fill out this part of the form.

Steps to Process

A. Complete the numbered instructions.

B. Record a copy of this form in every county where copies of the Certificate of Trustees' Powers and Abstract of Trust (LawForm #TR-2, see section 14.b) have been recorded.

C. Put a copy of this document in the safe file where you keep copies of all your trust documents.

AFFIDAVIT TERMINATING THE REVOCABLE LIVING TRUST

TR-7 © LawForms 6-90

1. I am over the age of 18 and otherwise competent to testify in a court of law of the United States or its several states and make this Affidavit without being under fraud, duress or undue influence from any person..

2. **Identification of Trust**. We are the Grantor(s) of the __Fennedy Family Trust__ ①, dated __1 January 1990__ ②, between __John K. Fennedy and Jacolyn O. Fennedy__ ③; as Grantors, and __John K. Fennedy and Jacolyn O. Fennedy__ ④, as Trustees.

3. The Beneficiary(ies) of the trust are:

John K. Fennedy, 1956 Massachusetts St., Scottsdale, AZ 85100
Jacolyn O. Fennedy, 1956 Massachusetts St., Scottsdale, AZ 85100
John K. Fennedy, Jr., 1956 Massachusetts St., Scottsdale, AZ 85100
Carolyn Fennedy, 1956 Massachusetts St., Scottsdale, AZ 85100

⑤

4. **Revocation**. The trust is hereby revoked:

[x] in accordance with paragraph 11.1 of the trust.(Power in Grantor During Lifetime of Grantor to Revoke)
[ ] as a result of all assets of the trust being distributed out of the trust.
[ ] pursuant to a court order, a copy of which is attached.

⑥

5. **Recorded Information on Trust**. The names and address of the grantor, trustees and beneficiaries of the trust, the identity of the trust and the relevant provisions of the trust have been disclosed in the Certificate of Trustees' Powers and Abstract of Trust which is recorded at:
__Maricopa County Recorders Office, Docket Number 12432, pages 27-35__ ⑦.

6. **Notice of Recording**. As evidence of such termination, a signed original of this Affidavit shall be recorded with the county Recorder's office in the following counties:

Pima, Arizona
Coconino, Arizona
Maricopa, Arizona

⑧

7. **Notice to Beneficiaries**. A copy of this Affidavit Terminating the Revocable Living Trust has been mailed to the above named beneficiaries this date of this Affidavit.

I have read the foregoing and know of my own knowledge that the facts stated therein are true and correct.

John K. Fennedy ⑨   _Jacolyn O. Fennedy_
Signature of Grantor   Signature of Grantor

STATE OF _Arizona_ COUNTY OF _Maricopa_ Date of Verification: _August 3, 1994_	Verification of Grantor. On this date, before me, a Notary Public, personally appeared: _John_ ⑩ _K. Fennedy_, who, being duly sworn upon oath, stated that he had read this document and knows of his own knowledge that the facts stated within are true and correct, except for those matters based on information which he believes to be true.	Signature of Notary Public: _Nora Notary_ Notary Expiration Date: _June 1, 1996_

SPECIAL WARRANTY DEED TO TRUST

Purpose of this Form: The Special Warrranty Deed is generally used to transfer your house or any other real (land) property to the Revocable Trust.

1. Return From Recording. Put the name and address of the person who is allowed to request this document from the recording agency. The person named is generally one of the trustees.

2. Office Space. Do **not** write in this space, it is for official use only.

3. Effective Date. Put the date of transfer in this space. Generally this is the date that you sign the document. Do not make it earlier than the date of the Trust.

4. Location of Property. Insert the name of the county and state where the property is located.

5. Grantor. Indicate the name and address of the person who is transferring interest in the property to the trust in the space provided.

6. Grantee. State the name and address of the trust following the names of the trustees. Be sure that the name of the trust includes the date it became effective.

7. Subject Real Property Address. Insert the best address for finding where the property is located.

8. Proof of Legal Description. The person who gives the legal description in instruction 9 must check to make sure that it is the same as the description on the original deed. Once the description has been checked, the proof reader(s) initial here. One person reads the legal description from the source of the description; the other checks it against the newly typed description. These persons initial that they did this.

9. Legal Description of Property. This is a "government survey", "meets and bounds", lots in a subdivision number, or other designated legal property description. You need to copy this from the original deed. All punctuation, letters and numbers must appear exactly as on the original deed.

This instrument was recorded at request of:

John K. Fennedy
1956 Massachusetts St.
Scottsdale, AZ 85100   (1)

(2)

The recording official is directed to return this instrument or a copy to the above person.

Space Reserved For Recording Information

SPECIAL WARRANTY DEED TO TRUST
TR-8 © LawForms 10-76, 12-85, 6-90

Effective Date: (3) 1 January 1990	County and State where Real Property is Located: (4) Maricopa, Arizona
Grantor (Name, Address and Zip Code): (5) John K. Fennedy & Jacolyn O. Fennedy 1956 Massachusetts St. Scottsdale, AZ 85100	Grantee (Name, Address and Zip Code): (6) John K. Fennedy & Jacolyn O. Fennedy as Trustees of the Fennedy Family Trust dated 1 January 1990 1956 Massachusetts St. Scottsdale, AZ 85100

Subject Real Property (Address or Location): 1956 Massachusetts St. (7) Scottsdale, AZ 85100	Legal Description Proofed by Persons Whose Initials Appear to the Right	1. (8)	2.	3.

Subject Real Property (Legal Description):

NE 1/4, SW 1/4, NW 1/4, SE 1/4 of Section 12, Township 2 North Range 4 West of the Gila and Salt River Base and Meridian, State of Arizona

(9)

(Continued on Reverse Side)

10. Recording Information. Put the recording information on your trust (where the Certificate of Trustees' Powers and Abstract of Trust is recorded for this property) here. This generally includes the name of the recording agency, the docket number and the pages of the docket where the Certificate of Trustees' Powers and Abstract of Trust is recorded. Be sure to include the date that the Abstract was recorded.

11. Signature of Grantor. Have the Grantors sign their names on the dotted lines.

12. Signatures of Witnesses. The witnesses of the Grantor(s)' signature(s) will sign here.

13. Notary. A notary must witness the signature(s) of the Grantor(s). Have the Grantor(s) sign in front of the witnesses and a notary, then the notary will fill out this part of the form.

Steps to Process

A. Complete the numbered instructions.

B. Have the form signed by the Grantor(s) in front of witnesses and a notary.

C. Record a Certificate of Trustees' Powers and Abstract of Trust (LawForm #TR-2, see section 14.b) in the county where the Special Warranty Deed is to be recorded..

D. After the Certificate of Trustees' Powers and Abstract of Trust is recorded, record this document in the county where the property is located.

E. Put a copy of this document in the safe file where you keep copies of all your trust documents.

1. **Recorded Information on Trust.** The names and addresses of the grantor, trustees and beneficiaries of the trust, the identity of the trust and the relevant provisions of the trust have been disclosed in the Certificate of Trustee's Powers and Abstract of Trust which is recorded at: ⑩ Maricopa County Recorders Office, Docket Number 12432, pages 27-35.

2. **Effect of Transfer.** Any transfers effectuated by this document transferring real property interests to a trust, involve the transfer of real property by the legal owners to a Revocable Living Trust, which will have the same IRS identification number as the transferor, and will not be an Irrevocable transfer until the death of the transferors and as such shall not warrant the triggering of "due on sale" clauses in any related documents, or the imposition of taxes, or tax reassessments, imposed when there is a completed transfer of real property ownership.

3. **Conveyance.** This Special Warranty Deed made by the assignor, hereby grants, sells and conveys the above described property to the above named assignee, for true and actual consideration in the amount of 10.00 dollars to have and to hold the same, with all appurtenances thereon, to assignee and assignee's heirs and assigns forever. I/We covenant that I/we convey and warrant specially the title against all persons claiming under me.

---

1. ⑪ *Harry Henderson*
2. *Tom Meyers*
Signatures of Witnesses

⑫ *John K. Fennedy*
Jacolynn O. Fennedy
Signatures of Grantor

STATE OF *Arizona*
COUNTY OF *Maricopa*
Date of Acknowledgement:
Jan. 1, 1990

Acknowledgement of Grantor. On this date, before me, a Notary Public, personally appeared: *John* ⑬ *K. Fennedy*, known to me or satisfactorily proven to be the person whose name is subscribed to this instrument and acknowledged that he executed the same. If this person's name is subscribed in a representative capacity, it is for the principal named and in the capacity indicated.

Signature of Notary Public:
Nora Notary
Notary Expiration Date:
June 1, 1996

STATE OF *Arizona*
COUNTY OF *Maricopa*
Date of Acknowledgement:
Jan. 1, 1990

Acknowledgement of Witnesses. On this date, before me, a Notary Public, personally appeared: 1. *Harry Henderson* 2. *Tom Meyers*, known to me or satisfactorily proven to be the person whose name is subscribed to this instrument and acknowledged that he executed the same. If this person's name is subscribed in a representative capacity, it is for the principal indicated.

Signature of Notary Public:
Nora Notary
Notary Expiration Date:
June 1, 1996

BILL OF SALE TO TRUST OF HOUSEHOLD GOODS AND EFFECTS

Purpose of this Form: This form transfers household goods and personal effects located at your place of residence, from you personally, to the Revocable Trust.

1. Return from Recording. Put the name and address of the person who is allowed to request this document from the recording agency. The person named is generally one of the trustees.

2. Office Space. Do **not** write in this space, it is for official use only.

3. Effective Date. Put the date of transfer in this space. Generally this is the date that you sign the document. Do not make it earlier than the date of the Revocable Trust.

4. Location of Property. Insert the name of the county and state where your residence is located.

5. Seller. Indicate the name and address of the person who is transferring the household goods and personal property to the trust in the space provided.

6. Buyer. State the name and address of the trust following the names of the trustees (Buyers). Be sure that the name of the trust includes the date it became effective.

7. Property Sold. Insert the address where your residence is located.

8. Address of Residence. Place the address of residence on the line.

9. Recording Information. Put the recording information on your trust (where the Certificate of Trustees' Powers and Abstract of Trust is recorded for this property) here. This generally includes the name of the recording agency, the docket number, and the pages of the docket where the Certificate of Trustees' Powers and Abstract of Trust is recorded. Be sure to include the date that the Certificate of Trustees' Powers and Abstract of Trust was recorded.

10. Signature of Seller. The Seller named in instruction 5 signs here.

11. Notary. A notary must witness the signature of the Seller(s). Have the Seller sign in front of the notary, then the notary will fill out this part of the form.

Steps to process

A. Record a Certificate of Trustees' Powers and Abstract of Trust (LawForm #TR-2, see section 14.6) in the county where this document is to be recorded.

B. Complete the numbered instructions.

C. Have the form signed by the Seller in front of a notary.

D. After the Certificate of Trustees' Powers and Abstract of Trust is recorded, record this document in the county where the property is located.

E. Put a copy of this document in the safe file where you keep copies of all your trust documents.

This instrument was recorded at request of:

John K. Fennedy
1956 Massachusetts St.
Scottsdale, AZ 85100

(1)

(2)

The recording official is directed to return this instrument or a copy to the above person.

Space Reserved For Recording Information

BILL OF SALE TO TRUST
(Household Goods and Personal Effects)

TR-9 © LawForms 10-71, 1-83, 7-87, 6-90

Effective Date: (3) 1 January 1990	County and State where property is located: (4) Maricopa, Arizona
Seller (Name, Address and Zip Code): John K. Fennedy & Jacolyn O. Fennedy 1956 Massachusetts St. Scottsdale, AZ 85100 (5)	Buyer (Name, Address and Zip Code): John K. Fennedy & Jacolyn O. Fennedy as trustees for the Fennedy Family Trust dated 1 January 1990 (6) 1956 Massachusetts St. Scottsdale, AZ 85100

Address and Location of Property Sold:

1956 Massachusetts St. (7)
Scottsdale, AZ 85100

Property Sold (List of Personal Property by Description, Serial Number and Other Identifying Characteristics):

All right, title and interest of Seller in, and to, all household furnishings, fixtures, equipment, works of art, silverware, chinaware, artifacts, collections, musical instruments, antiques, jewelry, furs and all personal property, and personal effects located in and about the residence of Sellers at __(8)__ 1956 Massachusetts St., Scottsdale, AZ 85100 _____ as of this date and as may be hereinafter acquired in this residence or in later acquired residences of Seller.

1. **Conveyance.** For valuable consideration, receipt of which is acknowledged, Seller sells and conveys to Buyer the Property Sold, to have and to hold the Property Sold to Buyer and the heirs, executors, administrators and assigns of Buyer forever, and Seller and the heirs, executors, administrators and assigns of Seller warrant to defend the sale of the Property sold unto Buyer and the heirs, executors, administrators and assigns of Buyer, against all and every person whomsoever lawfully claiming or to claim the same.

2. **Recorded Information on Trust.** The names and addresses of the grantor, trustees and beneficiaries of the trust, the identity of the trust and the relevant provisions of the trust have been disclosed in the Certificate of Trustee's Powers and Abstract of Trust which is recorded at: __(9)__ Maricopa County Recorders Office Docket Number 12432, pages 27-35 _____.

John K. (10) Fennedy
Signature of Seller

Jacolyn O. Fennedy
Signature of Seller

STATE OF *Arizona* COUNTY OF *Maricopa*	Acknowledgement of Seller. On this date, before me, a Notary Public, personally appeared: *John (11) K. Fennedy*, known to me or satisfactorily proven to be the person whose name is subscribed to this instrument and acknowledged that he executed the same. If this person's name is subscribed in a representative capacity, it is for the principal indicated.	Signature of Notary Public: *Nora Notary*
Date of Acknowledgement: *Jan. 1, 1990*		Notary Expiration Date: *June 1, 1996*

BILL OF SALE TO TRUST

Purpose of this Form: This form acts to transfer your interest in personal property to the trust. You can use this form to transfer most any item that you own except land and intangible property (money, bonds, stocks, tradenames, etc.).

1. Return from Recording. Put the name and address of the person who is allowed to request this document from the recording agency. The person named is generally one of the trustees.

2. Office Space. Do **not** write in this space, it is for official use only.

3. Effective Date. Put the date of transfer in this space. Generally this is the date that you sign the document. Do not make it earlier than the date of the Revocable Trust.

4. Location of Property. Insert the name of the county and state where the Bill of Sale items are located.

5. Seller. Indicate the name and address of the person who is transferring the Bill of Sale items to the trust in the space provided.

6. Buyer. State the name and address of the trust following the names of the trustees. Be sure that the trust includes the date it became effective.

7. Property Assigned. Insert the address or location where the Bill of Sale items are located.

8. Property Sold. List the items that you are transferring to the trust by Bill of Sale.

9. Recording Information. Put the recording information of your trust (where the Certificate of Trustees' Powers and Abstract of Trust is recorded for this property) here. This generally includes the name of the recording agency, the docket number, and the pages of the docket where the Certificate of Trustees' Powers and Abstract of Trust is recorded. Be sure to include the date that the Certificate of Trustees' Powers and Abstract of Trust was recorded.

10. Signature of Seller. The Seller named in instruction 5 signs here.

11. Notary. A notary must witness the signature of the Seller. Have the Seller sign in front of the notary, then the notary will fill out this part of the form.

Steps to Process.

A. Be sure to record a Certificate of Trustee's Powers and Abstract of Trust (LawForm #TR-2, see section 14.b) in the county where this document is to be recorded.

B. Complete the numbered instructions.

C. Have the form signed by the Seller in front of a notary.

D. After the Certificate of Trustees' Powers and Abstract of Trust is recorded, record this document, where the property is located.

E. Put a copy of this document in a safe file where you keep copies of all your trust documents.

This instrument was recorded at request of:

John K. Fennedy
1956 Massachusetts St.
Scottsdale, AZ 85100

(1)

(2)

The recording official is directed to return this instrument or a copy to the above person.

Space Reserved For Recording Information

BILL OF SALE TO TRUST
(General)

TR-10 © LawForms 10-71, 1-83, 7-87, 6-90

Effective Date: 10 January 1990 (3)	County and State where property is located: Maricopa, AZ (4)
Seller (Name, Address and Zip Code): John K. Fennedy 1956 Massachusetts St. (5) Scottsdale, AZ 85100	Buyer (Name, Address and Zip Code): John K. Fennedy and Jacolyn O. Fennedy trustees for the Fennedy Family Trust dated 1 January 1990 1956 Massachusetts St. (6) Scottsdale, AZ 85100

Address or Location of Property Sold:

Safety Deposit Box, First Bank International (7)

Property Sold (List of Personal Property by Description, Serial Number and Other Identifying Characteristics):

(8)

Vintage Baseball cards of the following players:
- Johnny Bench (1971)
- Mickey Mantle (1959)
- Joe Dimaggio (1967)

1. Conveyance. For valuable consideration, receipt of which is acknowledged, Seller sells and conveys to Buyer the Property Sold, to have and to hold the Property Sold to Buyer and the heirs, executors, administrators and assigns of Buyer forever, and Seller and the heirs, executors, administrators and assigns of Seller warrant to defend the sale of the Property sold unto Buyer and the heirs, executors, administrators and assigns of Buyer, against all and every person whomsoever lawfully claiming or to claim the same.

2. Recorded Information On Trust. The name and addresses of the grantor, trustees and beneficiaries of the trust, the identity of the trust and the relevant provisions of the trust have been disclosed in the Certificate of Trustee's Powers and Abstract of Trust which is recorded at: (9) Maricopa County Recorders Office, Docket Number 12432, pages 27-35.

John K Fennedy (10)
Signature of Seller

Signature of Seller

STATE OF _Arizona_
COUNTY OF _Maricopa_

Date of Acknowledgement:
January 10, 1990

Acknowledgement of Seller. On this date, before me, a Notary Public, personally appeared: _John K. (11) Fennedy_, known to me or satisfactorily proven to be the person whose name is subscribed to this instrument and acknowledged that he executed the same. If this person's name is subscribed in a representative capacity, it is for the principal indicated.

Signature of Notary Public:
Nora Notary

Notary Expiration Date:
June 1, 1996

DEED, BILL OF SALE AND ASSIGNMENT (OMNIBUS)

Purpose of this Form: This document transfers any items that accidently were not transferred to the trust. We have found that sometimes items which are meant to be transferred to the trust are somehow missed. These items cause needless probate costs which may be avoided by use of this form.

1. Return from Recording. Put the name and address of the person who is allowed to request this document from the recording agency. The person named is generally one of the Trustees.

2. Office Space. Do **not** write in this space, it is for official use only.

3. Effective Date. Put the date of transfer in this space. Generally this is the date that you sign the document. Do not make it earlier than the date of the Revocable Trust.

4. Location of Property. Insert the name of the county and state of your legal residence.

5. Assignor. Indicate the name and address of the person who is transferring property to the Trust in the space provided.

6. Assignee. State the name and address of the Trust following the names of the trustees. Be sure that the name of the trust includes the date that it became effective.

This instrument was recorded at request of:

Jacolyn O. Fennedy
1956 Massachusetts St.
Scottsdale, AZ 85100

The recording official is directed to return this instrument or a copy to the above person.

Space Reserved For Recording Information

DEED, BILL OF SALE AND ASSIGNMENT
(Omnibus)

TR-11 © LawForms 6-90

Effective Date: 1 January 1990	County and State where property is located: Maricopa, Arizona
Assignor (Name, Address and Zip Code): John K. Fennedy & Jacolyn O. Fennedy 1956 Massachusetts St. Scottsdale, AZ 85100	Assignee (Name, Address and Zip Code): John K. Fennedy & Jacolyn O. Fennedy as trustees for the Fennedy Family Trust, dated 1 January 1990 1956 Massachusetts St. Scottsdale, AZ 85100

1. Effort to Transfer. The Assignor has made every effort to transfer all assets belonging to Assignor to the above named Trust for the purpose of avoiding unnecessary costs or adverse consequences at time of Assignor's death, therefor the property assigned by this document is located wherever it may be at the time of Assignor's death, should it not have been previously assigned to the above named trust.

2. Conveyance. For valuable consideration receipt of which is acknowledged, assignor intends by this legal instrument to transfer to Assignee, as of the effective date, all right, title and interest in all property or property rights, tangible or intangible, which may now be owned or may hereafter accrue to Assignor unless there are written documents executed by Assignor stating a contrary intent in the language of the documents themselves dated after this date.

3. Transfer Without Additional Documents. Assignor intends that this document by itself shall effectuate the transfer without any necessity of additional transfer documents, and directs and consents that this document may be recorded or filed in any public agency to evidence the transfer of any property or property right which may vest title in the ownership of Assignor.

4. Power to Assignee to Make Transfer. However, if by reason of law, regulation, custom or other requirement, additional documents are necessary to mechanically evidence the transfer, the Assignee is given the express power by Assignor to prepare and sign, on behalf of both parties, whatever additional documents are necessary to mechanically carry out the intent of this omnibus transfer.

5. Purpose of Omnibus. The purpose of this document is to carry out the intent of Assignor that all Assignor's property (not otherwise transferred to a partnership, corporation, retirement plan or other trust) be owned by Assignee trust, in order to make unnecessary the costs, inconvenience and other adverse consequences of probate and other court proceedings which would otherwise be required if property is owned by Assignor at the time of Assignor's death.

6. Specific Examples. Specific examples of property to which this transfer applies would be: (1) causes of action in the nature of legal claims against other persons; (2) property rights accrued by reason of unwritten contracts or commitments; (3) inheritances which result in property being owned by Assignor by operation of law or documents that Assignor is not aware of; (4) devises from Wills of relatives; (5) distributions from trusts; and (6) real or personal tangible or intangible property that was inadvertently forgotten or omitted from transfer to Assignee.

(Continued on Reverse Side)

7. Recording Information. Put the recording information on your trust (where the Certificate of Trustees' Powers and Abstract of Trust is recorded for this property) here. This generally includes the name of the recording agency, the docket number, and the pages where the Certificate of Trustees' Powers and Abstract of Trust is recorded. Be sure to include the date that the Certificate of Trustees' Powers and Abstract of Trust was recorded.

8. Signature of Assignor. Have the assignor(s) sign their names on the dotted lines.

9. Notary. A notary must witness the signature(s) of the Assignor(s). Have the Assignors sign in front of a notary, then the notary will fill out this part of the form.

Steps to Process

A. Be sure to record a Certificate of Trustees' Powers and Abstract of Trust (LawForm #TR-2, see section 14.b) in the county and state where this document is to be recorded.

B. Complete the numbered instructions.

C. Have the form signed by the Assignor(s) in front of a notary.

D. After the Certificate of Trustees' Powers and Abstract of Trust is recorded, record this document where you plan to administer the trust.

E. Put a copy of this document in the safe file where you keep copies of all your trust documents.

7. Preparation of Documents. Assignee directs and consents that Assignee may prepare whatever document may be necessary to carry out the purpose and intent of this Deed, Bill of Sale and Assignment.

8. Recorded Information on Trust. The names and addresses of the grantor, trustees and beneficiaries of the trust, the identity of the trust and the relevant provisions of the trust have been disclosed in the Certificate of Trustee's Powers and Abstract of Trust which is recorded at: (7) Maricopa County Recorders Office, Docket Number 12432, pages 27-35 .

John K. Kennedy
Signature of Assignor

Jacolyn O. Kennedy
Signature of Assignor

STATE OF Arizona COUNTY OF Maricopa Date of Acknowledgement: January 1, 1990	**Acknowledgement of Assignor.** On this date, before me, a Notary Public, personally appeared: John (9) K. Kennedy , known to me or satisfactorily proven to be the person whose name is subscribed to this instrument and acknowledged that he executed the same. If this person's name is subscribed in a representative capacity, it is for the principal indicated.	Signature of Notary Public: *Nora Notary* Notary Expiration Date: June 1, 1996

LETTER OF INSTRUCTION FOR MOTOR VEHICLE DEPARTMENT, TITLE COMPANY, BANK, AND STOCK BROKER OF RIGHTS THAT FOLLOW CREATION OF TRUST

Purpose of these Letters: These letters are sent to inform the title company, bank, motor vehicle department, and stock broker that you have created a Revocable Trust. It also acts as instruction for transfer of title on your vehicles, bank accounts, title companies, mutual funds, and brokerage accounts.

1. Name of Trust. State the name or title of your trust here on all four letters.

1.1 The Letter on Banking with a Trust lets the bank know that your have established a trust. You need to let the bank know if the trust name will be on the face of the check. Just make an appointment with the accounts officer at your bank and let him know your decision regarding who will be listed on the face of the check.

1.2 Also in the Letter on Banking you should inform the accounts officer that safety deposit boxes will also be placed in the name of the trust. Plan to designate three authorized persons for the safe deposit boxes. This way if both spouses die at the same time the boxes may be opened conveniently. We recommend that the first successor trustees be added as signatories authorized to open the boxes.

2. Date of Trust. Put the date that the trust was created in the space provided.

2.1 Be sure to call and find out if there are any special forms or procedures required by the local motor vehicle department.

3. Names of Trustees. Place the names of all trustees on the line.

4. Signature of Trustee. All trustees should sign here on all four letters.

Steps to Process

A. Complete the numbered instructions.
B. Send the letters to your stock broker (Stock Broker letter), mutual fund account manager (Stock Broker letter), motor vehicle department (Motor Vehicle Department Letter), bank (Bank letter), and/or title company (Title Company Letter).
C. Put a copy of this letter in the safe file where you keep copies of all your trust documents.

LETTER OF INSTRUCTION TO MOTOR VEHICLE DEPARTMENT REGARDING TRANSFERRING ALL OF THE UNDERSIGN'S MOTOR VEHICLES INTO THE TRUST

TR-12a © LawForms 6-90

To whom it may concern:

This is a letter informing you of the formation by the undersigned Grantors of __the Fennedy Family__ Trust, dated ___1 January 1990___, with ___John K. Fennedy & Jacolyn O. Fennedy___ as trustees.

We are sending you this letter on the suggestion of LawForms, Inc. It has been drafted by the staff of attorneys which produce the LawForms product and is for the purpose of informing the Motor Vehicle Department of certain rights which are created by the formation of the Revocable Living Trust.

We want to make certain that there are no complications in making investments using the trust which we have implemented as part of our estate plan.

We provide you with all the relevant information pertaining to the trust in the Certificate of Trustee's Powers and Abstract of Trust which has been attached. This Certificate sets forth the "vital statistics" of the trust in an abbreviated form providing you with the information you need to deal with the trust -- much like a driver's license or passport is used to identify an individual:

1. **Owner of Automobiles.** Please change the title(s) of any vehicle(s) into the name of the above named Trust. The trustees will sign on behalf of the trust.

2. **Beneficiary Designations.** All beneficiary designations which may be necessary are set forth in the attached Certificate.

3. **Tax ID Numbers.** Revocable living trusts are not required to have a separate tax number and the social security numbers of the grantors/trustees may be used.

4. **Copies to Us.** We would appreciate your sending us copies of the documentation which evidences that the instructions set forth in this letter have been carried out.

5. **Further Information.** Should you require more information or explanation, please call us anytime. We would be happy to assist you.

It is our desire to make an easy transition of ownership and control to the Trust. We appreciate your help in making that possible.

Yours truly,

_____ _____
Signature of Grantor/Trustee   Signature of Grantor/Trustee

AFFIDAVIT OF TRUSTEE FOR TRANSFER OF MOTOR VEHICLE INTO NAME OF TRUST

Purpose of this Form: This document authorizes the motor vehicle department to transfer the title of the listed motor vehicle into the name of the Revocable Trust. You should send this document to the Motor Vehicle Department along with the Letter Transferring Title to the motor vehicle.

1. Name of State. Put the name of the state where you have residency here.

2. Name of Trust. Put the name or title of the Trust here.

3. Effective Date. Put the date that the trust was created in the space provided.

4. Name of Grantor. Put the names of the Grantors of the trust in this place.

5. Name of Trustee. Put the names of all current Trustees here.

6. Description of Automobile. Give the full description of the motor vehicle (year, make, model, and identification number) here.

7. Recording Information. Put the recording information on your trust (where the Certificate of Trustees' Powers and Abstract of Trust is recorded) here. This generally includes the name of the recording agency, the docket number and the pages of the docket where the Certificate of Trustees' Powers and Abstract of Trust is recorded. Be sure to include the date that the Certificate of Trustees' Powers and Abstract of Trust was recorded.

8. Signature of Trustee. Sign the Affidavit on the dotted line.

9. Notary. A notary must witness the signature of the Trustee. Have the Trustee sign in front of the notary, then the notary will fill out this part of the form.

Steps to Process

A. Complete the numbered instructions.
B. Have the form signed by the Trustee in front of a notary.
C. Send the Affidavit to the Motor Vehicle Department along with the "Letter of Instruction to the Motor Vehicle Department" (LawForm #TR-12a, see section 14.1.)
D. Put a copy of this document in the safe file where you keep copies of all your trust documents.

AFFIDAVIT OF TRUSTEE
FOR TRANSFER OF MOTOR VEHICLE
INTO NAME OF TRUST

TR-13 © LawForms 6-90

1. **Competency.** I am over the age of 21 years, a resident of the State of _____Arizona ①_____, and otherwise competent to testify in a court of law. I make this Affidavit without being under fraud, duress or undue influence from any person.

2. **Description of Trust.** I am a Trustee of the following-described revocable, living declaration of trust:

    Name of Trust: ② Fennedy Family Trust

    Date of Trust: ③ 1 January 1990

    Grantor: ④ John K. Fennedy & Jacolyn O. Fennedy

    Trustee: ⑤ John K. Fennedy & Jacolyn O. Fennedy

3. **Description of Motor Vehicle.** Concurrently with the submission of this Affidavit to the State Motor Vehicle Department, I have submitted an Application for Certificate of Title and Registration to transfer the ownership of the following-described motor vehicle to the above-described trust:

    1990 Mercedes 500D AS54310 ⑥

4. **Registration and Title.** This vehicle is to be titled and registered in the name of the family trust identified above and not in a business or commercial trust.

5. **Recorded Information on Trust.** The names and addresses of the grantor, trustees and beneficiaries of the trust, the identity of the trust and the relevant provisions of the trust have been disclosed in the Certificate of Trustees' Powers and Abstract of Trust which is recorded at
: Maricopa County Recorders Office Docket Number 12432, pages 27, 35 .

⑦

John K. Fennedy ⑧   _Jacolyn O. Fennedy_
Signature of Trustee   Signature of Trustee

STATE OF Arizona
COUNTY OF Maricopa
Date of Verification:
January 3, 1990

Verification of Trustee. On this date, before me, a Notary Public, personally appeared: _John_ ⑨ _K. Fennedy_, who, being duly sworn upon oath, stated that he had read this document and knows of his own knowledge that the facts stated within are true and correct, except for those matters based on information which he believes to be true.

Signature of Notary Public:
Nora Notary
Notary Expiration Date:
June 1, 1996

STOCK POWER AND ASSIGNMENT APART FROM CERTIFICATE TO TRUST

Purpose of this Form: This document transfers the power to vote, sell or otherwise control your stock to the Revocable Trust.

1. Effective Date. Put the date when the trust was established on this line.

2. County and State. Insert the name of the county and state where the stocks are located.

3. Assignor. Indicate the name and address of the person who is transferring the interest in the stocks to the trust in the space provided.

4. Assignee. State the name and address of the trustee for the Revocable Trust. Be sure that the name of the trust includes the date it became effective.

5. Stock Assigned. Put the name of the stock (which is listed as the name of the corporation) along with its classification (i.e. Class A voting, Class A non-voting, or Common stock), in the space provided. The corporate name and the classification will be on the stock certificates.

6. Number of Shares. Put the number of shares for each stock certificate here.

7. Certificate Number. Put the number that is listed in the upper left hand corner of the stock certificate here to correspond with the named stocks in instructions 5 and 6.

8. Attorney of Assignor. If you have authorized someone to process the stock certificate, then put the name of your attorney in fact in this box. If you have not appointed an attorney in fact, just insert "N/A".

9. Recording Information. Put the recording information on your trust (where the Certificate of Trustees' Powers and Abstract of Trust is recorded for these stock transfers) here. This generally includes the name of the recording agency, the docket number, and the pages of the docket where the Certificate is recorded. Be sure to include the date that the Certificate was recorded.

10. Name and Address of Signature Guarantor. You must have your signature guaranteed by a brokerage firm or bank which can verify the validity of this transaction. Go see an officer at your bank or a stock broker and ask if he is able to guarantor a signature. Put the name of the guarantor's institution along with the complete address in the space provided.

11. Signature of Assignor. The Grantor of the Revocable Trust who is transferring stock power to the Trust signs this document here. You must sign in the presence of the guarantor.

12. A Banker or Stock Broker will complete the rest of this document.

Steps to Process

A. Complete the numbered instructions.
B. Have the form signed by the Assignor in front of the Guarantor of your signature.
C. Send the original Stock Certificate and the Stock Power and Assignment to your stock broker for processing or to the transfer agent of the corporation whose stock you own.
D. Put a copy of this document in the safe file where you keep copies of your trust documents.

STOCK POWER AND ASSIGNMENT APART FROM
CERTIFICATE TO TRUST

TR-14 © LawForms 8-74, 6-90

Effective Date:	County and State:
4 January 1990 ①	Maricopa County, Arizona ②

Assignor (Name, Address and Zip Code):	Assignee (Name, Address and Zip code):
John K. Fennedy & Jacolyn O. Fennedy 1956 Massachusetts St. Scottsdale, AZ 85100 ③	John K. Fennedy & Jacolyn O. Fennedy as trustees of the Fennedy Family Trust, dated 1 January 1990 1956 Massachusetts St. Scottsdale, AZ 85100 ④

Stock Assigned (Corporation - Type)	Number of Shares	Certificate Numbers
ZATA Industries, Inc., a Delaware corporation, common stock, $1.00 par value: ⑤	75 ⑥	A 39412 ⑦

Attorney in Fact of Assignor (Name, Address and Zip Code):

N/A ⑧

---

1. Transfer of Stock. For value received, assignor assigns the stock carried in the name of assignor on the books of the designated corporation and appoints irrevocably the above named attorney-in-fact to transfer that stock on the books of the corporation, with full power of substitution in the premises, to assignee.

2. Recorded Information of Trust. The names and addresses of the grantor, trustees and beneficiaries of the trust, the identity of the trust and the relevant provisions of the trust have been disclosed in the Certificate of Trustee's Powers and Abstract of Trust which is recorded at: ⑨ Maricopa County Recorders Office Docket Number 12432, pages 27-35 .

3. Affirmation of Signature. I affix hereto my signature exactly as it appears on the certificates without alteration, change or enlargement.

Name, Address and Zip Code of commercial bank, trust company, or firm which guarantees signature of assignor:	⑪ *John K Fennedy*
⑩ Fealty Brokerage 1111 California Ave. NY, NY 10101	*Jacolyn O. Fennedy* Signature of Assignor

GUARANTY OF SIGNATURE

I am an officer of a commercial bank or trust company having its principal office OR a correspondent in the City of New York, Midwest, American or Pacific Coast Stock Exchanges, and I know and certify that the above signature is valid and guarantee it as the true signature of assignor.

Date of Guaranty of Signature	Signature and Title of Officer
January 4, 1990	⑫ *Dennis Jones President*

BOND POWER AND ASSIGNMENT APART FROM CERTIFICATE TO TRUST

Purpose of this Form: This document transfers the power to sell or otherwise control your bonds to the Revocable Trust.

1. Effective Date. Put the date when the trust was established on this line.

2. County and State. Insert the name of the county and state where the bonds are located.

3. Assignor. Indicate the name and address of the person who is transferring the interest in the bonds to the trust in the space provided.

4. Assignee. State the name and address of the trustee for the Revocable Trust. Be sure that the name of the trust includes the date it became effective.

5. Bonds Assigned. Put the name of the bond (which is listed as the name of the issuer) along with its type (i.e. revenue, etc.) in the space provided. The name of the issuer and the type of bond, will be on the face of the bond certificate.

6. Amount of Bond. Put the amount of the bond which is present on the face of the bond, in the space provided.

7. Certificate Number. Put the number that is listed in the upper left hand corner of the bond certificate here to correspond with the named bonds in instructions 5 and 6.

8. Attorney of Assignor. If you have authorized someone to process the Bond Certificate, then put the name of your attorney in fact in this box. If you have not appointed an attorney in fact, just insert N/A.

9. Recording Information. Put the recording information of your trust (where the Abstract is recorded for these bond transfers) here. This generally includes the name of the recording agency, the docket number, and the pages of the docket where the Abstract is recorded. Be sure to include the date that the Abstract was recorded.

10. Name and Address of Signature Guarantor. You must have your signature guaranteed by a brokerage firm or bank which can verify the validity of this transaction. Go see an officer at your bank or a stock broker and see if he is able to guarantor a signature. Put the name of the guarantors institution along with the complete address in the space provided.

11. Signature of Assignor. The Grantor of the Revocable Trust who is transferring bond power to the Trust signs this document here. You must sign in the presence of the guarantor.

12. A banker or stock broker will complete the rest of this document.

Steps to Process

A. Complete the numbered instructions.
B. Have the form signed by the Assignor in front of the Guarantor.
C. Send the original document to the company of the bond certificate.
D. Put a copy of this document in the safe file where you keep copies of your trust documents.

BOND POWER AND ASSIGNMENT
APART FROM CERTIFICATE TO TRUST
TR-15 © LawForms 8-74, 6-90

Effective Date: ① 4 January 1990	County and State: ② Maricopa, Arizona
Assignor (Name, Address and Zip Code): ③ John K. Fennedy Jacolyn O. Fennedy 1956 Massachusetts St. Scottsdale, AZ 85100	Assignee (Name, Address and Zip code): ④ John K. Fennedy & Jacolyn O. Fennedy as trustees for the Fennedy Family Trust dated 1 January 1990 1956 Massachusetts St. Scottsdale, AZ 85100

BONDS ASSIGNED (Issuer and Type)	Amount of bonds	Certificate Numbers
Maricopa County School Board Reserve Bond ⑤	$5,000.00 ⑥	007836 ⑦

Attorney in Fact of Assignor (Name, Address and Zip Code): ⑧
Steve H. Lawman 1070 Central Ave. Phoenix, AZ 85000

1. Conveyence of Bond Power. For value received assignor assigns the stock carried in the name of assignor on the books of the designated corporation and appoints irrevocably the above name attorney in fact to transfer that stock on the books of the corporation, with full power of substitution in the premises, to assignee.

2. Recorded Information. The names and addresses of the grantor, trustees and beneficiaries of the trust, the identity of the trust and the relevant provisions of the trust have been disclosed in the Certificate of Trustee's Powers and Abstract of Trust which is recorded at:
⑨ Maricopa County Recorders Office Docket Number 12432, pages 27-35 .

I affix hereto my signature exactly as it appears on the certificates without alteration, change or enlargement.

| Name, Address and Zip Code of commercial bank, trust company, or firm which guarantees signature of assignor:

⑩ Fealty Brokerage
1111 California Ave.
New York City, New York 10101 | ⑪ *John K. Fennedy*
Jacolyn O. Fennedy
Signature of Assignor |

GUARANTY OF SIGNATURE

I am an officer of a commercial bank or trust company having its principal office OR a correspondent in the City of New York, Midwest, American or Pacific Coast Stock Exchanges, and I know and certify that the above signature is valid and guarantee it as the true signature of assignor.

| Date of Guaranty of Signature:

January 4, 1990 | Signature and Title of Officer:

⑫ *Dennis Jones* President |

ASSIGNMENT OF PARTNERSHIP INTEREST TO TRUST

Purpose of this Form: This form transfers a partnership interest to the Revocable Trust.

1. Return from Recording. Put the name and address of the person who is allowed to request this document from the recording agency. The person named is generally one of the trustees.

2. Office Space. Do **not** write in this space, it is for official use only.

3. Effective Date. Put the date of transfer in this space. Generally this is the date that you sign the document. Do not make it earlier than the date of the Revocable Trust.

4. Location of Property. Insert the name of the county and state where the partnership is located. This is generally the primary place of business.

5. Assignor. Indicate the name and address of the person who is transferring the partnership interest to the Trust in the space provided.

6. Assignee. State the name and address of the trust following the names of the trustees. Be sure that the name of the trust includes the date it became effective.

7. Partnership Interest Documents. Insert the address or location where the partnership interest documents are located.

8. Percentage of Partnership. Insert the percentage of the partnership share or the number of units that is owned individually by the Assignor and is being transferred by this document.

9. Name of Partnership. Put the name of the partnership, of which an interest is being transferred, here.

10. State of Partnership. Put the state where the partnership was created on the line.

11. State Agency Partnership Number. Some state may require a partnership to be registered, if your partnership is registered by a state agency put the registration number here, if not, insert N/A.

12. Signatures of General Partners. Have all the General Partners of the partnership sign this form on the lines provided.

This instrument was recorded at request of:

John K. Fennedy
1956 Massachusetts St.
Scottsdale, AZ 85100

(1)

(2)

The recording official is directed to return this instrument or a copy to the above person.

Space Reserved For Recording Information

ASSIGNMENT OF PARTNERSHIP INTEREST TO TRUST
TR-16 © LawForms 10-71, 1-83, 7-87, 6-90

Effective Date: (3) 4 January 1990	County and State where property is located: (4) Maricopa County, Arizona
Assignor (Name, Address and Zip Code) John K. Fennedy & Jacolyn O. Fennedy 1956 Massachusetts St. Scottsdale, AZ 85100 (5)	Assignee (Name, Address and Zip Code) John K. Fennedy & Jacolyn O. Fennedy as trustees for the Fennedy Family Trust, dated 1 January 1990 1956 Massachusetts St. (6) Scottsdale, AZ 85100

Partnership Interests Assigned (Address or Location of Documentation of Articles of Partnership):

John K. Fennedy's office safe (7)

Partnership Interests Assigned (Legal Description):

All right, title and interest of Assignors in undivided percentage or units equal to __30 capital percent units__ (8) in the limited partnership, (9) __Lucky Mining Properties, LTD__, a partnership of the state of __California__ (10), __Certificate No. 1278__ (11), including all Assignor's right and interest in that partnership and any successor partnership and all Assignor's rights and interests in and under the partnership agreement relating thereto, and proceeds of any of the above.

1. General Partner Approval. By their signatures below, the General Partners of the limited partnership signify their approval of this assignment of interest on the dates set forth.

John K Fennedy (signature)
Signature of General Partner   Dated: Jan. 4, 1990

Jacolyn O. (12) Fennedy (signature)
Signature of General Partner   Dated: Jan. 4, (13) 1990

....
Signature of General Partner   Dated: _____

....
Signature of General Partner   Dated: _____

(Continued on Reverse Side)

13. Date of Partner Signatures. Put the date that each general partner signed the document accross from the signature.

14. Recording Information. Put the recording information of your trust (where the Abstract is recorded for this partnership) here. This generally includes the name of the recording agency, the docket number, and the pages of the docket where the Abstract is recorded. Be sure to include the date that the Abstract was recorded.

15. Signature of Assignor. The assignee named in instruction 6 signs here.

16. Notary. A notary must witness the signature of the Assignor. Have the Assignor sign in front of the notary, then the notary will fill out this part of the form.

Steps to Process

A. Be sure to record a Certificate of Trustees' Powers and Abstract of Trust (LawForm #TR-2, see section 14.b) in the county where this document is to be recorded.

B. Complete the numbered instructions.

C. Have the form signed by the Assignor in front of a notary.

D. Send an original and one certified copy of this to the General Partners to sign asking them to keep the certified copy for their files and return the oiginal to you.

E. Put a copy of this document in the safe file where you keep copies of all your trust documents.

2. Recorded Information on Trust. The names and addresses of the grantor, trustees and beneficiaries of the trust, the identity and the relevant provisions of the trust have been disclosed in the Certificate of Trustees' Powers and Abstract of Trust which is recorded at:
(14) Maricopa County Recorders Office Docket Number 12432, pages 27-35

3. Assumption of Partnership Agreement. Assignees below acknowledge that they have read and are familiar with the Agreement of Partnership and have received a copy of same, and agree to be bound by its terms as a limited partner.

4. Conveyance. For valuable consideration, receipt of which is acknowledged by Assignor, Assignor assigns all right, title, and interest of Assignor in the Partnership Interest assignment.

---

(15) *John K. Fennedy*
Jacolyn O. Fennedy
Signatures of Assignor

John K. Fennedy
Jacolyn O. Fennedy
Signatures of Assignee

STATE OF Arizona COUNTY OF Maricopa Date of Acknowledgement: Jan. 4, 1990	**Acknowledgement of Assignor.** On this date, before me, a Notary Public, personally appeared: John K. (16) Fennedy, known to me or satisfactorily proven to be the person whose name is subscribed to this instrument and acknowledged that he executed the same. If this person's name is subscribed in a representative capacity, it is for the principal named and in the capacity indicated.	Signature of Notary Public: *Nora Notary* Notary Expiration Date: June 1, 1996
STATE OF Arizona COUNTY OF Maricopa Date of Acknowledgement: Jan. 4, 1990	**Acknowledgement of Assignee.** On this date, before me, a Notary Public, personally appeared: Jacolyn O. Fennedy, known to me or satisfactorily proven to be the person whose name is subscribed to this instrument and acknowledged that he executed the same. If this person's name is subscribed in a representative capacity, it is for the principal indicated.	Signature of Notary Public: *Nora Notary* Notary Expiration Date: June 1, 1996

ASSIGNMENT AND BILL OF SALE OF SOLE PROPRIETORSHIP PROPERTY TO TRUST

Purpose of this Form: This form transfers the interest that you have in sole proprietorship property from you personally to the Revocable Trust which you have set up.

1. Return from Recording. Put the name and address of the person who is allowed to request this document from the recording agency. The person named is generally one of the trustees.

2. Office Space. Do **not** write in this space, it is for official use only.

3. Effective Date. Put the date of transfer in this space. Generally this is the date that you sign the document. Do not make it earlier than the date of the Revocable Trust.

4. Location of Property. Insert the name of the county and state where the sole proprietorship business is located.

5. Assignor. Indicate the name and address of the person who is transferring the sole proprietorship business to the trust in the space provided.

6. Assignee. State the name and address of the trust following the names of the trustees. Be sure that the name of the trust includes the date it became effective.

7. Property Assigned. Insert the address or location where the sole proprietorship is located.

8. Owners of Proprietorship. Put the name of the person(s) who owns and is transferring the sole proprietorship here.

9. Name of Business. Put the name of the sole proprietorship on the line.

10. Location of Business. Put the street address of the sole proprietorship here.

11. List of Tangible Assets. Mark the box with an "X" which indicates if you have listed the tangible property, and if so, where you have put that list.

12. Name of Business. Put the name of the sole proprietorship on the line.

13. Location of Business. Put the street address of the sole proprietorship here.

14. List of Intangible Assets. Mark the box with an "X" which indicates if you have listed the intangible property, and if so, where you have put that list.

This instrument was recorded at request of:

John K. Fennedy
1956 Massachusetts St.
Scottsdale, AZ 85100   ①

②

The recording official is directed to return this instrument or a copy to the above person.

Space Reserved For Recording Information

ASSIGNMENT AND BILL OF SALE
OF SOLE PROPRIETORSHIP PROPERTY TO TRUST
TR-17 © LawForm 10-71, 1-83, 7-87, 6-90

Effective Date: 1 January 1990 ③	County and State where property is located: Maricopa, Arizona ④
Seller/Assignor (Name, Address and Zip Code): John K. Fennedy & Jacolyn O. Fennedy 1956 Massachusetts St. Scottsdale, AZ 85100 ⑤	Buyer/Assignee (Name, Address and Zip Code): John K. Fennedy & Jacolyn O. Fennedy as trustees for the Fennedy Family Trust, dated 1 January 1990 1956 Massachusetts St. Scottsdale, AZ 85100 ⑥

Address or Location of Property Sold and Assigned:

1200 N. Wilson Ave., Mesa, AZ 85200   ⑦

Property Sold and Assigned (List of Property by Description, and/or Other Identifying Characteristics):   ⑧

All furniture and fixtures, equipment, personal property, and all other tangible assets of that certain sole proprietorship of _____ John K. Fennedy and Jacolyn O. Fennedy _____, known as __Fennedy Family Sporting Goods__ ⑨ , which are presently being used in the business or may be hereafter acquired, which are located at:
__1200 N. Wilson Ave., Mesa, AZ 85200__ ⑩ _____ and
which are: [-] listed hereafter [-] listed on attached inventory [x] contained at that location.
   ⑪

Intangible Property Assigned (files, customer lists):

All accounts receivable, notes receivable, funds receivable, good will, trade name, trademarks and all other intangible assets, both present and future, of that certain business which is known as __Fennedy Family Sporting Goods__ ⑫ located at _____
⑬ __1200 N. Wilson Ave., Mesa, AZ 85200__ as entered on the books, records, and files of said business and which are: [-] listed hereafter [-] listed on attached inventory [x] contained at that location.
   ⑭

(Continued On Reverse Side)

15. Recording Information. Put the recording information of your trust (where the Certificate of Trustees' Powers and Abstract of Trust is recorded for this property) here. This generally includes the name of the recording agency, the docket number, and the pages of the docket where the Certificate is recorded. Be sure to include the date that the Certificate was recorded.

16. Signature of Assignor. The Seller/Assignor named in instruction 5 signs here.

17. Notary. A notary must witness the signature of the Seller(s)/Assignor(s). Have the Seller/Assignor sign in front of the notary, then the notary will fill out this part of the form.

Steps to Process

A. Be sure to record a Certificate of Trustee's Powers and Abstract of Trust (LawForm #TR-2, see section 14.b) in the county where this document is to be recorded.

B. Complete the numbered instructions.

C. Have the form signed by the Seller/Assignor in front of a notary.

D. After the Certificate is recorded, record this document where the property is located.

E. Put a copy of this document in a safe file where you keep copies of all your trust documents.

1. **Conveyance of Tangible Property.** For valuable consideration, receipt of which is acknowledged by Seller, Seller sells and conveys to Buyer the tangible Property Sold, to have and to hold the Property Sold to Buyer and the heirs, executors, administrators and assigns of Buyer forever, and Seller and the heirs, executors, administrators and assigns of Seller warrant to defend the sale of the Property Sold unto Buyer and the heirs, executors, administrators and assigns of Buyer, against all and every person whomsoever lawfully claiming or to claim the same.

2. **Conveyance of Intangible Property.** For valuable considerations, receipt of which is acknowledged by Assignor, Assignor assigns all of his right, title and interest in the Property Assigned to Assignee.

3. **Recorded Information on Trust.** The names and addresses of the grantor, trustees and beneficiaries of the trust, the identity of the trust and the relevant provisions of the trust have been disclosed in the Certificate of Trustees' Powers and Abstract of Trust which is recorded at: (15)   Maricopa County Recorders Office Docket Number 12432, pages 27-35

John K Fenn (16)   *Carolyn O Fennedy*
Signatures of Assignor/Seller   Signatures of Assignor/Seller

STATE OF *Arizona*	Acknowledgement of Assignor/Seller. On this date, before me, a Notary Public, personally appeared: *John K.* (17) *Fennedy* known to me or satisfactorily proven to be the person whose name is subscribed to this instrument and acknowledged that he executed the same. If this person's name is subscribed in a representative capacity, it is for the principal indicated.	Signature of Notary Public: *Nora Notary*
COUNTY OF *Maricopa*		
Date of Acknowledgement: *January 1, 1990*		Notary Expiration Date: *June 1, 1996* 99

ASSIGNMENT AND ASSUMPTION OF LEASE

Purpose of this Form: This form acts to transfer your interest in a lease agreement to the trust. You may either be assigning an interest in rental monies or you may be assigning a lessor's interest in the property for a period of time.

1. Return from Recording. Put the name and address of the person who is allowed to request this document from the recording agency. The person named is generally one of the Trustees.

2. Office Space. Do **not** write in this space, it is for official use only.

3. Effective Date. Put the date of transfer of the lease in this space. Generally this is the date that you sign the document. Do not make it earlier than the date of the Revocable Trust.

4. Location of Property. Insert the name of the county and state where the leased property is located.

5. Assignor. Indicate the name and address of the person who is transferring the lease interest to the trust in the space provided.

6. Assignee. State the name and address of the trust following the names of the Trustees. Be sure that the trust name includes the date that it became effective.

7. Property Assigned. Insert the address or location where the lease property is located.

8. Proof of Legal Description. The person who gives the legal description in instruction 9 must check to make sure that it is the same as the description on the original lease. If the original lease does not have a legal property description, insert N/A here. Once the description has been checked, the proofreader(s) initials here. One person reads the legal description from the source of the description; the other checks it against the newly typed description. These persons initial that they did this.

9. Legal Description. This is a "government survey", "meets and bounds", lots in a subdivision number or other designated legal property description. You need to copy this from the original lease. All punctuation, letters, and numbers must appear exactly as on the original lease. If the original lease does not have a legal property description, insert N/A here.

10. Lessor's Name and Address. The Lessor is the person who pays money on the lease agreement, he/she has the right to use the property for a certain length of time. Put the Lessor's name and address in the space provided.

11. Lessee's Name and Address. The Lessee is the person who is paid money for the use of his/her property. Put the Lessee's name and address in the space provided.

12. Date of Lease. Indicate the date that the original lease became effective.

13. Recording Number. If the original lease agreement was recorded at a county recorder's office, put the recording agency's number here. If the original lease was not recorded insert N/A here.

14. Lessor or Lessee. If you are the Lessor named in instruction 10 mark the first box. If you are the Lessee named in instruction 11 mark the second box.

15. Recording Information. Put the recording information from the Certificate of Trustees' Powers and Abstract of Trust (LawForm #TR-2, see section 14.b) in this space. Generally this information includes the name of the recording agency, the docket number, and the pages of the docket where the Certificate was recorded. Be sure to include the date that the Certificate was recorded.

16. Signature of Lessor. The Lessor named in instruction 10 signs this form here.

17. Signature of Assignor. The Assignor named in instruction 5 signs this form here.

18. Signature of Lessee. The Lessee named in instruction 11 signs this form here.

19. Signature of Assignee. The Assignee name in instruction 6 signs this form here.

Steps to Process

A. Record a Certificate of Trustees' Powers and Abstract of Trust (LawForm #TR-2, see section 14.b) in the county where the Assignment and Assumption of Lease is to be recorded.

B. Complete the numbered instructions.

C. Have this form signed by the Lessor and Lessee in front of a notary public.

D. After the Certificate is recorded and this form is completed, record the Assignment and Assumption of Lease where the property is located.

E. Put a copy of this document in the safe file where you keep copies of all your trust documents.

This instrument was recorded at request of:

John K. Fennedy
1956 Massachusetts St.
Scottsdale, AZ 85100

(1)

(2)

The recording official is directed to return this instrument or a copy to the above person.

Space Reserved For Recording Information

ASSIGNMENT AND ASSUMPTION OF LEASE
TR-18 © LawForms 10-76, 12-85, 6-90

Effective Date: 1 January 1990 (3)	County and State where Real Property is Located: Maricopa County, Arizona (4)
Assignor (Name, Address and Zip Code): John K. Fennedy (5) Jacolyn O. Fennedy 1956 Massachusetts St. Scottsdale, AZ 85100	Assignee (Name, Address and Zip Code): John K. Fennedy & Jacolyn O. Fennedy as trustees for the Fennedy Family Trust, dated 1 January 1990 (6) 1956 Massachusetts St. Scottsdale, AZ 85100

Subject Leased Premises (Address or Location): 111 E. Worthy St. (7) Phoenix, AZ 85001	Legal Description Proofed by Persons Whose Initials Appear to the Right (8)	1.	2.	3.

Leased Premises Assigned (Legal Description of parcel on which leased premises are located):

NE 1/4, SW 1/4, NW 1/4, SE 1/4 of Section 12, Township 2 North Range 4 West of the Gila and Salt River Base and Meridian, State of Arizona (9)

Lessor (Name, Address, and Zip Code): Scott Rash (10) 121 Billet Blvd. New York, NY 10011	Lessee (Name, Address, and Zip Code): John K. Fennedy and Jacolyn O. Fennedy 1956 Massachusetts St. (11) Scottsdale, AZ 85100
Date of Lease: 7 December 1989 (12)	Recording Number if Recorded: N/A (13)

1. **Conveyance.** For valuable consideration, receipt of which is acknowledged, Assignor, Assignor assigns to Assignee all right, title and interest of Assignor as [-] Lessor [x] Lessee in the Lease Assigned and the property rights of Assignor in the Leased Premises assigned as prescribed in the Lease Assigned. (14)

2. **Assumption by Assignee.** Assignee assumes all terms of the Lease Assigned which were the obligations of Assignor as of the Effective Date. The below parties consent to this assignment.

3. **Recorded Information on Trust.** The names and addresses of the grantor, trustees and beneficiaries of the trust, the identity of the trust and the relevant provisions of the trust have been disclosed in the Certificate of Trustee's Powers and Abstract of Trust which is recorded at: __Maricopa County Recorders Office Docket Number 12432, pages 27-35__ (15)

Scott (16) Rash
Signature of Lessor

John K. (17) Fennedy
Signature of Assignor

Jacolyn O. (18) Fennedy
Signature of Lessee

John K. Fennedy (19)
Signature of Assignee

101

ASSIGNMENT OF PROMISSORY NOTE RECEIVABLE TO TRUST

Purpose of this Form: This form transfers the interest that you have in a promissory note, which secures the debt of another, from you personally to the Revocable Trust which you have set up.

1. Return from Recording. Put the name and address of the person who is allowed to request this document from the recording agency. The person named is generally one of the trustees.

2. Office Space. Do **not** write in this space, it is for official use only.

3. Effective Date. Put the date of transfer in this space. Generally this is the date that you sign the document. Do not make it earlier than the date of the Revocable Trust.

4. Location of Property. Insert the name of the county and state where the original promissory note document is kept.

5. Assignor. Indicate the name and address of the person who is transferring the promissory note interest to the trust in the space provided.

6. Assignee. State the name and address of the trust following the names of the trustees. Be sure that the name of the trust includes the date it became effective.

7. Property Assigned. Insert the address or location where the original promissory note document is kept.

8. Proof of Legal Description. Leave this area blank.

9. Promissory Note or Receivable. Mark the box with a "x" which indicates whether you are transferring a promissory note or receivable to your trust.

10. Date of Promissory Note. Put the date when the promissory note became effective here.

11. Amount of the Note. Put the amount of the promissory note in the space.

12. Name of Promisor. Put the name of the person who gave you the promissory note for purposes of security and owes the money to you.

13. Account Receivable Debtor. Insert the name of the account receivable debtor here.

14. Principle Sum of Account Receivable. Indicate the amount that the Account Receivable Debtor owes.

15. Evidence of Account Receivable. Indicate how you can demonstrate that the account receivable debt is owed. This can be a letter, receipt, or any other form of evidence of debt.

16. Recording Information. Put the recording information of your trust (where the Certificate of Trustees' Powers and Abstract of Trust is recorded for this property) here. This generally includes the name of the recording agency, the docket number, and the pages of the docket where the Certificate is recorded. Be sure to include the date that the Certificate was recorded.

17. Signature of Assignor. The Assignor named in instruction 5 signs here.

18. Notary. A notary must witness the signature of the Assignor. Have the Assignor sign in front of the notary, then the notary will fill out this part of the form.

Steps to Process

A. Be sure to record a Certificate of Trustees' Powers and Abstract of Trust (LawForm #TR-2, see section 14.b) in the county where this document is to be recorded.

B. Complete the numbered instructions.

C. Have the form signed by the Assignor in front of a notary.

D. After the Certificate is recorded, record this document where the promissory note is located. (Recording is Optional).

E. Put a copy of this document in the safe file where you keep copies of all your trust documents.

This instrument was recorded at request of:

John K. Fennedy
1956 Massachusetts St.
Scottsdale, AZ 85100

(1)

(2)

The recording official is directed to return this instrument or a copy to the above person.

Space Reserved For Recording Information

ASSIGNMENT OF PROMISSORY NOTE/RECEIVABLE TO TRUST
TR-19 © LawForms 10-71, 1-83, 7-87, 6-90

Effective Date: 4 January 1990 (3)	County and State where property is located: Maricopa, Arizona (4)
Assignor (Name, Address and Zip Code): John K. Fennedy & Jacolyn O. Fennedy 1956 Massachusetts St. Scottsdale, AZ 85100 (5)	Assignee (Name, Address and Zip Code): John K. Fennedy & Jacolyn O. Fennedy as trustees for the Fennedy Family Trust, dated 1 January 1990 1956 Massachusetts St. (6) Scottsdale, AZ 85100
Promissory Note / Receivable Assigned (Location of Original): 1956 Massachusetts St. Scottsdale, AZ 85100 (7)	Legal Description Proofed by Persons Whose Initials Appear to the Right (8)

(9)
[x] Promissory Note Assigned (Description):
All right, title and interest of Assignor in and to that certain Commercial Negotiable Promissory Note dated __24 July 1989__ (10) in the principal amount of __$75,000.00__ (11) by and between __Malcolm McDuck__ (12) as maker and Assignor as payee.

[x] Receivable Assigned (Description):
The Debt owing to Assignor by __Sam Snead__ (13) the Debtor for the principal sum of $ __1,000__ (14) which is evidenced by a:
(15)
Letter dated August 1, 1989 where Sam Snead promised to pay Assignor $1,000 if I beat him in golf

1. **Conveyance.** For valuable considerations, receipt of which is acknowledged by Assignor, Assignor assigns all of his right, title and interest in the Promissory Note / Receivable assigned to Assignee together with all liens, collateral or pledges which secure that debt.

2. **Recorded Information on Trust.** The names and addresses of the grantor, trustees and beneficiaries of the trust, the identity of the trust and the relevant provisions of the trust have been disclosed in the Certificate of Trustee's Powers and Abstract of Trust which is recorded at: (16) __Maricopa County Recorders Office Docket Number 12432, pages 27-35__.

John K. Fennedy (17)   _Jacolyn O. Fennedy_
Signature of Assignor   Signature of Assignor

| STATE OF _Arizona_
COUNTY OF _Maricopa_
Date of Acknowledgement:

January 4, 1990 | Acknowledgement of Assignor. On this date, before me, a Notary Public, personally appeared:
John K. Fennedy (18)
known to me or satisfactorily proven to be the person whose name is subscribed to this instrument and acknowledged that he executed the same. If this person's name is subscribed in a representative capacity, it is for the principal. | Signature of Notary Public:

Nora Notary
Notary Expiration Date:

June 1, 1996 |

103

ASSIGNMENT OF MORTGAGE TO TRUST

Purpose of this Form: This form transfers the interest that you have in a mortgage from you personally to the Revocable Trust which you have set up.

1. Return from Recording. Put the name and address of the person who is allowed to request this document from the recording agency. The person named is generally one of the trustees.

2. Office Space. Do **not** write in this space, it is for official use only.

3. Effective Date. Put the date of transfer in this space. Generally this is the date that you sign the document. Do not make it earlier than the date of the Revocable Trust.

4. Location of Property. Insert the name of the county and state where the original mortgage document is kept.

5. Assignor. Indicate the name and address of the person who is transferring the mortgage interest to the Trust in the space provided.

6. Assignee. State the name and address of the Trust following the names of the trustees. Be sure that the name of the trust includes the date it became effective.

7. Property Assigned. Insert the name of the county and state where the original mortgage document is kept.

8. Proof of Legal Description. The person who gives the legal description in instruction 12 must check to make sure that it is the same as the description on the original mortgage. Once the description has been checked, put the proof reader(s) initials here. One person reads the legal description from the source of the description; the other checks it against the newly typed description. These persons initial that they did this.

9. Date of Mortgage. Put the date when the mortgage became effective here.

10. Name of Mortgagor. Put the name of the person who gave you the mortgage for purposes of security or some other reason on the line.

11. Principle Amount. Put the amount of the loan which is secured by the mortgage on this line.

12. Legal Description. This is a "government survey", "meets and bounds", lots in a subdivision number or other designated legal property description. You need to copy this from the original mortgage. All punctuation, letters and numbers must appear exactly as on the original mortgage.

13. Recording Information. Put the recording information of your trust (where the Certificate of Trustees' Powers and Abstract of Trust is recorded for this property) here. This generally includes the name of the recording agency, the docket number, and the pages of the docket where the Certificate is recorded. Be sure to include the date that the Certificate was recorded.

14. Signature of Assignor. The assignor named in instruction 5 signs here.

15. Notary. A notary must witness the signature of the Assignor. Have the Assignor sign in front of the notary, then the notary will fill out this part of the form.

Steps to Process

A. Be sure to record a Certificate of Trustees' Powers and Abstract of Trust (LawForm #TR-2, see section 14.b) in the county where this document is to be recorded.

B. Complete the numbered instruction.

C. Have the form signed by the Assignor in front of a notary.

D. After the Certificate is recorded, record this document where the property is located.

E. Put a copy of this document in the safe file where you keep copies of all your trust documents.

This instrument was recorded at request of:

John K. Fennedy
1956 Massachusetts Street
Scottsdale, AZ 85100

(1)

(2)

The recording official is directed to return this instrument or a copy to the above person.

Space Reserved For Recording Information

ASSIGNMENT OF MORTGAGE TO TRUST
TR-20 © LawForms 10-71, 1-83, 7-87, 6-90

Effective Date: (3) 1 January 1990	County and State where property is located: (4) Maricopa, Arizona
Assignor (Name, Address and Zip Code): John K. Fennedy and Jacolyn O. Fennedy 1956 Massachusetts Street Scottsdale, AZ 85100 (5)	Assignee (Name, Address and Zip Code): John K. Fennedy & Jacolyn O. Fennedy as trustee for the Fennedy Family Trust, dated 1 January 1990 1956 Massachusetts Street (6) Scottsdale, AZ 85100
Mortgage Assigned (Address or Location of Real Property): 117 West Fitzgerald Street (7) Scottsdale, AZ 85100	Legal Description Proofed by Persons Whose Initials Appear to the Right (8)

Mortgage Assigned (Legal Description):

All right, title and interest of Assignor in and of that certain mortgage agreement dated (9) 6 February 1987, by and between John K. Fennedy, Jr. (10) as mortgagor and Assignors as mortgagee for the original principal amount of $ 75,000 (11) upon the following described real property:

NE 1/4, SW 1/4, NW 1/4, SE 1/4 of Section 12, Township Z North Range 4 West of the Gila and Salt River Base and Meridian, State of Arizona (12)

1. **Conveyance.** Any transfers effectuated by this document transferring real property interests to a trust, involve the transfer of real property by the transfer of real property by the legal owners to a Revocable Living Trust which will have the same IRS identification number as the transferor, and will not be an Irrevocable transfer until the death of the transferors, and as such shall not warrant the triggering of "due on sale" clauses in any related documents, or the imposition of taxes, or tax reassessments, imposed when there is a completed transfer of real property ownership.

2. **Assignment of Title.** For valuable considerations, receipt of which is acknowledged by Assignor, Assignor assigns all of his right, title and interest in the Property Assigned to Assignee.

3. **Recorded Information on Trust.** The names and addresses of the grantor, trustees and beneficiaries of the trust, the identity of the trust and the relevant provisions of the trust have been disclosed in the Certificate of Trustee's Powers and Abstract of Trust which is recorded at: (13) Maricopa County Recorders Office Docket Number 12432, pages 27-35

John K. (14) Fennedy _Jacolyn O. Fennedy_
Signature of Assignor   Signature of Assignor

| STATE OF Arizona
 COUNTY OF Maricopa
 Date of Acknowledgement:
 January 1, 1990 | Acknowledgement of Assignor. On this date, before me, a Notary Public, personally appeared:
 John K. (15) Fennedy <br> known to me or satisfactorily proven to be the person whose name is subscribed to this instrument and acknowledged that he executed the same. If this person's name is subscribed in a representative capacity, it is for the principal indicated. | Signature of Notary Public:
 Nora Notary
 Notary Expiration Date:
 June 1, 1996 |

DEED AND ASSIGNMENT OF INTEREST IN DEED OF TRUST TO TRUST

Purpose of this Form: This form transfers the interest in a Deed of Trust from the Grantor to the Revocable Trust.

1. Return from Recording. Put the name and address of the person who is allowed to request this document from the recording agency. The person named is generally one of the trustees.

2. Office Space. Do **not** write in this space, it is for official use only.

3. Effective Date. Put the date of transfer in this space. Generally this is the date that you sign the document. Do not make it earlier than the date of the Revocable Trust.

4. Location of Property. Insert the name of the county and state where the property described below is located.

5. Assignor. Indicate the name and address of the person who is transferring the beneficial interest to the Revocable Trust in the space provided.

6. Assignee. State the name and address of the Revocable Trust following the names of the Trustees. Be sure that the name of the trust includes the date it became effective.

7. Trustee. The Trustee cited here is not the same individual as the Trustee for the Revocable Trust. This is the Trustee named in the Deed of Trust document which you are now assigning to the Revocable Trust. Place the name and address of the Deed of Trust Trustee in the space provided.

8. Trust Date. This is the effective date of the Deed of Trust. Look on the Deed of Trust document, find the effective date, and place it in the space provided.

9. Original Trustor. The Trustor granting the benefit by Deed of Trust is named here.

10. Original Beneficiary. State the name of the beneficiary named in the Deed of Trust.

11. Location of Property. State the street address or location of the property on which the Deed of Trust was made here.

12. Proof of Legal Description. The person who gives the legal description in instruction 13 must check to make sure that it is the same as the description on the Deed of Trust. Once the description has been checked, put the proof reader(s) initial here. One person reads the legal description from the source of the description; the other checks it against the newly typed description. These persons initial that they did this.

13. Legal Description. This is a "government survey", "meets and bounds", lots in a subdivision number or other designated legal property description. You need to copy this from the Deed of Trust. All punctuation, letters and numbers must appear exactly as on the Deed of Trust.

14. Recording Information. Put the recording information of your trust (where the Certificate of Trustees' Powers and Abstract of Trust was recorded for this property) here. This generally includes the name of the recording agency, the docket number, and the pages of the docket where the Certificate is recorded. Be sure to include the date that the Certificate was recorded.

This instrument was recorded at request of:

Carolyn Fennedy
1956 Massachusetts St.
Scottsdale, AZ 85100   (1)

(2)

The recording official is directed to return this instrument or a copy to the above person.

Space Reserved For Recording Information

DEED AND ASSIGNMENT OF INTEREST IN DEED OF TRUST TO TRUST
(Special Warranty Deed)

TR-21 © LawForms 4-82, 1-89, 6-90

Effective Date: (3) 4 January 1990	County and State where Real Property is located: (4) Maricopa, Arizona
Assignor (Name, Address and Zip Code): John K. Fennedy (5) 1956 Massachusetts St. Scottsdale, AZ 85100	Assignee (Name, Address and Zip Code): John K. Fennedy & Jacolyn O. Fennedy as trustees for the Fennedy Family Trust dated 1 January 1990 (6) P.O. Box 17 Scottsdale, AZ 85100
Trustee of Deed of Trust (Name, Address and Zip Code): (7) John K. Fennedy Jacolyn O. Fennedy P.O. Box 17 P.O. Box 17 Scottsdale, AZ 85100 Scottsdale, AZ 85100	Deed of Trust Date: (8) 1 January 1990
	Name of Original Trustor: (9) J.L. Shern
	Name of Original Beneficiary: (10) John K. Fennedy
Subject Real Property (Address or Location): House and lot located at 5432 West St. Tucson, AZ 85700 (11)	Legal Description Proofed by Persons Whose Initials Appear to the Right (12)

Subject Real Property (Legal Description):

NE 1/4, SW 1/4, NW 1/4, SE 1/4 of Section 12, Township 2 North Range 4 West of the Gila and Salt River Base and Meridian, State of Arizona.

(13)

1. Recorded Information on Trust. The names and addresses of the grantor, trustee and beneficiaries of the trust, the identity of the trust and the relevant provisions of the trust have been disclosed in the Certificate of Trustee's Powers and Abstract of Trust which is recorded at: (14)   Maricopa County Recorders Office Docket Number 12432, pages 27-35 .

(Continued on Reverse Side)

107

15. Name of Trust. Put the name of your Revocable Trust here. Be sure to include the date that it became effective.

16. Trustor or Trustee Interest. Mark the first box if you are the trustor in the Deed of Trust. Mark the second box if you are the trustee in the Deed of Trust.

17. Signature of Assignor. The Assignor in instruction 5 signs here.

18. Signature of Assignee. The Assignee in instruction 6 signs here.

19. Signature of Witnesses. The Witnesses of the signatures of the Assignors and Assignees sign here.

20. Address of Witnesses. The address of each Witness is placed on the line opposite their signature.

21. Notary. A notary must witness the signature of the Assignor and Assignee. Have the Assignor and Assignee sign in front of a notary, then the notary will fill out this part of the form.

Steps to Process

A. Be sure to record a Certificate of Trustees' Powers and Abstract of Trust (LawForm #TR-2, see section 14.b) in the county where this document is to be recorded.

B. Complete the numbered instructions.

C. Have the form signed by the Assignor and Assignee in front of witnesses and a notary.

D. After the Certificate is recorded, record this document where the property is located.

E. Put a copy of this document in the safe file where you keep copies of all your trust documents.

2. Assignment. Assignor assigns to Assignee all right, title and interest of Assignor in that certain above described Deed of Trust of Subject Real Property.

3. Conveyance. For valuable consideration receipt of which is acknowledged, Assignor Specially Warrants to Assignee all right, title and interest of Assignor in Subject Real Property together with all rights and privileges appurtenant or to become appurtenant to Subject Real Property on effective date.

Assignee accepts this Deed and Assignment and receives ownership of the interest transferred as trustee for the ___Fennedy Family Trust___.

4. Effect of Transfer. Any transfers effectuated by this document transferring real property interests to a trust, involve the transfer of real property by the transfer of real property by the legal owners to a Revocable Living Trust which will have the same IRS identification number as the transferor, and will not be an Irrevocable transfer until the death of the transferors, and as such shall not warrant the triggering of "due on sale" clauses in any related documents, or the imposition of taxes, or tax reassessments, imposed when there is a completed transfer of real property ownership.

[x] This is an Assignment of the interest of the Beneficiary of the subject Deed of Trust. Assignee herein is granted the right to receive and accept any and all sums due under that agreement and to enforce that agreement according to its terms.

[ ] This is an Assignment of the interest of the Trustor of the subject Deed of Trust. Assignee herein assumes and accepts all obligations of that agreement and shall pay and fully discharge that agreement, holding Assignor harmless from any further liability thereon.

4. Special Warranty Deed. This special warranty deed made by the above named assignor, hereby grants, sells and/or conveys the above described property to the above named assignee, for true and actual consideration in the amount of 10.00 dollars, to have and to hold the same, with all appurtenance thereon, to assignee and assignee's heirs and assigns forever. I/We covenant that I/we convey and warrant specially the title against all persons claiming under me.

Signatures of Assignor: *John K Fennedy*	Signatures of Assignee: *John K Fennedy* / *Jacolyn O. Fennedy*

| 1. Signature of Witness: *Sally Newton* | Address of Witness: 12 W. Central Albuquerque, N. Mex |
| 2. Signature of Witness: *Irena Ragney* | Address of Witness: 3672 Whitten Blvd Ft Worth, TX |

STATE OF Arizona	Acknowledgement of Assignor. On this date, before me, a Notary Public, personally appeared: John K. Fennedy, known to me or satisfactorily proven to be the person whose name is subscribed to this instrument and acknowledged that he executed the same. If this person's name is subscribed in a representative capacity, it is for the principal named and in the capacity indicated.	Signature of Notary Public: *Nora Notary*
COUNTY OF Maricopa		Notary Expiration Date:
Date of Acknowledgement: January 4, 1990		June 1, 1996
STATE OF Arizona	Acknowledgement of Assignee. On this date, before me, a Notary Public, personally appeared: Jacolyn O. Fennedy, known to me or satisfactorily proven to be the person whose name is subscribed to this instrument and acknowledged that he executed the same. If this person's name is subscribed in a representative capacity, it is for the principal capacity indicated.	Signature of Notary Public: *Nora Notary*
COUNTY OF Maricopa		Notary Expiration Date:
Date of Acknowledgement: January 4, 1990		June 1, 1996

DEED AND ASSIGNMENT OF INTEREST IN REALTY AGREEMENT FOR SALE TO TRUST

Purpose of this Form: This document may be used to transfer the interest in a Realty Agreement to the Revocable Trust. If the assignor is purchasing property he assigns his interest in the Realty Agreement to buy the property to the trust. If the assignor is selling property he assigns his interest in the Realty Agreement to receive payment for the property to the trust. The example given is a Realty Agreement to buy property.

1. Return from Recording. Put the name and address of the person who is allowed to request this document from the recording agency. The person named is generally one of the Trustees.

2. Office Space. Do **not** write in this space, it is for official use only.

3. Effective Date. Put the date of transfer in this space. Generally this is the date that you sign the document. Do not make it earlier than the date of the Revocable Trust.

4. Location of Property. Insert the name of the county and state where the property described below (instruction 17) is located.

5. Assignor. Indicate the name and address of the person who is transferring the interest in the Realty Agreement to the Revocable Trust in the space provided.

6. Assignee. State the name and address of the Trustee for the Revocable Trust. Be sure that the name of the trust includes the date it became effective.

7. Realty Agreement Title. State the type of transaction and the parties to the agreement on the line.

8. Realty Agreement Date. Put the date that the realty agreement became effective here.

9. Realty Agreement Number. Put the number, if one is available, here for the Realty Agreement. Usually it will be a title company number.

10. Name of Seller. Insert the name of the person listed as the Seller (Buyer) or Grantor (Grantee) on the Realty Agreement.

11. Location of Property. State the street address or location of the property on which the Realty Agreement was made here.

12. Proof of Legal Description. The person who gives the legal description in instruction 13 must check to make sure that it is the same as the description on the Realty Agreement. Once the description has been checked, put the proof reader(s) initial here. One person reads the legal description from the source of the description; the other checks it against the newly typed description. These persons initial that they did this.

13. Legal Description. This is a "government survey", "meets and bounds", lots in a subdivisions number or other designated legal property description. You need to copy this from the Realty Agreement. All punctuation, letters and numbers must appear exactly as on the Realty Agreement.

This instrument was recorded at request of:

(1)

The recording official is directed to return this instrument or a copy to the above person.

(2)

Space Reserved For Recording Information

DEED AND ASSIGNMENT OF INTEREST IN REALTY AGREEMENT
FOR SALE OF REAL PROPERTY TO TRUST

(Special Warranty Deed)
TR-22 © LawForms 8-81, 6-90

Effective Date: January 1990 (3)	County and State where Real Property is Located: Maricopa, Arizona (4)
Assignor (Names, Address and Zip Code): John K. Fennedy (5) 1956 Massachusetts St. Scottsdale, AZ 85100	Assignee (Names, Address and Zip Code): John K. Fennedy & Jacolyn O. Fennedy as trustees for the Fennedy Family Trust dated 1 January 1990 (6) 1956 Massachusetts St. Scottsdale, AZ 85100 (as Trustee under Subject Trust)

Subject Realty Agreement For Sale:

Subject Realty Agreement For Sale is entitled: (7) Fennedy - Morgan Restaurant Contract

and is dated 3 April 1990 (8) and numbered (9) 312062 , if any, wherein the original Grantor/Seller is:

J. B. Morgan (10)

Subject Real Property (Address or Location): 1313 Mockingbird Lane (11) Flagstaff, AZ 86003	Legal Description Proofed by Persons Whose Initials Appear to the Right	1. (12)	2.	3.

Subject Real Property (Legal Description):

NE 1/4, SW 1/4, NW 1/4, SE 1/4 of Section 12, Township 2 North Range 4 West of the Gila and Salt River Base and Meridian, State of Arizona.

(13)

(Continued on Reverse Side)

14. Seller or Buyer Interest. Mark the first box if you are the Seller in the Realty Agreement. Mark the second box if you are the Buyer in the Realty Agreement.

15. Recording Information. Put the recording information of your trust (where the Certificate of Trustees' Powers and Abstract of Trust is recorded for this property) here. This generally includes the name of the recording agency, the docket number, and the pages of the docket where the Certificate was recorded. Be sure to include the date that the Certificate was recorded.

16. Signature of Assignor. The Assignor named in instruction 5 signs here.

17. Signature of Assignee. The Assignee named in instruction 6 signs here.

18. Signature of Witnesses. The witnesses of the signature of the Assignors and Assignees sign here.

19. Address of Witnesses. The address of each witness is placed on the line opposite their signature.

20. Notary. A notary must witness the signature of the Assignor and the Assignee. Have the Assignor and the Assignee sign in front of the notary, then the notary will fill out this part of the form.

Steps to Process

A. Be sure to record a Certificate of Trustees' Powers and Abstract of Trust (LawForm #TR-2, see section 14.b) in the county where this document is to be recorded.

B. Complete the numbered instructions.

C. Have the form signed in front of a notary.

D. After the Certificate is recorded, record this document where the property is located.

E. Put a copy of this document in the safe file where you keep copies of all your trust documents.

1. Interest Assigned. Assignor assigns to Assignee all right, title and interest of Assignor in subject Realty Agreement as follows:

[x] This is an Assignment of the interest of the Grantor/Seller of the subject Realty Agreement. Assignee herein is granted the right to receive and accept any and all sums due under that agreement and to enforce that agreement according to its terms.

(14)

[-] This is an Assignment of the interest of the Grantee/Buyer of the subject Realty Agreement. Assignee herein assumes and accepts all obligations of that agreement and shall pay and fully discharge that agreement, holding Assignor harmless from any further liability thereon.

2. Conveyance. Additionally and for valuable consideration, the above named Assignor conveys by special warranty deed hereby the following described property to the above named Assignee, for true and valuable consideration in the amount of 10.00 dollars, to have and to hold the same, with all appurtenances thereon to Assignee and Assignee's heirs and assigns forever. I covenant that I convey and warrant specially the title against all persons claiming under me.

3. Assignment. This assignment and deed is made to Assignee, as Trustee under Subject Trust, for Assignee to hold, sell, convey, mortgage or pledge, or otherwise handle as permitted and/or required under Subject Trust, and to do all things necessary or incidental for carrying out its purposes.

4. Recorded Information on Trust. The names and addresses of the grantor, trustees and beneficiaries of the trust, the identity and the relevant provisions of the trust have been disclosed in the Certificate of Trustees' Powers and Abstract of Trust which is recorded at:
(15) Maricopa County Recorders Office Docket Number 12432, pages 27-35

5. Effect of Transfer. Any transfers effectuated by this document transferring real property interests to a trust, involve the transfer of real property by the transfer of real property by the legal owners to a Revocable Living Trust which will have the same IRS identification number as the transferor, and will not be an Irrevocable transfer until the death of the transferors, and as such shall not warrant the triggering of "due on sale" clauses in any related documents, or the imposition of taxes, or tax reassessments, imposed when there is a completed transfer of real property ownership.

---

(16) *John K Kennedy*
Signatures of Assignor

(17) *John K Kennedy*
Jacolyn O. Kennedy
Signatures of Assignees

1. *Sally Newton*
Signature of Witness

12 W. Central Albuquerque, N. Mex
Address of Witness

2. (18) *Fiona Dewey*
Signature of Witness

(19) *3672 W. Whitten Blvd Ft Worth, Tx*
Address of Witness

	Acknowledgement of Assignor. On this date, before me, a Notary Public, personally appeared: *John K. Kennedy* (20), known to me or satisfactorily proven to be the person whose name is subscribed to this instrument and acknowledged that he executed the same. If this person's name is subscribed in a representative capacity, it is for the principal named and in the capacity indicated.	Signature of Notary Public: *Nora Notary*
STATE OF *Arizona* COUNTY OF *Maricopa* Date of Acknowledgement: *January 4, 1990*		Notary Expiration Date: *June 1, 1996*
STATE OF *Arizona* COUNTY OF *Maricopa* Date of Acknowledgement: *January 4, 1990*	Acknowledgement of Assignees. On this date, before me, a Notary Public, personally appeared: *Jacolyn O. Kennedy*, known to me or satisfactorily proven to be the person whose name is subscribed to this instrument and acknowledged that he executed the same. If this person's name is subscribed in a representative capacity, it is for the principal indicated.	Signature of Notary Public: *Nora Notary* Notary Expiration Date: *June 1, 1996*

DEED AND ASSIGNMENT OF INTEREST IN REALTY TRUST TO TRUST

Purpose of this Form: This Deed and Assignment of Interest in Realty Trust to Trust acts to transfer your interest in a realty trust to your trust.

1. Effective Date. Put the effective date of the Deed and Assignment of Interest in Realty Trust to Trust in this space. Generally this is the date that you sign the document. Do not make it earlier than the date of the Revocable Trust.

2. Location of Property. Insert the name of the county and state where the property is located.

3. Assignor. Indicate the name and address of the person who is transferring the property on the attached transfer document, to the trust in the space provided.

4. Assignee. State the name and address of the trust following the names of the Trustees. Be sure that the trust name includes the date that it became effective.

5. Property Assigned. Insert the address or location where the property to transfer is located.

6. Realty Trust Number. Put the number of the Realty Trust in the space provided. Usually it will be a title company number.

7. Realty Trust Date. Put the date that the Realty Trust became effective in this space.

8. First or Second Beneficiary. Indicate whether the assignor named in instruction 3 is the First Beneficiary (the person receiving the money) or the Second Beneficiary (the person paying the money) to the Realty Trust.

9. Status of Property Ownership. Mark the box which indicates how you held title to this property prior to transferring it to the trust.

**DEED AND ASSIGNMENT OF INTEREST
IN REALTY TRUST TO TRUST**

TR-23 © LawForms 4-82, 1-89, 6-90

Effective Date: 1 January 1990 ①	County and State where Real Property is located: Maricopa County, Arizona ②
Assignor (Name, Address and Zip Code): John K. Fennedy Jacolyn O. Fennedy ③ 1956 Massachusetts St. Scottsdale, AZ 85100	Assignee (Name, Address and Zip Code): John K. Fennedy & Jacolyn O. Fennedy as trustees for the Fennedy Family Trust, dated 1 January 1990 1956 Massachusetts St. ④ Scottsdale, AZ 85100
Property Assigned (Name, Address and Zip Code): Bank Of Parched ⑤ 103 Main Street Parched, AZ 85600	Trust Number: ⑥ Trust Date: ⑦ 22201 1 January 1990 Assignor Is: [x] First Beneficiary or Successor of First Beneficiary [-] Second Beneficiary or Successor of Second Beneficiary ⑧

1. Conveyance. For valuable consideration, receipt of which is acknowledged, Assignor conveys to Assignee all of Assignors right, title, interest, powers, privileges, and benefits created or reserved to Assignor in this Trust.

2. Acceptance of Trustee Actions. This Deed and Assignment of Interest is given and accepted with the understanding and agreement that Assignor and Assignee ratify, confirm, and approve all actions heretofore taken by Trustee and all disbursements heretofore made by Trustee, and is given and accepted with the understanding and agreement that the interest and the property held under this Trust which is conveyed and assigned is subject to all terms and conditions of this Trust Agreement, and subject to all obligations and liabilities under this Trust Agreement heretofore accrued or hereafter arising under the terms therof and the Assignee agrees to accept and be bound by all of the terms, conditions, stipulations and obligations thereof. Trustee is authorized to substitute the Assignee in place of Assignor under this Trust as of the effective date.

3. Assumption and Acceptance by Assignee. Assignee accepts this deed and assignment and approves all terms and conditions and agrees to be bound by and to comply with all obligations of the Trust, and receive ownership of the interest transferred as: [-] Sole and separate property; [x] Community Property; [-] Not as Community Property or as Tenants in Common but as Joint Tenants with Rights of Survivorship; Not as Community Property but as Tenants in Common. ⑨

4. Approval by Trustee. Trustee acknowledges and approves this assignment and receipts that a copy has been filed with the Trustee.

(Continued on Reverse Side)

10. Recording Information. Put the recording information from the Certificate of Trustees' Powers and Abstract of Trust (LawForm #TR-2, see section 14.b) in this space. Generally this information includes the name of the recording agency, the docket number, and the pages of the docket where the Certificate was recorded. Be sure to include the date that the Certificate was recorded.

11. Signature of Assignor. The Assignor named in instruction 3 signs this form here.

12. Assignee. The Assignee named in instruction 4 signs here.

13. Signature of Trustee. The Trustee signs this form here.

14. Notary. A notary must witness the signature of the Assignor and Trustee. Have the Assignor and Trustee sign in front of the notary. The notary will fill out this part of the form.

Steps to Process

A. Record a Certificate of Trustees' Powers and Abstract of Trust (LawForm #TR-2, see section 14.b) in the county where the Deed and Assignment of Interest in Realty Trust to Trust is to be recorded.

B. Complete the numbered instructions.

C. Have this form signed by the Assignor and Trustee in front of a notary public.

D. After the Certificate is recorded and this form is completed, give the original to the trustee and retain a certified copy signed by the trustee. This document does not need to be recorded.

E. Put a copy of this document in the safe file where you keep copies of all your trust documents.

5. **Recorded Information on Trust.** The names and address of the grantor, trustees and beneficiaries of the trust, the identity of the trust and the relevant provisions of the trust have been disclosed in the Certificate of Trustees' Powers and Abstract of Trust which is recorded at:

6. **Effect of Transfer.** Any transfers effectuated by this document transferring real property interests to a trust, involve the transfer of real property by the transfer of real property by the legal owners to a Revocable Living Trust which will have the same IRS identification number as the transferor, and will not be an Irrevocable transfer until the death of the transferors, and as such shall not warrant the triggering of "due on sale" clauses in any related documents, or the imposition of taxes, or tax reassessments, imposed when there is a completed transfer of real property ownership.

Maricopa County Recorders Office Docket Number 12432, pages 27-35

(10)

Signatures of Assignor	Signatures of Assignee	Signatures of Trustee
John K. Kennedy (11) / Jacolyn O. Kennedy	John K. Kennedy (12) / Jacolyn O. Kennedy	John K. Kennedy (13) / Jacolyn O. Kennedy

STATE OF Arizona COUNTY OF Maricopa Date of Acknowledgement: January 1, 1990	**Acknowledgement of Assignor.** On this date, before me, a Notary Public, personally appeared: John K. (14) Kennedy, known to me or satisfactorily proven to be the person whose name is subscribed to this instrument and acknowledged that he executed the same. If this person's name is subscribed in a representative capacity, it is for the principal named and in the capacity indicated.	Signature of Notary Public: Nora Notary Notary Expiration Date: June 1, 1996
STATE OF Arizona COUNTY OF Maricopa Date of Acknowledgement: January 1, 1990	**Acknowledgement of Assignee.** On this date, before me, a Notary Public, personally appeared: Jacolyn O. Kennedy, known to me or satisfactorily proven to be the person whose name is subscribed to this instrument and acknowledged that he executed the same. If this person's name is subscribed in a representative capacity, it is for the principal named and in the capacity indicated.	Signature of Notary Public: Nora Notary Notary Expiration Date: June 1, 1996
STATE OF Arizona COUNTY OF Maricopa Date of Acknowledgement: January 1, 1990	**Acknowledgement of Trustee.** On this date, before me, a Notary Public, personally appeared: John K. Kennedy, known to me or satisfactorily proven to be the person whose name is subscribed to this instrument and acknowledged that he executed the same. If this person's name is subscribed in a representative capacity, it is for the principal indicated.	Signature of Notary Public: Nora Notary Notary Expiration Date: June 1, 1996

CHANGE TO FINANCING STATEMENT

Purpose of this Form: This form will change a financing statement to indicate that a debt or secured interest has been assigned to your trust.

1. Return from Recording. Put the name and address of the person who is allowed to request this document from the recording agency. The person named is generally one of the Trustees.

2. Office Space. Do **not** write in this space, it is for official use only.

3. Effective Date. Put the date of the change to the financing statement in this space. Generally this is the date that you sign the document. Do not make it earlier than the date of the Revocable Trust.

4. Location of Financing Statement. Insert the name of the county and state where the financing statement is located.

5. Debtor. Indicate the name and address of the debtor on the original financing statement.

6. Secured Party. Indicate the name and address of the secured party on the original financing statement.

7. Secretary of State. Indicate the file number and the date that the original financing statement was filed with the Secretary of State.

8. Recorders Office. Indicate the name of the county, the docket number, and the date when the original financing statement was recorded with the County Recorder.

9. Assignment or Assumption. If you are the secured party on the original financing statement, and are assigning your secured interest to the trust, mark the box entitled ASSIGNMENT. If you are the debtor on the original financing statement, and are assigning the debt to the trust, mark the box entitled ASSUMPTION OF LIABILITY.

10. Trustee, Trust, and Address. Put the names of the Trustees, the name of the trust (including the effective date), and the address of the trust. The address of the trust is generally as the Grantor/Trustee.

11. Signature of Debtor. The debtor named in instruction 5 signs this form here.

12. Signature of Secured Party. The secured party named in instruction 6 signs this form here.

Steps to Process

A. Record a Certificate of Trustees' Powers and Abstract of Trust (LawForm #TR-2, see section 14.b) in the county where the document is to be recorded.

B. Complete the numbered instructions.

C. Have this form signed by the debtor and secured party.

D. After signing, send it for filing to the office in your state (usually the Secretary of State) which processes Uniform Commercial Code documents. You may find where to file it by calling your Secretary of State's office.

☐

UNIFORM COMMERCIAL CODE
CHANGE TO FINANCING STATEMENT
F-UCC-2 • LawForms 6-72, 7-82, 5-86, 7-88

This instrument was recorded at request of:

(1) John K. Fennedy
1956 Massachusetts St.
Scottsdale, Arizona 85100

(2)

The recording official is directed to return this instrument or a copy to the above person.

Space Reserved For Recording Information

Effective Date: (3) 3 January 1990	County and State of Transaction: Maricopa, Arizona (4)
DEBTOR (Name, Address and Zip Code) (5) John K. Fennedy 1956 Massachusetts St. Scottsdale, Arizona 85100	SECURED PARTY (Name, Address and Zip Code) (6) Edgar Dollarman 126 E. Bank St. Phoenix, Arizona 85000
This change refers to Financing Statement filed with the Secretary of State at: File No.: 173148 Date Filed: 3 January 1990 (7)	This change refers to Financing Statement recorded with the County Recorder of Maricopa County at: (8) Docket: 54132 Date Recorded: 3 January 1990 Pages: From 6 To 7

☐ CONTINUATION. Financing Statement described is continued.
☐ TERMINATION STATEMENT. Financing Statement described is terminated.
☐ ASSIGNMENT. The interest of Secured Parties under Financing Statement described has been assigned to Assignees whose names, addresses and zip codes appear below.
☐ AMENDMENT. Financing Statement described is amended as set forth below.
☐ RELEASE. Secured Party releases the collateral described below from Financing Statement described. (9)
☒ ASSUMPTION OF LIABILITY. The liability of Debtor under Financing Statement described has been assumed by the substitute Debtor whose name, address, and zip code appear below.

(10) John K. Fennedy and Jacolyn O. Fennedy as trustees for the Fennedy Family Trust dated 1 January 1990. 1956 Massachusetts St., Scottsdale, Arizona 85100

This form is executed and presented for filing or recording pursuant to State Statute.

(11) *John K. Fennedy*   (12) *Edgar Dollarman*

Signatures of Debtor   Signatures of Secured Party

Copy 1 – Filing   Copy 2 – Debtor   Copy 3 – Secured Party

AFFIDAVIT OF REVOCABLE LIVING TRUST DISCLOSURE

Purpose of this Form: This Affidavit may be used with transfers of real property to disclose the beneficiaries to a trust when attached to the transfer document. Use this when you do not have a recorded Certificate of Trustees' Powers and Abstract of Trust.

1. Return from Recording. Put the name and address of the person who is allowed to request this document from the recording agency. The person named is generally one of the Trustees.

2. Office Space. Do **not** write in this space, it is for official use only.

3. Effective Date. Put the effective date of the Affidavit in this space. Generally this is the date that you sign the document. Do not make it earlier than the date of the Revocable Trust.

4. Location of Property. Insert the name of the county and state where the property, named in the attached transfer document, is located.

5. Grantor. Indicate the name and address of the person who is transferring the property on the attached transfer document, to the trust in the space provided.

6. Trustee. State the name and address of the trust following the names of the Trustees. Be sure that the trust name includes the date that it became effective.

7. Trust Name. Insert the name of the Trust here.

8. Location of Trust Document. Put the name and address of the custodian of the trust document here.

9. Subject Real Property Address. Insert the best address for finding where the property is located.

10. Proof of Legal Description. The person who gives the legal description in instruction 11 must check to make sure that it is the same as the description on the original deed. Once the description has been checked, put the proof reader(s) initial here. One person reads the legal description from the source of the description; the other checks it against the newly typed description. These persons initial that they did this.

11. Legal Description. This is a "government survey", "meets and bounds", lots in a subdivision number or other designated legal property description. You need to copy this from the transfer document attached. All punctuation, letters, and numbers must appear exactly as on the transfer document attached. If the original lease does does not have a legal property description, insert N/A here.

12. Beneficiaries. Insert the names and addresses of all the primary beneficiaries of your trust. These are the persons listed in paragraph 1.2 of your trust document.

This instrument was recorded at request of:

John K. Fennedy
1956 Massachusetts St.
Scottsdale, AZ 85100   ①

②

The recording official is directed to return this instrument or a copy to the above person.

Space Reserved For Recording Information

AFFIDAVIT OF REVOCABLE LIVING TRUST DISCLOSURE

TR-25 © LawForms 10-76, 12-85, 6-90

Effective Date: 1 January 1990 ③	County and State where Real Property is Located: Maricopa County, Arizona ④
Grantor (Name, Address and Zip Code): John K. Fennedy & Jacolyn O. Fennedy 1956 Massachusetts St. Scottsdale, AZ 85100 ⑤	Trustee (Name, Address and Zip Code): John K. Fennedy & Jacolyn O. Fennedy as trustees for the Fennedy Family Trust, dated 1 January 1990 1956 Massachusetts St. Scottsdale, AZ 85100 ⑥
Trust Name (Exact Name as Set Forth in Trust): Fennedy Family Trust ⑦	Location of Trust. The Trust Document or Abstract Can be Located: At the above address of the trustee. ⑧

Subject Real Property (Address or Location): 1956 Massachusetts St. Scottsdale, AZ 85100 ⑨	Legal Description Proofed by Persons Whose Initials Appear to the Right	1.	2.	3.

Subject Real Property (Legal Description):

NE 1/4, SW 1/4, SE 1/4 of Section 12, Township 2 North, Range 4 West of the Gila and Salt River-River Meridian, State of Arizona ⑪

Beneficiaries (List all Beneficiaries and state their present Addresses and Zip Codes):

John K. Fennedy, 1956 Massachusetts St., Scottsdale, AZ 85100
Jacolyn O. Fennedy, 1956 Massachusetts St., Scottsdale, AZ 85100   ⑫
John K. Fennedy, Jr., 1956 Massachusetts St., Scottsdale, AZ 85100
Carolyn Fennedy, 1956 Massachusetts St., Scottsdale, AZ 85100

The above is a list of the Primary Beneficiaries. Additional, Contingent or Successor Beneficiaries may also be named in the Trust.

(Continued On Reverse Side)

13. Signature of Trustee. The Trustee named in instruction 6 signs this form here.

14. Notary. A notary must witness the signature of the Trustee. Have the Trustee sign in front of the notary. The notary will fill out this part of the form.

Steps to Process

A. Complete the numbered instructions.
B. Have this form signed by the Trustee in front of a notary public.
C. Record the Affidavit of Revocable Living Trust Disclosure where the property is located.
E. Put a copy of this document in the safe file where you keep copies of all your trust documents.

TERMS

1. **Intent.** In recording this Affidavit, it is Trustee's intent to comply with state requirements by placing in the records of the above described county the names of all Beneficiaries and their addresses and the identification of the Trust, as this information pertains to the above described Real Property. This Affidavit may serve to provide this information in relation to all past transactions concerning the Trust, or to the current transfer with which this Affidavit is recorded.

2. **Beneficiaries.** The above list sets forth the names and addresses of all Beneficiaries under this Trust. Depending on the nature and type of Trust, these Beneficiaries may be subject to change. However, as of the date of this Affidavit, the above list is a true and accurate list of the Beneficiaries under the Trust.

3. **Real Property.** The Subject Real Property completely describes all property held by the Trustee as Trustee pursuant to the Trust. This property may be comprised of all property transferred prior to this Affidavit, or the property which is being transferred under the Deed with which this Affidavit is being recorded.

4. **Trustee.** The below signed Trustee swears that: he has capacity to make this Affidavit; that he is the Trustee of the above described Trust, or is an Officer of the Trustee with the authority to execute such Affidavits on behalf of Trustee; and that all the information set forth in this Affidavit is true and correct to the best of Trustee's knowledge, information and belief.

John K. Fennedy (13) _Jacolyn O. Fennedy_
Signature of Trustee   Signature of Trustee

STATE OF Arizona COUNTY OF Maricopa Date of Acknowledgement: January 2, 1990	Acknowledgement of Trustee. On this date, before me, a Notary Public, personally appeared: _John K. (14) Fennedy_, known to me or satisfactorily proven to be the person whose name is subscribed to this instrument and acknowledged that he executed the same. If this person's name is subscribed in a representative capacity, it is for the principal indicated.	Signature of Notary Public: _Nora Notary_ Notary Expiration Date: June 1, 1996

ASSIGNMENT OF OWNERSHIP OF LIFE INSURANCE AND INSTRUCTIONS TO INSURER

Purpose of this Form: This transfers the Grantor's beneficial interest in a life insurance policy to the Revocable Trust. This completed form should be sent to your insurance agent along with a second completed original. Your agent should keep one and endorse and acknowledge the other one and send it back to you. You should then put it in your safe deposit box.

1. Effective Date. Put the date that you sign this form on the line.

2. County and State. Write or type the names of the county and state where you have the Revocable Trust in the space.

3. Insurer and Address. Place the name of your life insurance company followed by the address here.

4. Assignor. Put the name and address of the present policy owner in the space provided.

5. Policy Number. Put the policy number in the blank.

6. Face Amount. State the face value of your policy in this space. Call your life insurance company to get the current amount.

7. Life Insured. This is the name of the person whose life is insured by the insurance policy.

8. Assignee. Put the name of the Trust and the names of the Trustees of the Revocable Trust here. Indicate whether each person named is a Trustee or a Trustee/Grantor. Include the addresses of Trustee. Put the date of the creation of the Revocable Trust following the names of the Trust.

9. Owner's Designee. Put the name and address of the present policy owner in the space provided.

ASSIGNMENT OF OWNERSHIP OF LIFE INSURANCE
AND INSTRUCTIONS TO INSURER
TR-26 © LawForms 8-76, 6-90

Effective Date: 4 January 1990 ①	County and State of Transaction: Maricopa, Arizona ②
Insurer (Name, address and zip code): Signal Life Insurance Group 45 Colt Ave. Phoenix, AZ 85000 ③	Assignor (Present policy owner's name, address & zip code): John K. Fennedy & Jacolyn O. Fennedy 1956 Massachusetts Street Scottsdale, AZ 85100 ④

Policy Numbers: P109-1270 ⑤	Face Amount: 100,000.00 ⑥	Life Insured: John K. Fennedy ⑦

Assignee (New policy owner's name, address and zip code. If a trust, designate name of Trustee as Assignee with name, date and Grantors of Trust.):

John K. Fennedy & Jacolyn O. Fennedy
as trustees for the Fennedy Family Trust,
dated 1 January 1990
1956 Massachusetts Street ⑧
Scottsdale, AZ 85100

Owner's Designee Of Assignee (Name, address and zip code):

John K. Fennedy & Jacolyn O. Fennedy
1956 Massachusetts Street
Scottsdale, AZ 85100 ⑨

10. Signature of Assignor. The person whose name is listed in instruction 4 signs the document here.

11. Assignee. The person(s) named in instruction 8 should sign here.

12. Notary. A notary must witness the signature of the Assignor. Have the Assignor sign in front of the notary, then the notary will fill out this part of the form.

Steps to Process

A. Complete the numbered instructions.

B. Have the form signed in front of a notary.

C. Send an original and one certified copy of this document to your insurance agent to process and return original or certified copy signed by the insurance company agent.

D. Put the original of this document in the safe file where you keep copies of all your trust documents.

1. **Consideration.** For valuable consideration, the parties, all being of legal age, execute this Assignment according to the terms hereinafter set forth.
2. **Assignment.** Assignor assigns to Assignee all right, title and interest in the above-described insurance policies, and all dividends, benefits and advantages to be had or derived therefrom, subject to the conditions of the policies, the rules and regulations of Insurer, and any indebtedness to Insurer against the policies.
3. **Ownership.** Assignees shall hold ownership to these policies in trust.
4. **Owner's Designee.** Subject to Assignee's power to modify this designation, Assignee instructs Insurer that, in the event of Assignee's death before the death of the Insured, the persons designated as the Owner's Designee of Assignee shall become owner of the policies.
5. **Beneficiaries.** In connection with this Assignment, Insurer is notified that all previous beneficiary designations are revoked and new beneficiaries are set forth on the attached Change of Beneficiary.
6. **Insurance Premiums.** Assignee assumes all responsibility for all future payments and agrees that Insurer shall look solely to Assignee for payment of these premiums.
7. **Effect on Policy.** The other provisions of the policy shall remain in full force and effect. The right to change beneficiaries or to transfer or assign ownership is transferred to Assignee.
8. **More Than One Policy.** If more than one policy is involved, the changes effected shall apply to all policies listed by number and face amount.
9. **Endorsement of Change.** If the policies require Endorsement of Assignment, Assignor requests that Insurer waive all such requirements and attach a copy of this instrument to Insurer's file copy of the policy.
10. **Effective Date.** This Assignment, upon being filed with Insurer, will take effect as of the date of this notice, except as to any payment made by Insurer before the notice is received by Insurer.
11. **Instructions to Insurer.** One copy of this Assignment has been attached to Assignee's copy of the policy. Assignor requests that you attach this Assignment to your copy of the policy and otherwise record this change. You are also instructed to notify Assignor and Assignee immediately if additional procedures or documents are needed to effect this Assignment. Assignor and Assignee acknowledge that you are assuming no responsibility for the validity of this Assignment.
12. **Trust Terms and Revocation.** If a Trust is involved, Insurer shall not be obligated to inquire into the terms of the Trust and shall be fully discharged from all liability after the death proceeds are paid to the last designated beneficiary of Assignee.
13. **Verification of Trust.** In the event a Trust is involved, Trustee, by signing below as either Assignor or Assignee, certifies that the Trust as described above is in full force and effect.
14. **Assignee's Rights.** Nothing stated herein shall be construed to limit Assignee's right to change beneficiaries, assign his ownership interests, modify the Owner's Designee, or any other right or interest in these policies.
15. **Payment and Settlement Options.** Assignee expressly authorizes any beneficiary **after** death of insured, to elect any payment or settlement option that may be available under the terms of this policy. It is the intent of this provision to give the beneficiaries of the policy, after the death of the insured, the greatest amount of flexibility in dealing with the insurer when faced with the many and varied circumstances that the beneficiary may have at the time of the insured's death.
16. **Recorded Information on Trust.** The names and address of the grantor, trustees and beneficiaries of the trust, the identity of the trust and the relevant provisions of the trust have been disclosed in the Certificate of Trustees' Powers and Abstract of Trust which is recorded at:

DESIGNATION OF LIFE INSURANCE BENEFICIARY

Purpose of this Form: The Designation of Life Insurance Beneficiary informs your insurance company of who you have chosen as your primary and secondary beneficiaries of your insurance policies. This completed form should be sent to your insurance agent along with a second completed original. Your agent should keep one and endorse and acknowledge the other one and send it back to you. You should then put it in your safe deposit box.

1. Date. The date you wish this change of beneficiary to become effective.

2. County and State. Write or type the names of the county and state where you have the Revocable Trust in the space.

3. Insurer. The full name and address of your insurance company.

4. Policy Owner. Your full name and address.

5. Policy Number. The number of your insurance policy.

6. Face Amount. The dollar amount of the policy.

7. Life Insured. The name of the person whose life is insured.

8. New Beneficiaries. The names, addresses and relation to you of your primary and contingent beneficiaries. Always put the trust (with its effective date) as the primary beneficiary.

9. Witness. The name and mailing address and signature of the witness to your signature.

10. Signature of Policy Owner. Your signature.

11. Notary. A notary must witness the signature of the Policy Owner. Have the Policy Owner sign in front of the notary, then the notary will fill out this part of the form.

Steps to Process

A. Complete the numbered instructions.

B. Have the form signed in front of a notary and a witness.

C. Send an original and certified copy of this document to your insurance agent to process and return the original or certified copy signed by the insurance company.

D. Put the original of this document in the safe file where you keep copies of all your trust documents.

DESIGNATION OF
LIFE INSURANCE BENEFICIARY
(GENERAL)

TR-27 © LawForms 8-74, 12-82, 7-87, 6-90

Effective Date: 1 January 1990 ①	County and State of Transaction: Maricopa County, Arizona ②
Insurer (Name, Address & Zip Code): Famous Brands ③ 3147 W. Greenway Phoenix, AZ 85024	Policy Owner (Name, Address & Zip Code): John K. Fennedy & Jacolyn O. Fennedy as trustees for the Fennedy Family Trust, dated 1 January 1990 1956 Massachusetts St. ④ Scottsdale, AZ 85100

Policy Number: 20937-8-669 ⑤	Face Amount: $50,000 ⑥	Life Insured (Name of Policy Owner): John K. Fennedy ⑦

New Beneficiaries (Name, Relation [if any] and Address):

Primary: Fennedy Family Trust, dated 1 January 1990, 1956 Massachusetts St., Scottsdale, AZ 85100

⑧

1st Contingent: Jacolyn O. Fennedy, 1956 Massachusetts St., Scottsdale, AZ 85100

2nd Contingent: Charlene Johnson, 1921 W. Indian School, Phoenix, AZ 85000

INSTRUCTIONS: UNLESS OTHERWISE PROVIDED, surviving beneficiaries in the same class will share equally. Terms like "share and share alike" are not necessary. It is not necessary to name beneficiaries in each class above.

---

1. **Revocation and Change.** All previous beneficiary designations under each policy numbered above are revoked. All proceeds shall be paid to the "new beneficiaries".
2. **Effect On Policy.** The other provisions of the policy shall remain in full force and effect. Any ownership or assignments of the policy previously transferred or held are not to be affected. Unless otherwise provided, the right to change beneficiaries or to transfer or assign ownership is reserved to the policy owner.
3. **More Than One Policy.** If more than one policy number is listed above, the changes effected shall apply to all such policies.
4. **Endorsement Of Change.** If the policy requires endorsement of change of beneficiary, I/we request that the Insurer waive all such requirements.
5. **Effective Date.** This revocation and change of beneficiary, upon being filed with the Insurer, will take effect as of the date of the notice, except as to any payment made by the Insurer before the notice is received by the Insurer.
6. **Additional Procedures.** One copy of this document has been attached to my copy of the policy. I/We request that you attach this to your copy and otherwise record this change. The Insurer is requested to notify the policy owner immediately if additional procedures or documents

---

Signature of Witness ⑨
Name: _____
Address: _____

Signature of Policy Owner ⑩

STATE OF Arizona
COUNTY OF Maricopa

Acknowledgement of Policy Owner. On this date, before me, a Notary Public, personally appeared: John K. ⑪ Fennedy, known to me or satisfactorily proven to be the person whose name is subscribed to this instrument and acknowledged that he executed the same. If this person's name is subscribed in a representative capacity, it is for the principal indicated.

Date of Acknowledgement: January 1, 1990

Signature of Notary Public: Nora Notary

Notary Expiration Date: June 1, 1996

129

EMPLOYEE'S DESIGNATION OF BENEFICIARIES FOR RETIREMENT PLAN TRUST

Purpose of this Form: The Employee's Designation of Beneficiaries for Retirement Plan Trust allows you to designate the Revocable Trust as your beneficiary to your retirement plan or I.R.A. (Individual Retirement Account), Keogh plan, or profit-sharing plan. This completed form should be put in a safe deposit box until needed.

1. Name of Corporation. Your employer's name.

2. Name of Retirement Plan Trust. The name of your trust plan.

3. Employee. Your full name and mailing address.

4. Primary Beneficiary. The full name or title and mailing address of the person who you want to receive the benefits of the trust. This generally is your spouse.

5. Contingent Beneficiaries. This may be the full name or title and mailing address of your second choice which is usually your Revocable Living Trust.

6. Check Appropriate Box. Whether you want the shares of your second choice to belong only to them (per capita) or also to their children (per stirpes) if the beneficiary should predecease you. We recommend that you check per stirpes so that heirs of the beneficiaries of the trust may get the benefit if all named beneficiaries of the Trust predecease prior to the trust coming due.

EMPLOYEE'S DESIGNATION OF BENEFICIARIES
FOR RETIREMENT PLAN TRUST

TR-28 © LawForms 8-74, 12-82, 7-87, 6-90

Name of Corporation (Employer): Fennedy Family Sporting Goods ①	Name of Retirement Plan Trust: Ajax Bowl Investment Trust ②
Employee (Name, Address & Zip Code): John K. Fennedy ③ 1956 Massachusetts St. Scottsdale, AZ 85100	Primary Beneficiary (Name, Address & Zip Code): Jacolyn O. Fennedy ④ 1956 Massachusetts St. Scottsdale, AZ 85100 Relationship to Employee: Wife

Contingent Beneficiaries (Names, Addresses, Zip Codes and Relationship to Employee):

1st Contingent: Fennedy Family Trust, dated Jan 1 1990, 1956 Massachusetts St., Scottsdale, AZ 85100

⑤

2nd Contingent: None

---

1. Primary Beneficiary. I designate the above name Primary Beneficiary to receive the death benefits to which I am entitled under the above named Retirement Plan Trust.

2. Contingent Beneficiaries. In the event the Primary Beneficiary should predecease me, or in the event that our deaths should occur simultaneously, or in a common disaster or calamity, then, I designate the above named Contingent Beneficiaries to receive the amount to which I am entitled under the Trust. If more than one Contingent Beneficiary is named, they shall benefit equally, if no designation is given to the contrary. Should a Contingent Beneficiary not survive me, then the share of such person shall be distributed as follows:

[-] Per Capita, in its entirety, to the surviving Contingent Beneficiary, if there be only one; in equal shares to the surviving Contingent Beneficiaries, if there be more than one.   ⑥

[x] Per Stirpes, equally by right of representation, to the living descendants of the deceased Contingent Beneficiary; but if there are none, then equally to the remaining Contingent Beneficiaries, if any, or if any be deceased, then equally by right of representation to the living descendants of the other deceased Contingent Beneficiaries.

3. No Beneficiary Surviving Employee. If, at the time of my death, none of the above name beneficiaries survive me, then my trust share shall be distributed as provided in the Trust.

4. Right To Revoke Or Change Beneficiary. I reserve the right to revoke or change the designation of any beneficiary, but such revocation or change shall be in writing to the Advisory Committee, and no such revocation or change shall be effective unless, and until, received by the Advisory Committee prior to my death.

5. Effect Of Marriage Or Divorce. I understand that my marriage or divorce after the effective date of this document shall be deemed to revoke the above designations, if written notice of such marriage or divorce is received by the Advisory committee before payment of the amount to which I am entitled under the Trust is made in accordance with such designations. I understand that I should file a new Designation of Beneficiaries following such marriage or divorce.

6. Affidavits And Other Evidence. The Advisory Committee may require an affidavit or other evidence, in form satisfactory to the committee, from any Primary or Contingent Beneficiary as proof of such beneficiary's right to receive benefits from the Trust. Payments made by the Trustee, upon directive of the Advisory Committee, in good faith reliance upon such affidavit or other evidence, shall relieve the Trustee and Advisory Committee from further liability.

(Continued on Reverse Side)

7. Employee's signature. Sign your full name here.

8. Witness. Have a witness to your signature sign and put his/her address here.

9. Spouse's signature. Have your spouse sign his/her full name here.

10. Witness. Have a witness to your spouse's signature sign and put his/her mailing address here.

11. Acceptance of Designation. Your employer fills this out with date of signing, the signature of the retirement plan representative and his/her title.

12. Advisory Committee Signature. Have an officer of your business sign this form and put their title below.

13. Notary. A notary must witness the signatures of you and your spouse (if you have one). You and your spouse will sign this form in front of witnesses and a notary, then the notary will fill out this part of the form.

Steps to Process

A. Complete the numbered instructions.

B. Sign this form in front of witnesses and a notary.

C. Send an original and a certified copy of this document to the corporation or business named in instruction 1 asking that they return the original or certified copy with the signature of the advisory committee member acknowledging the document.

D. Put the original of this document in the safe file where you keep copies of all your trust documents.

7. Rights Subject To The Trust. Rights of the designated beneficiaries shall be subject to the terms and conditions of the Trust and all rules and regulations formulated thereunder.

8. Release And Discharge. Payment of any credits or funds in my Trust Account to any beneficiary designated above shall be a full and complete release and discharge of the Trustee, the Advisory Committee and the Employer to the extent of such payment.

9. Revocation Of Prior Designations. I hereby revoke all prior designations of beneficiaries made by me before the effective date of this document.

John K. Kennedy (7)	*Jacolyn O. Kennedy* (9)
Employee's Signature	Spouse's Signature
John Smith	*Good Johnson*
Signature of Witness	Signature of Witness
Name: John Smith (8)	Name: Good Johnson (10)
Address: 1 West Avenue, Phoenix, AZ 85050	Address: 2 West Avenue, Phoenix, AZ 85050

Acceptance Of Designation. The above Designation of Beneficiaries is hereby accepted this date: **1 January 1990** (11)

THE ADVISORY COMMITTEE

By ....(12)................

Title: Advisory Committee Chairman

STATE OF Arizona	**Acknowledgement of Employee.** On this date, before me, a Notary Public, personally appeared: *John K. (13) Kennedy*, known to me or satisfactorily proven to be the person whose name is subscribed to this instrument and acknowledged that he executed the same. If this person's name is subscribed in a representative capacity, it is for the principal named and in the capacity indicated.	Signature of Notary Public: *Nora Notary*
COUNTY OF Maricopa		Notary Expiration Date:
Date of Acknowledgement: January 4, 1990		June 1, 1996
STATE OF Arizona	**Acknowledgement of Spouse.** On this date, before me, a Notary Public, personally appeared: *Jacolyn O. Kennedy*, known to me or satisfactorily proven to be the person whose name is subscribed to this instrument and acknowledged that he executed the same. If this person's name is subscribed in a representative capacity, it is for the principal indicated.	Signature of Notary Public: *Nora Notary*
COUNTY OF Maricopa		Notary Expiration Date:
Date of Acknowledgement: January 4, 1990		June 1, 1996

CERTIFICATE OF TRUE COPY

Purpose of this Form: This form can be attached to any photo copy of your trust or transfer documents and notarized to authenticate the attached document. You use this form if you are having a problem with people accepting your documents.

1. Notary Name. The notary will fill in his/her name here.

2. Title of Certified Document. Put the title of the document which you are going to attach to this form on the line.

3. Date of Document. Put the effective date of the document which you are going to attach here.

4. Name of Transferring Party. Put the names of the Grantors of the trust here.

5. Capacity of Grantors. Indicate the capacity that you acted in with the attached certified document. This will be either the Trustor, Assignor, Grantor, or Seller.

6. Name of Receiving Party. Put the names of the Trustees here.

7. Capacity of Trustees. Indicate the capacity that you acted in with the attached certified document. This will be either the Trustee, Assignee, or Buyer.

8. Location of Original Document. List the location of the original document which you are having certified here.

9. Notary. The notary will fill out the rest of this form.

Steps to Process

A. Complete the numbered instructions.
B. Show notary public the original document with the photo copy allowing him/her to verify that the photo copy is a recplica of the original.
C. Have the notary attach the Certificate of True Copy to the photo copy and sign as notary and impress the notary seal or notary stamp on all pages of the photo copy.
D. Use the photo copy as an original.

CERTIFICATE OF TRUE COPY

TR-29 © LawForms 6-90

1. I, __Jack Notorious__ ①, the undersigned Notary Public, hereby certify that the attached is a true, complete and correct copy of that certain document titled: ② __Certificate of Trustees' Powers and Abstract of Trust__

2. The above named document is dated: __1 January 1990__ ③.

3. The above named document is by and between __John K. Fennedy and Jacolyn O. Fennedy__ ④ as __Grantors__ ⑤, and __John K. Fennedy and Jacolyn O. Fennedy__ ⑥ as __Trustees__ ⑦.

4. An original of the above named document is on file at: __John K. Fennedy's office safe in his study__ ⑧.

5. I am a notary of the State of __Arizona__ ⑨, and the county of __Maricopa__.

IN WITNESS WHEREOF, I have hereunto set my hand and seal this date: __1-1-90__.

Notary Expiration Date: __8-19-94__

Signature of Notary Public: _Jack Notorious_

135

15. Appendix A -- Examples of Sample Paragraphs of Final Distribution of Principal to Children

2.6 OPTION A
(Percentage Over Fixed Years)

Final Distribution of Principal (Percentage Over Fixed Years). The principal of each separate trust share established for a child of Grantor shall be distributed as follows: When or after a beneficiary has graduated from an accredited college or university or has reached the age of 25, whichever occurs first, or upon division of the trust estate into shares if such beneficiary has already reached such age or has graduated from an accredited college or university, Trustee shall distribute to such beneficiary, upon written requests of that beneficiary, any amount up to *one-fourth* in value of the principal of his or her respective share then held hereunder.

Thereafter, when a beneficiary has evidenced to Trustee *three* years tenure of education, gainful employment or training in or for a business or profession or as a homemaker, Trustee shall distribute to that beneficiary, upon written requests of that beneficiary, any amount up to *one-third* in value of the remaining principal of his or her respective share then held hereunder.

Thereafter, when a beneficiary has evidenced to Trustee an additional *three* years tenure of education, gainful employment or training in or for a business or profession or as a homemaker, Trustee shall distribute to that beneficiary, upon written requests of that beneficiary, any amount up to *one-half* in value of the remaining principal of his or her respective share then held hereunder.

And when or after a beneficiary has evidenced to Trustee an additional *three* years tenure of education, gainful employment or training in or for a business or profession or as a homemaker, Trustee shall distribute to that beneficiary, upon written requests of that beneficiary, any or all the balance of his or her respective share then held hereunder.

The value of the share shall be determined as of the first exercise of each withdrawal right. Unless Trustee has determined that the beneficiary has not met the above distribution requirements, payments shall be made without question upon the beneficiary's written request. The right of withdrawal shall be a privilege which may be exercised only voluntarily and shall not include an involuntary exercise.

If any principal is not distributed, the beneficiary shall retain a life estate in such property. On the death of such beneficiary, the property shall be distributed as provided in paragraph 2.6.d (Deceased Child).

The above rights to distributions are intended to be cumulative. For instance, if a beneficiary is 31 years of age at the time of Grantor's death or otherwise qualifies for the second distribution at a different age, that beneficiary shall be entitled to any amount up to *three-fourths* in value of the principal of the beneficiary's trust share the *one-fourth* share the beneficiary would have received at age *25*, the *one-third* share of the balance the beneficiary would have received at age *28*, and the *one-half* share of the balance the beneficiary is entitled to at age *31*.

2.6 OPTION B
(Fixed Period of Years From Death of Grantor)

Final Distribution of Principal (Fixed Period of Years from Death of Grantor). All or any portion of the principal of each separate trust share established for a child of Grantor may be distributed to the beneficiary *three* years from the date of Grantor's death. Payments shall be made without question upon the beneficiary's written request. The right of withdrawal shall be a privilege which may be exercised only voluntarily and shall not include an involuntary exercise.

If any principal is not distributed, the beneficiary shall retain a life estate in such property. On the death of such beneficiary, the property shall be distributed as provided in paragraph 2.6.d (Deceased Child).

2.6 OPTION C
(Lifetime)

<u>Final Distribution of Principal (Lifetime)</u>. All or any portion of the principal of each separate trust share established for a child of Grantors may be distributed at any time after the beneficiary has reached the age of 65 years. Upon beneficiary reaching 65 years of age, the Trustee shall either purchase a lifetime annuity on the life of the beneficiary with the funds in that beneficiary's trust share or distribute those funds to the beneficiary in equal monthly payments amortized based upon annuity tables then available to Trustee, or Trustee may elect for other reasons to merely continue the interim distributions as set forth in 2.6.b (Interim Distributions of Income and Principal from Children's Separate Trusts) and withhold the distribution of principal to the beneficiary.

2.6 OPTION D
(When Requested)

<u>Final Distribution of Principal (When Requested)</u>. All or any portion of the principal and any undistributed income of each separate trust share established for a child of Grantor may be distributed at any time or times upon written request to Trustee by that child. Payments shall be made by Trustee without question upon such child's written request. The right of withdrawal shall be a privilege which may be exercised only voluntarily and shall not include an involuntary exercise.

If any principal or income is not distributed, the child shall retain a life estate in such property. On the death of such child, the property shall be distributed as provided in paragraph 2.6.d (Deceased Child).

2.6 OPTION E
(Fixed Age of Child)

<u>Final Distribution of Principal (Fixed Age of Child)</u>. All or any portion of the principal of each separate trust share established for a child of Grantor may be distributed at any time after the beneficiary has reached the age of *35* years. Payment shall be made without question upon the beneficiary's written request. The right of withdrawal shall be a privilege which may be exercised only voluntarily and shall not include an involuntary exercise.

In the event that any principal is not distributed, the beneficiary shall retain a life estate in such property. On the death of such beneficiary, the property shall be distributed as provided in provision 2.6.d (Deceased Child).

2.6 OPTION F
(Generation Skipping --
Spendthrift -- Dynasty)

<u>Final Distribution of Principal (Generation Skipping)</u>. The principal of each separate Trust established for each child shall be held in trust for the benefit of each child for life. The child shall receive all net income and additional amounts in the sole discretion of the Trustee for the child's care, maintenance, support and education as long as the beneficiary shall live and secured loans to assist the child with professional and business opportunities and the establishment of a comfortable, safe home. On the death of the child, the remaining principal shall be distributed as provided for in paragraph 2.6d (Distribution on Death of Child).

* *Italics indicate your options of distribution to beneficiaries at different times, ages, and percentages of principal.*

16. Appendix B -- Examples of Sample Paragraphs of Final Distribution of Principal to Grandchildren

2.7 OPTION A
(Percentage Over Fixed Years)

Final Distribution of Principal (Percentage Over Fixed Years). The principal of each separate trust share established for a grandchild of Grantor shall be distributed as follows: When or after a grandchild has graduated from an accredited college or university or has reached the age of *25*, whichever occurs first, or upon division of the trust estate into shares if such grandchild has already reached such age or has graduated from an accredited college or university, Trustee shall distribute to such grandchild, upon written request of that grandchild, any amount up to *one-fourth* in value of the principal of his or her respective share then held hereunder.

Thereafter, when a grandchild has evidenced to Trustee *three* years tenure of education, gainful employment or training in or for a business or profession or as a homemaker, Trustee shall distribute to that grandchild, upon written requests of that grandchild, any amount up to *one-third* in value of the remaining principal of his or her respective share then held hereunder.

Thereafter, when a grandchild has evidenced to Trustee an additional *three* years tenure of education, gainful employment or training in or for a business or profession or as a homemaker, Trustee shall distribute to that grandchild, upon written requests of that grandchild, any amount up to *one-half* in value of the remaining principal of his or her respective share then held hereunder.

And when or after a grandchild has evidenced to Trustee an additional *three* years tenure of education, gainful employment or training in or for a business or profession or as a homemaker, Trustee shall distribute to that grandchild, upon written requests of that grandchild, any or all the balance of his or her respective share then held hereunder.

The value of the share shall be determined as of the first exercise of each withdrawal right. Unless Trustee has determined that the beneficiary has not met the above distribution requirements, payments shall be made without question upon the grandchild's written request. The right of withdrawal shall be a privilege which may be exercised only voluntarily and shall not include an involuntary exercise.

If any principal is not distributed, the grandchild shall retain a life estate in such property. On the death of such grandchild, the property shall be distributed as provided in paragraph 2.7.d. (Distribution on Death of Grandchild).

The above rights to distributions are intended to be cumulative. For instance, if a grandchild is *31* years of age at the time of Grantor's death or otherwise qualifies for the second distribution at a different age, that grandchild shall be entitled to any amount up to *three-fourths* in value of the principal of the grandchild's trust share the *one-fourth* share the grandchild would have received at age *25*, the *one-third* share of the balance the grandchild would have received at age *28*, and the one-half share of the balance the grandchild is entitled to at age *31*.

2.7 OPTION B
(Fixed Age of Grandchild)

Final Distribution of Principal (Fixed Age of Grandchild). All or any portion of the principal of each separate trust share established for a grandchild of Grantor may be distributed at any time after the beneficiary has reached the age of *35* years. Payment shall be made without question upon the grandchild's written request. The right of withdrawal shall be a privilege which may be exercised only voluntarily and shall not include an involuntary exercise.

In the event that any principal is not distributed, the beneficiary shall retain a life estate in such property. On the death of such grandchild, the property shall be distributed as provided in provision 2.7.d (Distribution on Death of Grandchild).

2.7 Option C
(Fixed Period of Years From Death of Grantor)

Final Distribution of Principal (Fixed Period of Years from Death of Grantor). All or any portion of the principal of each separate trust share established for a grandchild of Grantor may be distributed to the beneficiary *three* years from the date of Grantor's death. Payments shall be made without question upon the beneficiary's written request. The right of withdrawal shall be a privilege which may be exercised only voluntarily and shall not include an involuntary exercise.

If any principal is not distributed, the beneficiary shall retain a life estate in such property. On the death of such beneficiary, the property shall be distributed as provided in paragraph 2.7.d (Deceased Grandchild).

2.7 OPTION D
(When Requested)

Final Distribution of Principal (When Requested). All or any portion of the principal and any undistributed income of each separate trust share established for a grandchild of Grantor may be distributed at any time or times upon written request to Trustee by that grandchild. Payments shall be made by Trustee without question upon such grandchild's written request. The right of withdrawal shall be a privilege which may be exercised only voluntarily and shall not include an involuntary exercise.

If any principal or income is not distributed, the grandchild shall retain a life estate in such property. On the death of such grandchild, the property shall be distributed as provided in paragraph 2.7.d (Deceased Grandchild).

* Italics indicate your options of distribution to beneficiaries as different times, ages, and percentages of principal.

17. Appendix C -- Examples of Designation of Successor Trustees.

1.3 OPTION A
(Single Successor Trustee)

Designation of Single Successor Trustee. References in the trust instrument to Trustee shall be deemed to include not only the original Trustee but also any additional or successor Trustee or Co-Trustee, and all the powers and discretion vested in Trustee shall be exercisable by any such additional or successor Trustee or Co-Trustee. If the primary Trustees dies or otherwise ceases to function as Trustee, the following persons shall serve as Successor Trustees in the order of priority hereafter set forth:

1.3.a <u>Successor Co-Trustees.</u>
(1) John K. Fennedy, Jr., 1956 Massachusetts st., Scottsdale, Az. 85100
(2) Carolyn Fennedy, 1956 Massachusetts st., Scottsdale, Az. 85100
(3) Steve Austene, 6 Million Dollar Avenue, Majors, WI, 73490

1.3.b Upon the death, resignation, disqualification, or removal of all but the last one designated Successor Trustee, the last remaining Successor Trustee shall select a replacement in the event that he or she ceases to be a Trustee, so that the trust will always have one Trustee.

1.3c <u>Selection Procedure.</u> Selection shall be made by a written Affidavit of Succession mailed to the (a) then serving Co-Trustee, (b) to all beneficiaries of their representatives, and (c) recording a duplicate original where the trust has its situs.

1.3 OPTION B
(Family and Disinterested Successor Trustee)

Designation of Family and Disinterested Successor Trustee. References in the trust instrument to Trustee shall be deemed to include not only the original Trustee but also any additional or successor Trustee or Co-Trustee, and all the powers and discretion vested in Trustee shall be exercisable by any such additional or successor Trustee or Co-Trustee. On the death or incapacity of Grantor/Trustee, the trust shall have two or more Successor Co-Trustees, one or more of whom shall be a person or persons familiar with the wants, needs and conditions of the family and its members and who shall be called to Family Co-Trustee; and the other one or more of whom shall be a competent and objective person or corporation and shall be called the Disinterested Co-Trustee. The Successor Co-Trustee are designated below in their order of priority.

1.3.a <u>Family Co-Trustee</u>.
1. John K. Fennedy, Jr., 1956 Massachusetts st., Scottsdale, Az. 85100
2. Carolyn Fennedy, 1956 Massachusetts st., Scottsdale, Az. 85100
3. Steve Austene, 6 Million Dollar Avenue, Majors, WI, 7349
4. A member of Grantor's family or a friend of Grantor's family designated as the Family Co-Trustee by the last surviving Family Co-Trustee designated above with the approval of the then disinterested Trustee. If the last surviving Family Co-Trustee designated above does not designate a family member or friend to serve as the Family Co-Trustee, the then serving Disinterested Co-Trustee shall designate a family member or friend to serve as Family Co-Trustee with the approval of a majority of the adult beneficiaries and the guardians of the minor beneficiaries.

1.3.b <u>Disinterested Co-Trustees</u>.

1. Bob Beasly, Certified Public Accountant, 1 Acabas, NY, NY, 11001

2. John Jaques, Attorney, 24 Cour de Droit, New Orleans, Louisiana, 58603

3. Saint John's bank and Trust.

4. A competent and objective person or corporation designated as the Disinterested Co-Trustee by the last surviving Disinterested Co-Trustee. If the last surviving Disinterested Co-Trustee designated does not designate a competent and objective person or corporation to serve as Disinterested Co-Trustee, the then serving Family Co-Trustee shall designate a competent and objective person or corporation to serve as Disinterested Co-Trustee with the approval of a majority of the adult beneficiaries and the guardians of the minor beneficiaries.

1.3c. <u>Selection Procedure.</u> Selection shall be made by written Affidavit of Succession mailed to the (a) then serving Co-Trustee, (b) to all beneficiaries or their representatives, and (c) recording a duplicate original where the trust has its situs.

1.3 OPTION C
(Board of Trustees)

<u>Designation of Successor Trustee.</u> References in the trust instrument to Trustee shall be deemed to include not only the original Trustee but also any additional or successor Trustee or Co-Trustee, and all the powers and discretion vested in Trustee shall be exercisable by any such additional or successor Trustee or Co-Trustee.

1.3.a <u>Board of Trustees</u>. On the death or incapacity of the Primary Trustee, a Board of Trustee shall serve as the Trustees of this trust. The Board of Trustees shall be comprised of the following persons:

1. Bob Beasly, Certified Public Accountant, 1 Acabas, NY, NY, 11001

2. John Jaques, Attorney, 24 Cour de Droit, New Orleans, Louisiana, 58603

3. Steve Austene, 6 Million Dollar Avenue, Majors, WI, 7349

1.3.b <u>Nomination by Trustee</u>. Should one of these persons die or otherwise remove himself/herself as Trustee before the termination of this Trust, the retiring Trustee, before he/she retires may designate a Successor Trustee by sending a written nomination to the attorney serving as attorney for the Trust.

1.3.c <u>Nomination by the Board</u>. If that person fails to nominate a Successor to serve in his or her position as Trustee on the Board, the other Trustees may nominate in writing, in like fashion, a Substitute Successor Trustee who may either be a member of the family of Grantor or a banker or qualified fiduciary.

1.3.d <u>Structure of the Board</u>. The Board of Trustees shall meet on or before *1 December* each year to set policies for the Trust and to elect a Managing Trustee and a Secretary Trustee to serve for the next calendar year. Thereafter the Managing Trustee shall have all the rights to act as Trustee of the Trust as if the Managing Trustee were the sole Trustee for the period of his/her tenure. However, to be effective, all legal documents for and on behalf of the Trust shall be signed by both the Managing Trustee and the Secretary Trustee.

1.3.e <u>Removal of Board Officers</u>. At any time during the tenure of any Managing Trustee and Secretary Trustee, either or both may be removed by a vote of three-fourths of the Board of Trustees and a new Managing Trustee or Secretary Trustee elected at a special meeting called for that purpose.

1.3.f <u>Selection Procedure</u>. Selection shall be made by a written Affidavit of Succession mailed to the (a) then serving Co-Trustee, (b) to all beneficiaries or their representatives, and (c) recording a duplicate original where the trust has its situs.

GLOSSARY

Affidavit - This form is a statement of truth. The person who signs it is swearing that he or she is telling the truth. If that person is found to be lying, he or she will be guilty of perjury and may be fined or put in prison.

Asset - Anything owned that has a dollar value, including any interest in real or personal property that can be used for payment of debt.

Assign (assignment) - This is a transfer of one's interest in property (assets), contract, or other rights to another person.

Attorney Fees - This is the amount charged by an attorney for his or her services.

Beneficiaries - These are the people who will receive money or property from your trust. Beneficiaries can be the Grantors, Trustees, Family of the Grantors, Friends of the Grantors, charities, or any person to whom the Grantor wants to give property.

Certify - To certify something it to state that it is true and correct.

Creditor - A creditor is the person who is owed money by the debtor.

Debt - This is a legal obligation to pay money to a creditor. When you owe someone money it is a debt, he or she is the creditor and you are the debtor.

Debtor - This is the person who owes money to the creditor.

Deed - A deed is the paper that gives the legal right to real property. This is the title to real estate.

Estate - The estate is all the property that you have in your possession at any point in time. This includes real, personal, and intangible property. When you die this property will be taxed by the state with what are called estate taxes. You can avoid these taxes through the use of a Living Trust.

Executor - This is the person who will distribute your money and property after you die, in the event you do not have a Living Trust.

File (Filing) - In filing your trust documents you give the document to the county recorder and he or she puts it in the county records.

Filing Fee - This is the money that the county recorder will charge to process your documents that you want to have filed.

Grantor - This person is also called the Trustor. It is this person that puts his/her property into the trust to avoid estate taxes and probate.

Indicate - A person indicates something by doing some action. You can indicate your name by writing it on a piece of paper.

Judgment - A judgment is a court decision on the rights of certain parties. Generally this includes an order to pay money from one person to another.

Liability - This is an obligation to pay money. A liability indicates that money is owed. A liability is the opposite of an asset. A liability can also mean responsibility for you own actions.

Lien - A charge, hold, claim, or encumbrance on property as security for some debt is called a lien. This does not transfer the title to the property, but it does cloud the title and will make it hard to sell the property.

Notary (Notary Public) - A notary is a person who is registered by the state as an official signature witness. The signature of a notary verifies that the person who signs a legal form has signed on the date has stated, and that he or she has identified themself as the actual person signing.

Notarize - To have a document signed by a notary is to notarize the document.

Personal Property - This is movable items, as distinguished from real property or things attached to real property. However, things attached to real property may be considered personal property if, by their nature, they can be removed without injury to the real property. An example would a lamp attached to a wall of a house on a piece of property. If the lamp could be removed without hurting the house it is personal property. The house which is attached to the land is considered real property, and the land is real property. If the lamp could not be removed without doing serious damage to the house then it too would be considered real property.

Probate - This is a court procedure which is used to retitle property after someone dies. A probate action determines who has the title to what property after you die. Probate is very costly, and is to be avoided if possible. You can avoid probate by using a Living Trust.

Real Property - This is land and buildings, mineral rights that are attached to property, and permanent fixtures to the buildings, such as carpeting. Real property is also called real estate.

Realty - Realty is another word for real estate or real property.

Secured Debt - Debt which is covered by some type of collateral is called secured debt. An example would be the lien that a credit company holds on a car, if the payments are not made on time the secured creditor can take the car.

Secured Creditor - This is a person who is owed a debt which is secured by mortgages, deeds, assignments, and liens.

Transfer Document - This document acts to transfer the right to property into another's name. A transfer document transfers the title to property from one person or entity to another.

Trust - This is the document which you will be preparing to avoid estate taxes and probate. It has possession of your property, and a system for caring for the property, both before and after your death.

Trustee - This is the person who will administer the trust. Generally this will also be the Grantor before the Grantor's death.

Trustor - This person is also called the Grantor. It is this person that puts his/her property into the trust to avoid estate taxes and probate.

Unsecured Debt - An unsecured debt is a promise to pay which has no collateral attached.

Verify - To verify something is to state that it is true and correct.

Witness - A person who verifies that he or she has seen some activity. A witness may see someone write their signature on a transfer document, they will then sign their own name to certify that they witnessed the signature.